A SENSE OF TALES UNTOLD

A SENSE OF TALES UNTOLD

Exploring the Edges of Tolkien's Literary Canvas

PETER GRYBAUSKAS

The Kent State University Press ⬛ KENT, OHIO

© 2021 by The Kent State University Press, Kent, Ohio 44242
All rights reserved
First paperback edition, 2024

ISBN 978-1-60635-490-2 (paper)
ISBN 978-1-60635-430-8 (cloth)
Manufactured in the United States of America

Cataloging information for this title is available at the Library of Congress.

28 27 26 25 24   5 4 3 2

IN MEMORY OF

ANGELINE F. EVANGELISTA

(1931–2017)

A story must be told or there'll be no story,
yet it is the untold stories that are most moving.
—J. R. R. Tolkien, *The Letters of J. R. R. Tolkien*

What did Odin whisper in the ear of his son,
Ere Baldr on bale was laid?
—*The Poetic Edda*

the beginning and end of a story is to it like the edges of the canvas
—J. R. R. Tolkien, *Smith of Wootton Major*

CONTENTS

ACKNOWLEDGMENTS
AND PERMISSIONS

ACKNOWLEDGMENTS

This book has been many years in the making. Its germination dates back an Age or more to undergraduate work in Maryland with Dr. Verlyn Flieger. It grew in starts and stops and after several transplants; since those undergraduate days it has been to Rome, to Oxford, and back to Maryland again. No doubt it retains something of the character of these times and places.

In bringing this project to fruition, I have had much help along the way. I am most grateful to Verlyn Flieger for her many years of mentorship, friendship, and good conversation. Thanks also go to friends from school days: Kannan Mahadevan and Adam Baker, and classmates at UMD, especially Rob Wakeman. For much encouragement, thanks to the TolkTalkers of Maryland—Michelle Markey Butler, Eleanor Simpson, Carl Hostetter, and Chip Crane. Thanks to Robin Anne Reid for her work on the Tolkien track at the PCA National Conference and to fellow conference-goers, organizers, and panelists over the years—at UVM, Kalamazoo, and Modena, too. *Grazie mille* to Roberto Arduini and my friends in the Associazione Italiana Studi Tolkieniani. And thanks also to my students over the years in ARHU158K, ENGL101, and ENGL391.

Thanks to Catherine McIlwaine and to Cathleen Blackburn for help navigating the Tolkien material at the Bodleian Library, and to Chris Smith and Jack Baker at HarperCollins Publishers. Thanks to Susan Wadsworth-Booth, Mary Young, and the staff at the Kent State University Press; to Valerie Ahwee for her editorial assistance; and to my anonymous readers whose generous reports helped make this book better. Thanks to my parents, who (meaning no harm) first encouraged me in letters. For good company and cheer on the road, thanks to my wife, Marie, and our broodlings, Bruno and Flavia.

PERMISSIONS

Portions of chapter 1 are revised from "Untold Tales: Solving a Literary Dilemma" in *Tolkien Studies* Vol. 9, West Virginia University Press, 2012.

Portions of chapter 2 are revised from "'Now Often Forgotten': Gollum, the Great War, and the Last Alliance," which first appeared in *Baptism of Fire: The Birth of the Modern British Fantastic in World War I*, ed. Janet Brennan Croft, Mythopoeic Press, 2015.

Portions of chapter 4 are revised from "A Portrait of the Poet as a Young Man: Noteworthy Omission in *The Homecoming of Beorhtnoth Beorhthelm's Son*" in *Tolkien Studies* Vol. 17, West Virginia University Press, 2020.

Quotations from Tolkien's unpublished writings are printed here with the kind permission of the Tolkien Estate.

Quotations from Tolkien's published writing are reprinted by permission of HarperCollins Publishers Ltd.:

The Hobbit © The Tolkien Estate Limited 1937, 1965
Farmer Giles of Ham © The Tolkien Estate Limited 1949
The Homecoming of Beorhtnoth © The Tolkien Estate Limited 1953, 1966, 1980
The Lord of the Rings © The Tolkien Trust 1954, 1955, 1966
The Adventures of Tom Bombadil and Other Verses from the Red Book © The Tolkien Estate Limited 1961
Leaf by Niggle © The Tolkien Trust 1964
Smith of Wootton Major © The Tolkien Trust 1967
Sir Gawain and the Green Knight, Pearl and Sir Orfeo © Tolkien Estate Limited 1975
The Silmarillion. © Tolkien Estate Limited and C. R. Tolkien 1977
Unfinished Tales of Númenor and Middle-earth. © Tolkien Estate Limited and C. R. Tolkien 1980
The Letters of J. R. R. Tolkien © The Tolkien Trust 1981
Finn and Hengest © The Tolkien Trust 1982
The Book of Lost Tales, Part I © The Tolkien Estate Limited and C. R. Tolkien 1983 "The Monsters and the Critics" *and Other Essays* © The Tolkien Estate Limited and the Tolkien Trust 1983

ABBREVIATIONS FOR WORKS BY TOLKIEN

Shaping *The Shaping of Middle-earth*
SK *The Story of Kullervo*
SWM *Smith of Wootton Major*
TI *The Treason of Isengard*
TL *Tree and Leaf*
TOFS *Tolkien on Fairy-Stories*
TT *The Two Towers*
UT *Unfinished Tales of Númenor and Middle-earth*
VT *Vinyar Tengwar*
WJ *The War of the Jewels*
WR *The War of the Ring*

INTRODUCTION

Of the many charming treasures unveiled in the recent *Tolkien: Maker of Middle-earth* exhibition and catalog, the first Silmarillion map, drawn by J. R. R. Tolkien in the 1920s on an "unused page from an examination booklet from the university of Leeds," is one that might be said to stand out (McIlwaine 2018, 222–23). How could it not? The experience of unfolding one of Tolkien's maps is a formative one in many readers' lives, perhaps even the first remembered instance of not just literary but bibliophilic pleasure, the map unfolded on a bedroom rug or spread across a kitchen table. And, of course, the maps of Middle-earth confirm some of our most cherished ideas about Tolkien: that he is first and foremost a world-builder, or "sub-creator" as he puts it in his essay "On Fairy-stories"—probably the finest of the twentieth century.

But this map tells other stories, too. Near the top left can be read the words—not in Tolkien's hand, but stamped with administrative authority— "Do not write on this margin." Perhaps it is a story of wartime paper shortages and financial crunches, of the conflicts between professional duties and private hobbies, or of the idle fancies of bored academics. Whatever the case, it remains a fascinating and even funny little window into a humble moment in the creation of a literary oeuvre that has gone on to shake the world. But neither of these are the subject of this book.

This is a book instead all about the margins of Tolkien's work, what I call (as an umbrella term) his untold tales: the frames, the edges, allusions, lacunae, the borders between story and un-story, gaps and spaces between vast Ages and miniscule periods in an ellipsis. Surely every reader of Tolkien's fantasies could rattle off a "pet" untold tale: whether it be the surefooted Cats of Queen Berúthiel, the wanderings of the Blue Wizards, or the bar menu at the *Forsaken Inn*. My own for many years, and I suppose ultimately the germ of this project, was the narrator's grotesquely detailed hypothesis as to Shelob's recovery and return to action after her run-in with Sting. This ghastly digression is, then, as if our anonymous narrator's editor has finally stepped in, cut savagely short: "this tale does not tell" (*TT*, IV, x, 730). (Citations from *The Lord of the Rings* follow this format: volume, book, chapter, page.)

Now in the case of the first Silmarillion map, Tolkien has not heeded the stern warning against violation of the marginal space at all: the contours of his map seem to spill over uninterrupted, unfazed by the warning and its bold typeface.[1] He treats the boundary more as provocation than prohibition. And this sense of intrepid boundlessness, of an excess of invention, has also become indicative of popular views of Tolkien—both laudatory and critical.

Admirers remind us that Tolkien did more than tell stories and make maps: he crafted trees of branching languages (some have even verbs!), genealogies, annals, writing systems, and verse traditions for imagined cultures. "The allusions in *The Lord of the Rings*," notes Christopher Tolkien, the author's youngest son and literary executor, in the first of his twelve-volume *History of Middle-earth,* a manuscript study of his father's life's work, "are not illusory" (*BLT I*, 3).[2] The world he built has become like his classic description of the Faërian otherworld in "On Fairy-stories": it is "wide and deep and high and filled with many things" (*MC*, 109). His oft-cited, "overweening" ambition outlined for potential publisher Milton Waldman—to create his own "body of . . . legend . . . linked to a majestic whole"—is not so absurd, it would seem (*Letters,* 144–45).

As for critics, Tolkien has his fair share; inevitably perhaps, for one whose work has taken on such staggering popularity. *The Lord of the Rings* is by now a classic according to most standards, even the Twainian sort: "a book which people praise and don't read." I give just a few high-profile samples, for I think they touch on a tension between world-building and the "economy" of writing that is central to this study. Harold Bloom's introduction to his *Modern Critical Interpretations* volume on *The Lord of the Rings* calls the text "inflated, over-written, tendentious, and moralistic in the extreme" (2008, 1). "Nobody ever read Tolkien for the writing," adds Salman Rushdie in the *Guardian,* as if he had first stumbled upon his work in the pages of *Playboy* magazine.[3] Edmund Wilson's infamous 1956 review of *The Lord of the Rings* follows up the legendary zinger of "juvenile trash" with an unfavorable comparison of Tolkien and James Branch Cabell. Cabell, Wilson boasts, "can cover more ground in an episode that lasts only three pages than Tolkien is able to in one of his twenty-page chapters, and he can create a more disquieting impression by a reference to something that is never described than Tolkien through his whole demonology" (1965, 332). In this way, Wilson's review is not only hilariously bad, it actually anticipates (by antithesis) the central argument of this book.

Tolkien himself was quite capable of dishing out a few roasts in his critical work. In the 1936 lecture, "*Beowulf*: The Monsters and the Critics," he conjured up a parable of a man who long ago built a tower for its splendid view of the sea, while those who came after him dismantle (and dismiss) it without bothering to climb its stairs—an allegory for the sad state of *Beowulf* scholarship, a critical conversation that failed to understand or emphasize the poem's essence: its poetry (*MC*, 7–8).

Turn the allegory of the tower inside out a bit and we have a decent picture of a Bloom, Rushdie, or Wilson picking apart Tolkien's own work.[4] His was a vivid imagination, they would say, a knack, maybe, for world-building—it's a pity that he couldn't write. But Tolkien's tower—his prose tales, sometimes interspersed with chunks of verse—is what grants us the sweeping view of a world in the distance, just out of reach. And untold tales, we might say, are the weep holes in this edifice, integral to its craftsmanship and stability.

The title of this book, glimpsed in the third epigraph above, is taken from an unpublished essay Tolkien wrote to accompany the last prose tale he published during his lifetime, *Smith of Wootton Major* ([1967] 2005), about six years prior to his death in 1973. This fairy tale, which recounts a man's adventures in Faërie and his final (somewhat bitter) surrendering of the magic star, which has been his passport to the perilous realm, invites a reading as a kind of swan song, Tolkien's last comment (the author himself referred to it as an "old man's book") on the fantasy realms in which he traveled throughout his life (*Letters*, 389). The essay likewise might be seen as a return to some of the theoretical precepts of fantasy writing first explored in "On Fairy-stories." The passage reads thus:

> The beginning and end of a story is to it like the edges of the canvas or an added frame to a picture. . . . It concentrates the . . . attention . . . on one small part of the country. But there are . . . no real limits: . . . in the remote and faintly glimpsed distances, and in the unrevealed regions on either side, there are things that influence the very shape and colour of the part that is pictured. Without them it would be quite different, and they are really necessary to understanding what is seen. (*SWM*, 92–93)

Tolkien takes a similarly pictorial view in reflecting on the success of *The Lord of the Rings* in a letter drafted in 1971: it "emerged as a Frameless Picture . . . surrounded by the glimmer of limitless extensions in time and space" (*Letters*, 412).

Such a picture is consistent with Tolkien's long-held belief in the importance of a story's "impression of depth," yet it is in the *Smith* essay that Tolkien finally qualifies the nature of this importance, suggesting as he does that the untold stories that ring all about the frame of a tale are more than artful window dressing; they are in fact "really necessary to understanding" the story proper.[5] And so this book seeks to explore the edges of Tolkien's literary canvas, and to inquire how these untold tales color, inform, and enrich the reading of his work. In the chapters that follow, I argue that untold tales are nothing short of a defining feature of his subcreation.

Chapter 1, "Tolkien and the 'Fundamental Literary Dilemma,'" introduces untold tales through a survey of the author's long engagement with the theories and practices of the literary impression of depth and situates his work within the contexts of his sources of inspiration and his contemporaries.

The following three chapters offer close readings across Tolkien's body of work, seeking to illuminate his technique and to highlight the profound influence that untold tales exert on his stories.

Chapter 2, "Great Matters Grown Dim: The Allusive Web of the Last Alliance," reexamines the famous "impression of depth" in *The Lord of the Rings* by way of the vast and tangled web of allusions to the Last Alliance, the legendary precursor to the War of the Ring. While Tolkien's many verifiable references to unpublished but preexisting legends are often celebrated, this chapter highlights a no less important side of Tolkien's world-building founded instead on a nebulous conception of the Second Age of Middle-earth.

Chapter 3, "'Strange Lumber': Faded Tradition in the Túrin Saga," turns its attention to the First Age and is devoted to the nexus of tales concerning Tolkien's tragic hero, Túrin Turambar. It argues that the Túrin legend, one of those "vast backcloths" that shroud *The Lord of the Rings*, possesses its own peculiar sense of depth. In his frequent retellings of the Túrin tragedy, Tolkien found a lifelong playground for untold stories.

The fourth chapter, "A Portrait of the Poet as a Young Man: Omission in *The Homecoming of Beorhtnoth*," shifts away from the study of Middle-earth, examining an omission—perhaps the purest form of untold tale—in *The Homecoming of Beorhtnoth Beorhthelm's Son*, Tolkien's dramatic coda to the Old English fragment, *The Battle of Maldon*. Drawing on the manuscript history of the text and comparison to Ernest Hemingway's Iceberg Theory, it argues that in deliberately excising a line from the text but not rejecting its implications, Tolkien asks his readers, à la Hemingway, to "feel something more than they understand."

The fifth and final chapter, "Destroying Magic, Kindling Fire: Untold Tales and Tolkien's Legacy," considers the place of untold tales in Tolkien's legacy and "afterlives," touching on modern fantasy literature, film, and, ultimately, focusing on their interfacing with fantasy video gaming.

Chapter One

TOLKIEN AND THE "FUNDAMENTAL LITERARY DILEMMA"

Heard melodies are sweet, but those unheard / Are sweeter;
—John Keats, "Ode on a Grecian Urn"

Where the stream is clear, not too much scriveners' preciseness:
vomit up ink to trouble the waters.
—E. R. Eddison, *Mistress of Mistresses*

In January 1945, near the end of World War II and about midway through the long gestation period of *The Lord of the Rings*, J. R. R. Tolkien wrote to his son Christopher describing a "fundamental literary dilemma":[1] "A story must be told or there'll be no story, yet it is the untold stories that are most moving. I think you are moved by *Celebrimbor* because it conveys a sudden sense of endless *untold* stories: mountains seen far away, never to be climbed, distant trees . . . never to be approached—or if so only to become 'near trees'"[2] (*Letters*, 110–11). "How to tell the untold," as Vladimir Brljak puts it—or, perhaps, untell the told—"was Tolkien's fundamental literary dilemma" (2010, 19).[3] Throughout his career, Tolkien brought to this challenge an impressive playbook of tools, tricks, and devices that, with a nod to the letter, I call untold tales: the gaps, enigmas, allusions, digressions, omissions, ellipses, and loose ends that pepper his narratives.

The mid-1940s was not a time of idle chitchat between father and son. Writing to his aunt Jane Neave years later, Tolkien reflects on the period in which he wrote of his dilemma to Christopher—a dark one historically as well as a challenging one for Tolkien the writer and father. *The Lord of the Rings* was "revealing endless new vistas—and I wanted to finish it, but the world was threatening. And I was *dead stuck.* . . . It was not until Christopher was carried off to S. Africa that I forced myself to write Book IV" (*Letters,* 321). By making peace in a sense with untold tales—seeking a resolution to his fundamental dilemma—Tolkien found a way to keep his story going.

In addition to the name Celebrimbor, the letter to Christopher also cites some of Gandalf's remarks about the Palantír as examples that were evidently successful in evoking a feeling of untold stories with its attendant "heart-racking sense of the vanished past." Later in this chapter, I will briefly consider them both as a foundation on which to build the more robust investigations of particular untold tales in later chapters.

But before delving into these examples, this chapter will first explore the contexts in which untold tales develop, their theoretical foundations in Tolkien's scholarly work and other writings, and some significant models and contemporaries. In the first place, it should be noted that Tolkien's efforts to resolve the paradox of the untold story certainly predate his work on *The Lord of the Rings*—indeed they persist throughout his entire legendarium.[4] From the early work of *The Book of Lost Tales* and the first extant texts of the legend of Beren and Lúthien, we might note Tinúviel's song, with its invocation of a catalog of name-dropped wonders (both known and unknown): "the beards of the Indrafangs, the tail of Carcaras, the body of Glórund the drake, the bole of Hirilorn, and the sword of Nan she named" (*BLT II,* 19).

The Hobbit, too, shows a marked interest in the problem.[5] C. S. Lewis's review in the *Times Literary Supplement* highlighted its sense of "a world that seems to have been going on long before we stumbled into it," as well as its impression that the author withholds much about his invented world and its denizens ([1937] 2013). Professor Tolkien, he wrote, "obviously knows much more about them than he needs for this tale."[6] Lewis cites no examples, but it does not take much to find them: from Gandalf's mysterious "other business (which does not come into this tale)," to Bilbo's delight in carrying a sword from Gondolin, made "for the goblin-wars of which so many songs had sung" (*H,* 178, 66).[7]

Lewis's enthusiastic and insightful review touches on what is perhaps the mainspring of Tolkien's literary project—its sense of hidden depth, which has been the subject of a good deal of scholarly attention in the intervening years. Chief among these commentators has been T. A. Shippey, who declared that "the literary quality Tolkien valued above all was the 'impression of depth'" (2003, 228). Shippey clarifies how this sense of depth is largely "Beowulfian" in inspiration, drawing from Tolkien's lifelong professional engagement and personal enjoyment of the Old English *Beowulf.* Shippey's groundbreaking work on Tolkien dates at least as far back as his article "Creation from Philology in *The Lord of the Rings,*" where he notes "that the lore with which the trilogy is studded works overwhelmingly to produce that sense of depth and consistency" so unique to Tolkien's writing (1979, 299).

Other scholars, too, have taken up the study of depth in Tolkien's works. Gergely Nagy's (2003) "The Great Chain of Reading" is a remarkable consideration of intertextuality across versions of the Túrin legend, shedding a light on Tolkien's mythopoeic ambitions and effects. Michael D. C. Drout, Namiko Hitotsubashi, and Rachel Scavera (2014) turn to corpus analysis and empirical data for their study of "Tolkien's Creation of the Impression of Depth." Along the way they offer a concise summary of four factors generally accepted as ingredients in Tolkien's recipe for depth:

> (1) the vast size and intricate detail of the background Tolkien created for his imagined world; (2) the ways he refers to this background material through seemingly casual and incomplete allusion; (3) the logical gaps and apparent inconsistencies in the stories; and (4) the variations in style within given texts. (167)

This project makes for a fascinating companion to Nagy's work, though it differs from my own work in its emphasis on verifiable allusions rather than untold tales as well as "distant" rather than close reading.

The subject of untold tales more specifically has not altogether escaped scholarly attention. John D. Rateliff's "And All the Days of Her Life Are Forgotten: *The Lord of the Rings* as Mythic Prehistory" lays important groundwork for the elegiac effects of Tolkien's preoccupation with lost tales, noting that "a sense of loss is always pervasive in all Tolkien's work. . . . As a medieval scholar and above all as a philologist, Tolkien was keenly aware of just how much we have lost of our cultural heritage" (2006, 80).

Rateliff, in "'A Kind of Elvish Craft,'" has also studied Tolkien's prose style and its ability to engage the reader imaginatively, suggesting that "Tolkien deliberately withholds . . . detail . . . so that the reader is nudged into providing it" (2009, 6). Likewise, Steve Walker, in *The Power of Tolkien's Prose,* argues that the "deliberate construction of fictive blank spaces . . . might be the consummate touch of Tolkien's artistic encouragement of reader subcreation. Omission in his fiction becomes not passive but provocative, a sort of ultimate understatement" (2009, 165–66).

The present work owes a debt to all these scholars and more. Besides focusing particularly on those liminal spaces I call untold tales, my project distinguishes itself by its focus on the dialogue outlined in my introductory discussion of Tolkien's theory of the edges of the canvas. While we have a foundation for *what* the impression of depth is—and what inspires and engenders it in Tolkien's work—there is work to be done still to understand *how* this sense of depth colors and transforms our reading. This book will seek to fill some of these gaps, but it will do so selectively—a complete theory of and guide to untold tales is beyond my skill, and would possibly run counter to the spirit of the project. In the end, maybe the best words come from Paul Kocher, who, without recourse to any of the vast catalog of posthumous publications edited by Christopher Tolkien, noted, quite rightly: "The art of fantasy flourishes on reticence" (1977, 5).

Despite his celebrated/lambasted attention to minutiae, Tolkien understood when to check his pen and create space for untold tales. This opening chapter surveys Tolkien's lifelong engagement with the theory and practice of untold tales, argues for the centrality of this engagement, and places Tolkien's efforts in this regard within the broader context of his medieval models and contemporaries.

Perhaps anticipating the sort of critical responses he would receive for producing a work of fantasy for adults, Tolkien on several occasions demonstrated a feel for the tension between elaboration and economy, and a cognizance of the dangers of bloated prose, expressing doubts about the habit of overelaboration. In a letter written to Naomi Mitchison in April 1954, just prior to the publication of *The Fellowship of the Ring,* Tolkien probed the "clash" between a desire for exhaustive detail and what he came to understand as an equally important need to suppress it: "As a story, I think it is good that there should be a lot of things unexplained (especially if an explanation actually exists). . . . even in a mythical Age there must be some enigmas, as there always are" (*Letters,* 174).

Some months later, in a letter to Hugh Brogan of September 1954, he returned to the subject, noting that much "of the 'fascination' [of *The Lord of the Rings*] consists in the vistas of yet more legend and history, to which this work does not contain a full clue" (*Letters,* 185). Then, in a letter of March 1955 to publisher Rayner Unwin, Tolkien once more expressed an awareness of the tension, this time with regard to the supplementary material to accompany *The Return of the King.* He warned that readers "who enjoy the book as an 'heroic romance' only, and find 'unexplained vistas' part of the literary effect, will neglect the appendices, very properly." While he confessed that indulgence in ancillary detail was for him (and, judging by the fan letters, for many others) "fatally attractive," still he was unsure whether "the tendency to treat the whole thing as a kind of vast game is really good" (*Letters*, 210).

Many such examples of this fatal attraction, for Tolkien and his readers, follow in the collected *Letters*. Amid a lengthy treatise drafted in response to a question on the gift-giving practices of Hobbits, Tolkien wryly notes that "the giving of information always opens still further vistas,"[8] before rambling on for several more pages on the (somewhat) related subject of familial structures in Hobbit society (*Letters*, 293).

The clamoring for lore—and the attendant frustration when it is withheld—is frequently dramatized in *The Lord of the Rings* as well. Merry confesses to having seen Bilbo's "secret book," lamenting, "But I have only had one rapid glance, and that was difficult to get. . . . I should like another look" (*FR*, I, v, 105). An exasperated Gandalf seems a mouthpiece for Tolkien facing the steady stream of fan inquiries: "Mercy! . . . If the giving of information is to be the cure of your inquisitiveness, I shall spend all the rest of my days in answering you. What more do you want to know?" (*TT*, III, ii, 599).

Tolkien remained a generous writer of letters and revealed—or even developed—much previously unpublished lore therein. Yet in his fiction, the laconic narrators and lore-masters harness the power of suggestion and exploit the payoff of untold tales. In this regard, his training as a philologist and a scholar well versed in old literatures stood him in good stead.

DEEP ROOTS: TOLKIEN'S SCHOLARLY INTEREST IN UNTOLD TALES

Sadly, Tolkien never made a definitive study of literary depth or untold tales, though he does appear to flirt with the idea in his work on *Sir Gawain and the Green Knight*: brief musings on "this flavor, this atmosphere, this virtue that such rooted works have" are tantalizingly cut off—this "is not the kind of thing about which I wish to speak today" (*MC*, 72). Yet his sustained interest in the subject is unquestionable, and we can, with some labor, trace through his work a number of insights into his thinking on untold tales.

Chief in this regard must be Tolkien's extended explorations of literary depth, beginning with "*Beowulf*: The Monsters and the Critics." *Beowulf*, Shippey notes, not coincidentally, is a poem "absolutely full . . . of . . . 'lost tales'" (2010). Tolkien's lecture to the British Academy, which argued for the poem's artistic value and asserted the legitimate merit of the monsters at its center, is seen as a turning point in the field. Drout has suggested that the argument may have been *too* successful, and that in fact Tolkien might very well regret some of its impact on the field, particularly in squashing inquiry into the "outer edges," the historical and legendary references that were peripheral to the main action of the poem but had received the lion's share of attention before Tolkien's entrance into the conversation.[9] Drout's clarification is an important point for a study of untold tales: for what Tolkien really suggests is not that the lost tales of *Beowulf* are unimportant but that their value is much greater when read not for their own sake but in terms of their relation to the fairy story at the heart of the poem. Tolkien's own untold tales, as I hope to demonstrate throughout this book, were not world-building for world-building's sake alone but are often shaped to suit the purposes of the stories to which they are attached.

In the lecture, Tolkien memorably describes *Beowulf*'s as "illusion of surveying a past . . . that itself had depth and reached backward. . . . This impression of depth is an effect and a justification of the use of episodes and allusions to old tales" (*MC,* 27). Elsewhere in the text, Tolkien depicts the primary and subsidiary action of the poem in spatial terms; it is a "great scene, hung with tapestries woven of ancient tales of ruin" (2006, 18). In additional lecture commentary on the poem, this sense of depth in *Beowulf* crosses both time and space: it is "like a play in a room through the windows of which a distant view can be seen over a large part of the English traditions about the world of their original home" (*B,* 254).

Such depth is compounded by layers: the *Beowulf* poet and his audience are looking back on days already long gone, "they are memories already in that day of a far past caught and coloured in the shells and amber of tradition, and refashioned by the jeweler of a later day" (*BC,* 74–75).

And for modern readers the experience is twice removed, though not, perhaps, less poignant: Beowulf's funeral is for us "a memory brought over the hills, an echo of an echo" (*MC,* 33).

A fascination with depth appears also in "On Fairy-stories," which had its start as an Andrew Lang lecture at the University of St. Andrews in 1939, revised and published in 1947. The essay mounts a defense of fairy tale (and fantasy) in part by redefining the genre as one built not on a quota of magical creatures but around the imaginary world of Faërie, the perilous realm. Tolkien emphasizes throughout the essay the concept of sub-creation, his own peculiar brand of world-building. Vastness and depth are hallmarks of the world conjured up by a sub-creator: "The realm . . . is wide and deep and high" (*MC,* 109). One of the desires satisfied by these tales "is to survey the depths of space and time"; the successful fairy-story, Tolkien argues, opens a "door on Other Time" (116,

129). Yet full satiety of these primordial desires is not granted us, for as Tolkien makes clear from the beginning of the essay, the reader is only a wanderer "(or trespasser)" in the otherworld of Faërie, whose "gates should be shut and the keys be lost" if we ask too many questions (109).

Some two decades later, with *The Lord of the Rings* long in the rearview mirror, Tolkien returns in his *Smith of Wootton Major* essay to grapple with many of the technical fine points first explored in "On Fairy-stories." Naturally, the depth of Faërie and the experience of traveling through it are reconsidered here. Tolkien muses: "And when it comes to Fairy-land! That has no known limits, and no maps. Travellers have to do without them—probably the best thing" (*SWM*, 92).

Returning to "The Monsters and the Critics," Tolkien stresses that this sense of boundless depth is largely illusory: "The illusion of historical truth and perspective . . . is largely a product of art. . . . The lovers of poetry can safely study the art, but the seekers after history must beware lest the glamour of Poesis overcome them" (*MC*, 7). This caution—beware the glamour of Poesis—recalls the conflicts described by Tolkien to his publishers in preparing the appendices for publication.

To put it another way, the impression of depth is in large part founded on withholding information. Tolkien had singled out the following lines from the conclusion of the *Kalevala* (1835), Elias Lönnrot's collection of Finnish folklore, as far back as his undergraduate essay in appreciation of that text: "E'en the waterfall when flowing / Yields no endless stream of water; / Nor does an accomplished singer / Sing till all his knowledge fail him" (*SK*, 108). It is much the same sentiment echoed in Lewis's review of *The Hobbit*—Tolkien had taken a page from the folk singers enshrined in the *Kalevala*.

As a philologist first, whose inspirations were often linguistic, it is not surprising to find Tolkien touching upon similar themes in his writing on the serious play of language creation. There is, for example, an art of illusion at work in imbuing invented languages with a sense of depth. In the essay "A Secret Vice," he highlights the importance of a language's "hypothetical historical background (a necessary thing . . . for the giving of an illusion of coherence and unity . . .)" (*MC*, 210). He clearly had his own invented languages in mind. Discussing the origins in Quenya or Sindarin of the proper names in his tales, he noted in his letter to Milton Waldman that his robust invented languages grant "a certain character (a cohesion, a consistency of linguistic style, and an illusion of historicity) to the nomenclature" (*Letters*, 143).

While Tolkien frequently demonstrates a sympathetic ear for an individual poet's genius, he also knew that there may be more than art at work in producing the illusion of depth. *Sir Gawain and the Green Knight,* he muses, "has deep roots in the past, deeper even than its author was aware. It is made of tales often told before and elsewhere, and of elements that derive from remote times, beyond the vision or awareness of the poet" (*MC,* 72).

The poet inherits a tradition—working in, against, and overtop it—but it is not always kept tidily on a leash. It may be beyond the full grasp even of an accomplished craftsman and a well-versed audience. It was a hypothesis Tolkien evidently felt very early on in his career, for in the undergraduate essay on the *Kalevala* he contrasted what he felt to be a freshness in Lönnrot's collection with the more familiar Welsh legends, with their "thick dust of a no longer understood tradition lying on them; . . . names and allusions . . . that were already nonsense for the bards who related them" (*SK,* 107). The traditions behind the Welsh *Mabinogion,* he went on to suggest, lend a feeling of "long years of development" as well as "of decay which has resulted . . . in the cumbering of the tale with forgotten traditional names and matter" (*SK,* 109).[10]

Then, too, this loss or confusion could not wholly be chalked up to the forgetful or unstudied poet but to the ravages and accidents of history and time. Water, fire, war, sun—these are all the enemies of delicate manuscripts—not to speak of the fragility of oral traditions. Tolkien's professional work would have offered a daily reminder of this sense of loss. In his New Year's Day 1938 lecture to children about dragons, Tolkien spun some of his favorite dragon yarns out of the legendary past, and as he did so he attempted to impress on the young audience the physical frailty of these stories and the challenges of studying them. In his brief retelling of the *Beowulf* legend, he highlights some of the damage done to that famous manuscript, "all blotted and spoilt just at the most exciting part" (*D,* 51). Tolkien would transfer some of this professional knowledge to the fictive manuscripts of Middle-earth, most notably in the sample pages out of the Book of Mazarbul, read aloud to the company hastily, haltingly—and thrillingly—by Gandalf in the Mines of Moria. For what Tolkien understood about *Beowulf,* and dramatized for millions of readers in the Book of Mazarbul, was that such loss carried with it a kind of romance, and the felt absence a strong impression of depth.

For Tolkien, romance is felt most poignantly at a distance. It was true of *Beowulf*'s tantalizing glimpses of a vast and vanished world of story. And it is true also of *The Lord of the Rings:* in a letter from September 20, 1963, Tolkien returns to the tensions between telling and untelling explored earlier in this chapter, highlighting the unique aesthetic of *The Lord of the Rings* and the challenges he faced in preparing *The Silmarillion* for an audience hungry for more. Its appeal is "like that of viewing far off an unvisited island, or seeing the towers of a distant city gleaming in a sunlit mist. To go there is to destroy the magic, unless new unattainable vistas are again revealed" (*Letters*, 333).

Both the special attraction of *The Lord of the Rings* and the subsequent doubts about how to present the earlier legends are partly due to Tolkien's unusual publication history. Tolkien's initial attempts to publish *The Silmarillion*—first in lieu of the sequel to *The Hobbit* requested by his publishers, and then, at least alongside *The Lord of the Rings*—had been thwarted. An audience for *The Silmarillion* could only be found after the great success of *The Lord of the Rings*, and the problems posed by efforts to publish it afterwards, where it would inevitably be viewed as a kind of prequel, proved ultimately intractable for Tolkien in his lifetime.[11] Despite the devastation Tolkien felt at being unable to publish his life's work, he himself was well aware that the great unseen body of myth and legend looming behind *The Lord of the Rings* made for a uniquely indelible impression of depth. Allusions to the First and Second Ages—to Beren and Lúthien, Húrin and Túrin, Fëanor and Morgoth, Númenor and the Far West— were "caught and coloured in the shells and amber of tradition, and refashioned by the jeweler" of the Third.

This romance of distance—and its redoubtable foil, the ironic disappointment of "going there"—is frequently dramatized in Tolkien's fiction. Consider, for example, Gollum's hope of "great secrets buried" at the mountains' roots (*FR*, I, ii, 54). Yet, with his head down, worming his way into the hills and out of memory, the reality sets in: those great secrets "turned out to be just empty night: there was nothing more to find out" (55). Or, even more plainly, there is Michael George Ramer, describing Faërian dream experiences to his friends in the abandoned time travel story *The Notion Club Papers:* "The whole stories are often not particularly good . . . the charm of the fragment is often largely in being unfinished" (*SD*, 189).

This conflict is explored in more complicated ways in the late and unfinished tale of Númenor, "Aldarion and Erendis." Aldarion's insatiable sealonging—the desire to sail "to coasts and havens unguessed"—makes him a man "at war with" himself, with his father (the King), and with Erendis his wife (*UT*, 169, 171). King Meneldur cautions him of the diminishing returns for a mariner not tied to his own shores: he may go "further, but not with more profit" (172). The king furthermore fears that the "grace of the Lords of the West" on the Númenórean ships "may wane" or be withdrawn from "those who risk themselves without need upon the rocks of strange shores" (172). But Aldarion counters: "To what purpose then is the gracing of our ships . . . if they are to sail to no shores, and may seek nothing not seen before?" (172). Both Númenor and Middle-earth are changed forever by Aldarion's search for far Faërian shores. He will always be restless, and will lose his wife and his daughter, but these losses are also complicated by the friendship and political ties established with Gil-galad—a connection that will take us all the way through the Downfall of Númenor and up to the Last Alliance.

Tolkien's explorations of literary depth are often couched in pictorial terms, drawing attention to the relationship between picture and frame. In "On Fairy-stories," he suggests that stories framed as dreams ultimately cheat the achievement of Secondary Belief that is so central to Tolkien's definition of the genre. Such a story is, he suggests, "like a good picture in a disfiguring frame" (*MC*, 116). A similar debate rages in *The Notion Club Papers,* where one member of the titular club claims that a story's frame is irrelevant—"'But it's just like you . . . to pick on the frame . . . and say nothing about what's inside it'"—while another responds by reasserting the frame's integral value: "A picture-frame is not a parallel. . . . It's part of the picture, even if it's only in a marginal position" (*SD*, 163). While Tolkien cautions here and elsewhere against straight biographical interpretation (he notes that likenesses to the Inklings are in *The Notion Club Papers* seen through a cracked mirror), it is fair to see the latter perspective in this case near his own.

For Tolkien, the frame marks a kind of boundary between a story and the untold stories all about it—but this boundary could be a porous one. *Eucatastrophe,* the sudden upswing in fortune described in "On Fairy-stories" as the highest function of the genre, grants "a piercing glimpse of joy . . . that for a moment passes outside the frame" (*MC*, 154).

Endnote H to "On Fairy-stories" considers further the stock beginnings and endings of fairy tale in terms of the frame. The genre's myriad end-phrases, including "happily ever after," he suggests, "are to be compared to the margins and frames of pictures, and are no more to be thought of as the real end of any particular fragment of the seamless Web of Story than the frame is of the visionary scene" (161). Whatever their design, these cuts "in the endless tapestry" gesture toward a boundless "World of Story" (161). And even the commonplace beginning of "once upon a time," Tolkien proclaims, "produces at a stroke the sense of a great uncharted world of time" (161). One might say something similar of his own stock formula for untold tales; even the blunt and explicit "no tale tells" may be an irresistible provocation to the reader, a challenge to further explore the endless tapestry.

Ultimately Tolkien came to see a symbiotic relationship between frame and picture—or tale and untold tale. It was not enough to say that the frame is "part of the picture, even if it's only in a marginal position," for "it may seriously affect all that's inside" (*SD*, 163). *The Notion Club* may have little value as autobiography, but it certainly does provide a clear antecedent to the passage from the *Smith* essay discussed in this book's introduction: those things beyond the "edges of the canvas . . . are really necessary to understanding what is seen" (92–93).

This sense of symbiosis is also demonstrated in Tolkien's scholarship on medieval literature. That dusty tradition framing the legends of the *Mabinogion* was not all detrimental, for it also "produced a field of . . . subtly varied colours against which the figures of the actors stand out" (*SK,* 109). Likewise, the rooted, multidimensional depth of *Sir Gawain*—"Behind our poem stalk the figures of elder myth, and through the lines are heard the echoes of ancient cults"—could also be put in service of the poem itself: the poet's "story is not *about* those old things, but it receives part of its life, its vividness, its tension from them" (*MC,* 73).

It is through these examples—the poet's power of illusion, Faerie's often inaccessible extensions in space and time, the relationship between frame and picture—that Tolkien found the clues by which he might endeavor to resolve his fundamental literary dilemma, to tell a story without spoiling the untold ones, and to marry the appetite for untasted dainties with the refined enjoyment of the main course. So, while it's a pity that Tolkien never dedicated a lengthy study to untold tales, much can still be pieced together. And, as this book seeks to demonstrate, we might say that the whole of his legendarium functions as a practical demonstration of these principles.

THE BEOWULF POET

Having strung together this loose theory of literary depth and untold tales as it emerges across Tolkien's scholarly interest in medieval literature and fairy tale, we can now turn to a closer look at his primary inspiration. If, as Shippey and others have argued, *Beowulf* serves as Tolkien's aspirational benchmark in depth-making, it follows unsurprisingly that the *Beowulf* poet's technique would be the chief model for Tolkien's own creative work. The 2002 publication of *Beowulf and the Critics,* and especially the 2014 edition of Tolkien's *Beowulf* translation and commentary,[12] provide a far more comprehensive picture of Tolkien's work on the poem than can be gleaned from his famous 1936 lecture alone. In particular, his discussion of digressions, lost traditions, differentiation, and sedimentation in *Beowulf*—and the readerly detective work needed to appreciate these facets of the poem—offer a lens through which we can begin to engage Tolkien's own untold tales.

Tolkien lavished great care on evaluating the artistry of the poem's many digressions. He felt that the poet's genius was one of arrangement, not invention; he went about "enriching the whole poem with references to other cycles of story" (*B*, 254). Offering up the text of two dragon poems (written by Tolkien and C. S. Lewis) amid his commentary on *Beowulf* sparked the quip that readers will see the move as an "unpardonable digression in the manner of the poor Beowulf-poet" (*BC*, 91). Even as he praised the fantastic monsters at the heart of the poem, he was a staunch defender of the artistic purpose of its many digressions. His fierce belief that this ancillary material mattered and made sense, even if that sense eludes us today, is perhaps best summed up in a single line from Tolkien's painstaking work in *Finn and Hengest* to reconstruct a lost story by comparing evidence from *Beowulf* and the Old English "Finnesburg Fragment": "though it may seem a digression it is essential" (*FH*, 54).

Indeed, Tolkien suggests that many such segments of the poem could hardly be called digressions at all, as in the case of Ingeld and Freawaru: "it is . . . essential. . . . [I]t completes the picture . . . [and] links the Danish and Geatish halves of the scene . . . and it gives a peculiarly realistic touch to the whole background" (*B*, 324). Even in a "lay within a lay," as he describes the allusions to Sigemund and Heremod made by the *scop* within the poem, the mark of the author's craft is clear; his selection is not "random" but had "point for his purposes in his poem as a whole" (*B*, 285). Tolkien's commentary on the poem's digressions repeatedly demonstrates the trust he had in its author's craftsmanship. Here he muses on the poet's brief reference to Sigemund the dragon-slayer: "*Beowulf* is threaded . . . with remarks, references, and allusions, for the full understanding of which the whole poem must be taken into account," and while Tolkien cannot say whether the irony of such remarks amounts to an in-joke or to common knowledge, it is "impossible to believe that it is accidental (*B*, 287). In the chapters that follow, I hope to lavish the same care—and uncover the same degree of artistry—on Tolkien's untold tales.[13]

While we cannot readily appreciate the poet's use of irony in his digressions and references, Tolkien suggests that *Beowulf* affords the modern reader a different sort of pleasure in its wistful whiff of lost tradition. "There were clearly traditions about these names," he affirms, "which the author did not invent; his allusive references being certainly to things that (many of) his audience would know about" (*B*, 198). The poet's "tantalizingly allusive way" leaves us today "in doubt" (258). For Tolkien, the writer's craft is again beyond reproach, and through it we glimpse the faint outline of that which is long gone: "he was not . . . a mere dragger-in of old tales," though "our ignorance of that great nexus of interwoven 'historial [*sic*] legend' . . . which he possessed" may limit appreciation of the art (317). Tolkien's work in *Finn and Hengest* gropes for the elusive "stuff of the mental storehouse of the author of *Beowulf*, as of other poets now lost" (*FH*, 37). In all this impossible tangle of tradition, Tolkien attends to the individual voice of the poet, and reminds us that tradition is not aped statically or blindly; it invites riffing. The Sigemund reference in *Beowulf* might be "'aberrant' . . . it could omit matter which in his time was normally included . . . or it could add incidents that had not so far been usually added to the tale" (*B*, 290).

Beowulf then presented a unique challenge and pleasure to a careful modern reader, and Tolkien approaches the poem as a kind of detective engaged in the "guesswork" of untangling history from legend and locating the poet's position in a longer tradition. Without such investigative work, we cannot, for example, "understand the 'flyting' of Beowulf and Unferth, or fully appreciate the *use* our poet has made of the situation" (*B*, 211). What may have been "well-known" to an audience of the poet's own time now requires that we "piece much scattered evidence together to make out now what it is all about" (325). But we see again here something of that symbiosis between the tale and the untold tales behind it—the fullest appreciation will depend on a sensitivity to the edges of the canvas.

In his commentary on *Finn and Hengest*, Tolkien notes that questions "ramify into puzzling intricacy . . . we are attempting to unravel the echoes" (37). Though the way is hard, Tolkien maintains that it is a worthy endeavor: Arduous though the process may be, "there is not so much left of the heroes of ancient English traditions that we should scorn the attempt . . . to piece together all the scraps" (50).

What confidence we take from the hypotheses of such detective work relies once more on the warrant of the *Beowulf* poet's design and skill. One's confidence in this guesswork "will depend on the degree of respect you have for the artistry (or at least for the thoughtful care) with which *Beowulf* was composed" (*B*, 285). Tolkien saw a kind of breadcrumb method to the *Beowulf* poet's madness. Denying other scholars' claims of discrepancy and inconsistency in the poem, he characterizes the poet's practice as one of circling back and slow unfolding: his narrative repetitions with variation are not signs of. We learn more, in due course" (228). It is a technique Tolkien later identifies as the poet's "enlivening the double account."

He lets slip certain crumbs in "the narrative and others in the report" (346). Such a tactic is familiar to readers of *The Lord of the Rings*. Consider the slow unfolding of lore on the Last Alliance, or the double accounts of the journey on the Paths of the Dead in book V.

These sorts of varied repetition touch upon another element of Beowulfian craft that Tolkien admired very much: its quality of "differentiation" (*BC*, 105). The poem is in a sense polyphonic; the voices, viewpoints, and knowledge of its characters are distinct. Interpretation thus depends on a grasp of the dramatic and rhetorical situation of a given scene. Such differentiated narrative texture also opens up the reflexive possibilities of stories within stories—a depth working both within and without the frame. Returning to the interpretive puzzle of the dragon-slayer allusion, Tolkien notes that the passage concerning "Sigemund and Heremod, is a story (or stories) within a story (the eulogy) within a story (*Beowulf*). It is therefore 'cursory' to us, who would like to know more; but no doubt it picks out the 'high lights' for those who *knew*: every phrase had a point" (*B*, 284). Tolkien frequently sets up this sort of "lore gap" in his legendarium.[14] The situation in *The Hobbit* and *The Lord of the Rings* is accentuated further by the presence of the Hobbits as surrogate readers, desperately playing catch-up.

One final point of interest pertains less to design and more to Tolkien's thoughts on the writing process and his remarkably keen ear for the incidental side of "rootedness" that he identified in the old stories. In

> this early part of *Beowulf* our poet is sticking very close to some old material. . . .
> Or . . . he may . . . have improved and enlarged his own earlier, simpler, more plain fairy-story drafts. Such things do happen. (*B*, 162–63)

It is a remarkably apt description of the sedimentation that developed over six decades of starts, stops, and revisions in the history of the writing of his legendarium.

OTHER PRACTITIONERS

Undoubtedly the *Beowulf* poet was only one of many sources of the ancient world to inspire Tolkien's craft. There was Virgil, certainly, and the Gawain-poet, too.[15] The *Battle of Maldon* poet, with his stirring fragment of verse and dubious place in tradition, is treated at some length in chapter 4. The sagas of Norse literature are a well-documented mine for Tolkien's imagination, and no doubt he could not help but admire the earthy temerity of the narrator in chapter 145 of *Njal's Saga*: "some of the things that happened are related here, but there were far many more that have not been reported" (317). Source study remains a profitable field, but it is not the principal aim of this book.

More interesting, maybe, is a look at some of Tolkien's contemporaries. It is an unfortunate thing that Tolkien is more often read in conversation with the writers of antiquity than with other major authors of the twentieth century. I know of no other modern writer for whom this sense of untold depth was more keenly felt and whose literary bag of tricks was so finely tuned to suggest it. Yet Tolkien was neither the first nor the only twentieth-century writer—of fantasy or otherwise—engaging with this fundamental dilemma. I offer here a brief discussion of three writers—two fantasists (Lord Dunsany and E. R. Eddison) and one modernist (Ernest Hemingway)—whose preoccupations with the illusions of literary depth dovetail with Tolkien's.

Lord Dunsany's story collections (probably admired by Tolkien) effectively capture fantastic glimpses of distant dreamscapes lost to Time. While his tales lack much of the inner consistency and intertextual coherence that Tolkien so carefully cultivates, Dunsany exploits the short story form in its tantalizing ability to suggest further depth without taking the reader there. "The Sword of Welleran" ([1908] 2000) depicts a city defended only by the legendary reputation of its former heroes. It is a story about the power of old stories—a good deal of whose force lies in being untold. The city's inhabitants are wholly ignorant "of the lands . . . that lay all round about them . . . save that they were the theatre of the terrible deeds of Welleran, that he had done with his sword" (130). As for their enemies in those lands beyond, the traumas of the legendary past are so deeply ingrained in them that they believe these heroes to be immortal: "Surely men that have escaped so many swords and so many sleety arrows shall escape the years and Time" (131). This tale finds an intriguing corollary in the shadow of the past cast by the Last Alliance in *The Lord of the Rings,* or in the blades out of Gondolin that still strike fear into the hearts of the orcs many thousands of years after that city's fall.

Tolkien's connection to E. R. Eddison is marked by a degree of ambivalence.[16] The two met personally on at least two occasions, when Eddison was invited to Oxford by C. S. Lewis. In spite of their differences, however, Eddison manages to earn from Tolkien a book cover blurb to rule them all: "the greatest and most convincing writer of 'invented worlds'" (*Letters,* 258). That Eddison could earn such praise from Tolkien as a world-builder may at first glance seem puzzling in light of Tolkien's criticism of his "silly 'philosophy'" and "nomenclature slipshod and often inept"—two elements (language and moral philosophy) often seen as bedrock principles of Tolkien's own literary projects (258).

One possible explanation for Tolkien's ability to overlook such shortcomings is in Eddison's own engagement with untold tales. Eddison's *The Worm Ouroboros* ([1922] 1991) is in a sense all about the romance of distance and the ironic prohibition Tolkien expressed in his letter quoted earlier in this chapter: "to go there is to destroy the magic." The consummate turncoat, Lord Gro (one of Eddison's characters whom Tolkien evidently admired) is afflicted by "a strange enamourment with lost causes," or, as the Demon Lord Juss puts it, he "perversely affecteth ever the losing side if he be brought into any quarrel; and this hath dragged him ofttimes to misfortune" (284, 104). Gro's waffling stirs up the pot, keeps heroes and villains both on their toes, and prolongs and redirects the adventure in surprising ways. He sets out his philosophy eloquently after abandoning the Witches in the hour of their victory:

> But because day at her dawning hours hath so bewitched me, must I yet love her when glutted with triumph she settles to garish noon? Rather turn as now I turn to Demonland, in the sad sunset of her pride. And who dares call me turncoat, who do but follow now as I have followed this rare wisdom all my days: to love the sunrise and the sundown and the morning and the evening star? Since there only abideth the soul of nobility, true love, and wonder, and the glory of hope and fear. (Eddison [1922] 1991, 286)

The fierce beauty of uncertainty, chance, danger, movement, adventure: Here Gro lays out not only his personal ethos but the central concern of *The Worm Ouroboros*, most memorably taken up in its first and last chapters. Although Tolkien appears to find Eddison's personal philosophy wanting, it seems to me that he has more than a passing affinity for the literary philosophy epitomized in Gro.

Near the end of the tale, Eddison's Demonlords, through their unparalleled strength in arms, come to feel as if their own untold stories are not indeed endless, but have been utterly exhausted, and they, too, understand Gro's reluctance to celebrate the "garish noon," even if their metaphor for stagnation and the death of romance takes on a mistier form, one certainly redolent of Tolkien's standby of mountains in the distance:

> Juss spake saying, "O Queen Sophonisba, hast thou looked ever, on a showery day in spring, upon the rainbow flung across earth and sky, and marked how all things of earth beyond it, trees, mountain-sides, and rivers, and fields, and woods, and homes of men, are transfigured by the colours that are in the bow?"
>
> "Yes," she said, "and oft desired to reach them."
>
> "We," said Juss, "have flown beyond the rainbow. And there we found no fabled land of heart's desire, but wet rain and wind only and the cold mountain-side. And our hearts are a-cold because of it." (Eddison [1922] 1991, 391–92)

Eucatastrophe, in Eddison's fantasy, is the marvelous loop, symbolized by the Worm that eateth its own tail: to go there and to *reboot* the magic.

Eddison's later tales of Zimiamvia, the perilous paradise that the Demon lords only glimpse from afar in their story, were not to the taste at least of C. S. Lewis, who found the imagined world and its emphasis on Eddison's philosophical speculations wanting when compared to the heroic romance of *The Worm*. Yet here, too, Eddison demonstrates a grasp of the finer points of suggestive storytelling. Take, for example, this exchange from *Mistress of Mistresses* between the Vicar Horius Parry and his cousin, Lord Lessingham, held captive in the Vicar's dungeons:

> The Vicar . . . gave a short laugh. "Let me remember you . . . of Prince Valero, him that betrayed Argyanna a few years since to them of Ulba and led that re-volt against me. The Gods delivered him into my hand. Know you the manner of his end, cousin? No: for none knew it . . . and I have told no man of it until now. Do you see that hook in the ceiling?" and he swung the light to show it. "I'll not weary you with particulars, cousin. I fear 'twas not without some note and touch of cruelty. . . . But we've washed the flagstones since."
>
> "Well," he said, after a silence. (Eddison 2014, 183)

In awe of Eddison's craft but skeptical of his message, we might well imagine Tolkien voicing Lessingham's retort: "'Well,' said Lessingham, and from now he held the Vicar constantly with his steel-cold eye: 'I have listened to your story. Your manner of telling of it does you credit: not so greatly the substance of it'" (2014, 183). It is tempting to read the whole exchange as one of those evening discussions between the two authors in Lewis's Magdalen College rooms transmuted in the Zimiamvian otherworld.

The comparisons to Dunsany and Eddison as groundbreaking fantasy writers are made, I think, on solid ground, but one further writer who deserves mention here, though he seldom comes into the same conversations as Tolkien, is Ernest Hemingway. While I am not aware of any evidence that the two contemporaries ever read one another's work, the American Nobel Prize winner's now legendary Iceberg Theory—his belief that a story's effect on its reader is greatly enhanced by material its author has intentionally omitted—endures as the most famous formulation of a literary theory of depth and untold stories, not to mention a remarkably valuable analogue to the "impression of depth" so essential to Tolkien's whole literary project. Call them strange bedfellows. The development of Hemingway's theory is considered at greater length in chapter 4.

A number of Hemingway's short stories are celebrated chiefly for this sparse but highly suggestive mode of narration—dialogue circles around a topic or an event that never appears on the page but is nonetheless conveyed clearly and movingly. And, in spite of his reputation for terseness, he was not above slipping in some surprisingly playful digressions; the epigraph to the 1936 "The Snows of Kilimanjaro" ends on a puzzler: "Close to the western summit there is the dried and frozen carcass of a leopard. No one has explained what the leopard was seeking at that altitude" (39).

Lost stories were a frequent preoccupation for Hemingway, as well. The loss of his own early manuscripts, misplaced by his wife on a train, appears to have haunted his later fiction. The writer protagonist of "The Snows of Kilimanjaro," dying of a gangrenous wound, reflects on all the stories he will never have time to finish; while the dragon does not come for David Bourne in the posthumously published *The Garden of Eden,* his wife Catherine does, burning his press clippings and unpublished stories alike.

RESOLVING THE DILEMMA

Having set the stage with this brief overview of the theory and broader context for untold tales, this chapter concludes with a brief practical demonstration of Tolkien's tricks of the trade. I will begin with the two examples—"Gandalf's words about the Palantir"[17] and Celebrimbor—noted in Tolkien's letter on the fundamental literary dilemma introduced at the beginning of this chapter.

It is difficult to determine precisely which of Gandalf's words are referred to, as the subject of the palantíri—the seven Seeing Stones—is broached quite often by the wizard once he has discovered Saruman's use of one of the Stones at Orthanc. There is also the added complication that Tolkien's letter to Christopher refers to drafts of the text sent via airmail—it does not necessarily reflect the text as published a decade later. Still, keeping in mind that the words are said at least to evoke an elegiac "heart-racking sense of the vanished past," it is Gandalf's conversation with Pippin in book III: "The Palantír" that seems to me the best fit. Unfortunately, Christopher Tolkien makes no mention of the letter from his father in his notes on the evolution of the chapter in *The War of the Ring.* He does, however, include some alternate versions of Gandalf's words to Pippin that differ somewhat from the published text and are worth examining as further demonstrations of the range of effect Tolkien produces through his untold tales.

While most of what carries an elegiac tone in the conversation between Gandalf and Pippin is preserved in the final form of the text, Gandalf's rumination in one draft about the lost location of two of the Stones—"I do not know where, for no rhyme says. Maybe they were at Fornost, and with Kirdan at Mithlond in the Gulf of Lune where the grey ships lie"—is ultimately excised (*WR*, 77). The full force of the remote fictive past is delivered in not-so-subtle terms; the mystery of the stones' locations is explicitly untold—"no rhyme says." Another wrinkle of interest is introduced by the use of dialogue over plain narrative description. It is a gesture toward the kind of differentiation Tolkien admired in *Beowulf*, although from the perspective of a loremaster such as Gandalf, the words bear an authority (almost) rivaling that of omniscient narration. The wizard's wistful, hypothetical "maybe" and the names of distant lands and characters that readers would have little knowledge of contribute also to the sense of loss, wonder, and melancholy.

What Tolkien ultimately decides to include of Gandalf's words in published form maintains the elegiac tone of the drafts while evoking the sublime as well. The scene weaves in references to his wider body of myth while impressing on readers Gandalf's extensive, yet ultimately limited knowledge. The discussion of the Palantír begins with Gandalf muttering rhymes to himself as he and Pippin ride toward Minas Tirith. The rhyme Pippin overhears ends with "*Seven stars and seven stones / And one white tree*" (*TT*, III, xi, 597). Songs and poems are often used throughout Tolkien's narrative to convey a sense of oral history and depth—verses like the Rhymes of Lore suggest layers of prior history and legend, preserved fragments.[18] The remote appeal of the Rhyme catches Pippin's attention, prompting his inquiries about the origins of the Palantír. Gandalf's reply exemplifies the emotion Tolkien considered closest to his heart, and it is the most reasonable candidate for the vague reference to "Gandalf's words" in the letter. The wizard tells Pippin, "Fëanor himself, maybe, wrought them, in days so long ago that the time cannot be measured in years" (*TT*, III, xi, 597). Whether or not we are familiar with the legendary craftsman, Gandalf's words leave us with a powerful sense of a measureless abyss of time.

This is again the impression when Gandalf later expresses his longing to gaze into the Stone, "to look across the wide seas of water and of time . . . and perceive the unimaginable hand and mind of Fëanor at their work" (*TT*, III, xi, 598). It is a poignant image of longing and regret, though we might understand little of what Gandalf says, and its beauty and sadness are only heightened by the fact that the time is irretrievably lost—even Gandalf, sage and scholar, finds the work of Fëanor almost "unimaginable." It should be noted that much of the history of Fëanor, at least, is recounted in *The Silmarillion,* thus setting this episode somewhat apart from the many completely "ungrounded" untold tales. Yet even if we have had the privilege of reading *The Silmarillion* (those reading prior to 1977 certainly had no such recourse), the element of confusion is only slightly effaced; Gandalf is justified in expressing uncertainty about the origins of the stones, as Fëanor is not explicitly linked to them in any other writings. The wizard's words, as Tolkien rightly indicates in the letter to Christopher, grant the reader a brief glimpse of the vanished past, at once revealing and baffling.

The untold story of another legendary Elvish smith is the subject of Tolkien's second example in the letter to Christopher. If his reference to the Palantír was somewhat vague, Celebrimbor proves even more troublesome. Although a renowned craftsman and in fact the maker of the Three Elven Rings of Power (a feat of obvious import to the events of the Third Age), Celebrimbor is mentioned only three times in all *The Lord of the Rings.* We know he is the "maker of the Three" and that he wrote the "signs" on the door to the entrance of Moria, but little else (*FR,* II, ii, 253; *FR,* II, iv, 306). It seems an oversight that so little is said of the smith who had such an important hand in the events leading up to what transpires in *The Lord of the Rings,* but this may be precisely Tolkien's point in the letter; the name alone imparts a sense of untold stories, as the deeds of Celebrimbor are almost entirely obscured in the fictional past.[19] What little that remains, however, is shaped for maximum effect.

During "The Council of Elrond," a chapter so densely weighted with historical revelation that Tolkien himself expressed some misgivings, the history concerning Celebrimbor at least is delivered in a manner that showcases the importance of the paradox of the untold story. As the Council progresses, we are tantalized by the thought of "Elrond in his clear voice" telling the full tale of Sauron and the Rings, but such dialogue is withheld in favor of a kind of terse summation by the narrator, dashing any hopes of a thorough account: "But Celebrimbor was aware of him, and hid the Three which he had made; and there was war, and the land was laid to waste, and the gate of Moria was shut" (*FR,* II, ii, 242).

Here are present many of the hallmarks of Tolkien's untold tales, which grant his prose narratives the ability to solve his "fundamental literary dilemma." The condensed, polysyndetic summation, combining stark and striking images with the passive voice, recalls Christopher Tolkien's description of *The Silmarillion*'s "epitomising form," which, "with its suggestion of ages of poetry and 'lore' behind it, strongly evokes a sense of 'untold tales,' even in the telling them; 'distance' is never lost" (*BLT I,* 4). In "The Adapted Text:

The Lost Poetry of Beleriand," Gergely Nagy elaborates further on this point, demonstrating how certain elements of style in *The Silmarillion* contribute to a sense of depth by suggesting (and at times revealing) verse adaptation. In "the textual world," Nagy argues, these stylistic elements often "mark central scenes, climaxes, or privileged points in the narrative" (2004, 25). As the Celebrimbor passage suggests, this phenomenon is not limited to *The Silmarillion*. Crucial events in *The Lord of the Rings,* whether "historical" or in the narrative present, are often treated indirectly or elliptically through mediating storytellers who withhold from telling the whole tale.

The following paragraph provides another shift, and we are further removed from the action, with all but the duration of Elrond's speech, indirectly measured by the sun's path through the sky, omitted. The description of the passing day is reminiscent of the excuse used by Aeneas in book I of Virgil's *Aeneid*: "Goddess, should I recount / From their first source, and wert thou free to hear, / Our sorrow's sad recital, eve would first / Put day to sleep, and shut the gates of heaven." But Tolkien does not stop at simply robbing the reader of the full story. He then offers the blunt, dead-end provocation that, because this text can be accessed in Elrond's library ("elsewhere recounted"), the details of the tale are "not here recalled" (*FR*, II, ii, 242). As in the examples from *Beowulf* discussed earlier in this chapter, we have a situation in which, maybe, the "high lights" are hit for those who know (i.e., those with institutional access to Rivendell's collections), but for the reader, the account is beyond cursory. We are left with a powerful and lasting impression of this legend out of the fictive past, but any sense that our curiosity has been satisfied quickly gives way to the realization that it is merely being tickled into the realm of further inquiry.

FADED TRADITIONS, ALLUSIVE WEBS, AND OUTRIGHT OMISSIONS

The examples above stood out to Tolkien—at least at a particular moment in the many-staged development of *The Lord of the Rings,* and as representatives of a particularly elegiac effect—but they are, of course, only two of the hundreds we find when reading Tolkien's work. A full taxonomy of untold tales is, as I have noted, beyond the scope of this chapter, or indeed this book.[20] There are, however, three major "types" of untold tales that I wish to introduce here, as they are wound up with the major investigations of the next three chapters.

The first of these, and the most closely aligned with Nagy's work, I would call the suggestion of *faded tradition,* a move generated chiefly through cursory summary or by intertextual reference and retelling. The summary offers a whiff of rootedness that is difficult to grasp—yet when grasped, it destabilizes and delivers in force the "heart-racking sense of the vanished past." Celebrimbor can take comfort, maybe, that he is not the only figure of history largely forgotten. As an example of Tolkien's play with faded tradition, consider the summary of the events described in *The Lord of the Rings* as recontextualized for the 1977 *Silmarillion* in "Of The Rings of Power and the Third Age": "Here let it be said that . . . the Heir of Isildur . . . took the shards of the sword of Elendil, and in Imladris they were reforged. . . . the Heir of Isildur led the host of the West to the Black Gates of Mordor. . . . There at the last they looked upon death and defeat, and all their valour was in vain; for Sauron was too strong" (303). So far so good, though certainly more redolent of a *Saga of Aragorn Arathorn's Son* than of the Hobbit-centric text we know—certainly there is a marked omission here in the special motive of ironic distraction played by the saber-rattling of the Captains of the West (*Letters*, 258). Things take a more drastic turn, however, as the unexpected victory is described: "Frodo the Halfling, it is said, . . . took on himself the burden, and alone with his servant . . . came at last in Sauron's despite even to Mount Doom; and there into the Fire . . . he cast the Great Ring of Power" (303–4). Thus we make the awkward discovery that the historian or scribe behind this text has fallen into the same trap as many readers of *The Lord of the Rings* have: as Tolkien emphasizes both in the book and in his letters, "very few seem even to have observed" that Frodo fails (*Letters*, 252). The discrepancies here—an unnamed Sam, a final heroic gesture from Frodo, and a Gollum completely erased from history—are cause for reflection, if not alarm. Are these indeed elements of some other text and tradition, like the hypothetical *Saga of Aragorn?* What else might be missing from this source? Or from the story as we know it? The sense of loss, confusion, and puzzlement resulting from rewritings or the comparisons of divergent texts is a focal point of chapter 3, which examines Tolkien's lifelong preoccupation with retelling the story of Túrin Turambar, becoming a kind of sandbox for the infinite play of untold tales.

Gollum features prominently in chapter 2, remedying somewhat the slight paid him in "Of the Rings of Power." There I take up the shadow of the past and the nebulous allusions to the Last Alliance. These form what we might call an *allusive web:* a series of references dancing around the outer edges of a story that never fully comes into view. We learn more, in due course, as Tolkien said of the *Beowulf* method—but not too much more. The Last Alliance is, I believe, the supreme example of this move in Tolkien's fiction, but there are certainly many others. Take, for instance, the web initiated during the journey along the Paths of the Dead. We would expect Aragorn and company to continue straight through, satisfying the immediate needs of both Gondor and the narrative, but Tolkien instead takes them on a short detour to highlight something quite far removed from the pressing concerns of the War of the Ring or the Oathbreakers. "Something glittered in the gloom" and Aragorn goes to investigate: "Before him were the bones of a mighty man. He had been clad in mail. . . . His belt was of gold and garnets, and rich with gold was the helm upon his bony head. . . . He had fallen near the far wall of the cave . . . and before him stood a stony door closed fast: his finger-bones were still clawing at the cracks. A notched and broken sword lay by him, as if he had hewn at the rock in his last despair" (*RK*, V, ii, 787).

The ranger sighs, taking a moment to reflect by the body, yet he is resigned to his ignorance of the man's purpose, knowing that the Company must press on. He leaves the fallen warrior, pondering the locked door: "Whither does it lead? Why would he pass? None shall ever know" (787). It is a moment full of puzzling mystery, not unlike Hemingway's leopard near the summit of Kilimanjaro. Yet it is not a one-off allusion but the first in a trail of breadcrumbs that leads not to a completely rounded story but a fractured glimpse of Rohan's old heroic legends, and, importantly, a pointed contrast to the courageous necessity of Aragorn's decision to remember the Paths of the Dead. Hints of the lost story of Baldor the hapless (for that is his name as we learn later) take us through several chapters, in the appendices of *The Lord of the Rings,* and finally, for those with a subscription, the linguistic journal *Vinyar Tengwar.* Here, in an unfinished essay of the late 1960s, Tolkien writes in a footnote that the "special horror" of the shut door "was probably due to the fact that the door was the entrance to an evil temple hall to which Baldor had come, probably without opposition up to that point. But the door was shut in his face, and enemies that had followed him silently came up and broke his legs and left him to die in the darkness, unable to find any way out" (2001b, 22). The excitement at discovering the "conclusion" to this enigmatic episode within a footnote of an etymological essay is tempered also by some disappointment, and we may prefer in the end the elliptical web spun throughout *The Lord of the Rings.* This is ultimately no fitting conclusion at all—nor is it marketed as such. What did Baldor seek? Why did these enemies treat him so? Baldor clutching at the closed door of the evil temple is in a sense a fitting symbol for the Dark Ages of Middle-earth and a distant echo of the worship of the Dark and the first fall of Man in Tolkien's invented world.[21]

"There cannot be any 'story' without a fall," Tolkien wrote to Milton Waldman in the résumé of his sub-creation as it stood in the early 1950s (*Letters,*

147). Though in the next paragraph he also remarks that the fall of Man "nowhere appears—Men do not come on the stage until all that is long past." Thus the fall of Man might be said to be an example of the last, and perhaps the most surprising, of the three types of untold tales I will focus on in this book: outright *omission*.

Most interesting of all, for the study of technique, are those that we know Tolkien to have written but ultimately excised from his published texts. Probably the most well-known omission is that of the epilogue to *The Lord of the Rings*.

Drafts of this intended final chapter, in which the manuscript conceit of the Red Book of Westmarch reappears, and Sam, in fielding questions from his children years after Frodo's departure, wraps up a few loose ends, were posthumously published in *Sauron Defeated*. Tolkien expressed some ambivalence about the decision to cut the chapter, and its omission brings us round to the beginnings of this chapter, and the conflict between economy and elaboration. Here, at any rate, economy wins the day. As he once remarked on the decision to remove the epilogue: "One must stop somewhere" (*Letters*, 179).

The epilogue, however, is not the focus of chapter 4 and its study of omission. Instead, this chapter signals a return to the scholarly roots of untold tales with analysis of Tolkien's *The Homecoming of Beorhtnoth*, a text published only a year before *The Lord of the Rings*, and one that unsurprisingly resonates throughout Tolkien's sub-creation.

At their best, Tolkien's untold tales rival the sublime depth attributed to Niggle's Parish in *Leaf by Niggle*. The reader can "approach it, even enter it, without its losing that particular charm" because there is always the sensation of "new distances" unfolding, "doubly trebly, and quadruply enchanting" (*TL*, 157–58). "To walk into the distance without turning it into mere surroundings"—this was the great challenge behind much of his literary project, and its achievement one of the great lessons in twentieth-century storytelling and world-making.

Chapter Two

GREAT MATTERS GROWN DIM

The Allusive Web of the Last Alliance

There were wars among the mighty of Middle-earth,
of which only the echoes now remain.
—J. R. R. Tolkien, *The Lost Road and Other Writings*

In other cases you can't even tell a true war story.
Sometimes it's just beyond telling.
—Tim O'Brien, *The Things They Carried*

A cursory scan of J. R. R. Tolkien's major fiction reveals a world riven by war. Like our own, Middle-earth's history, geography, and chronology are—despite all their fantasy—defined and measured by great conflicts: wars of jewels and wars of rings; of great victories, fruitless ones, and unnumbered tears; of sudden flame and torrential water; battles between five armies and sometimes just two. Many early readers of *The Lord of the Rings* understandably took the work to be a comment on the recent and catastrophic World War II. Tolkien, in the foreword to the second edition of the text (1965), had evidently had enough, dismantling this allegorical reading of his tale and alluding to his own tragic history in the Great War: "as the years go by it seems now often forgotten that to be caught in youth by 1914 was no less hideous an experience than to be involved in 1939 and the following years. By 1918 all but one of my close friends were dead" (*FR*, xxii). Tolkien found this sort of amnesia troubling—that a mere quarter century on, the experience of the Great War "seems now often forgotten"—and the implications of his reflection cut through the foreword and deep into the heroic romance that follows it.[1]

For in moving beyond cursory scan into careful perusal of *The Lord of the Rings,* we might say that it is not so much a story about war as it is about war stories: telling them, reading them, remembering and reflecting on them.[2]

Certainly no war story in the text exerts a more pronounced or problematic influence than that of the War of the Last Alliance of Elves and Men, which ends the Second Age of Middle-earth. Fearing, maybe, the same kind of forgetfulness that Tolkien laments in his foreword, Isildur, one of the great figures of that war, left a scroll in Gondor that proclaims: *"The Great Ring shall . . . be an heirloom of the North Kingdom; but records . . . shall be left in Gondor . . . lest a time come when the memory of these great matters shall grow dim"* (*FR,* II, ii, 252; italicized in original). The scroll, it would seem, sat unread for three millennia.

A sort of mythic preamble to the War of the Ring, the Last Alliance predates Bilbo's long-expected birthday party by some 3,000 years, a point that might account for—if not entirely excuse—the hazy and fragmentary nature of its renderings within *The Lord of the Rings.*[3] In spite of—or perhaps because of—its uncertain and fraught legacy, the Last Alliance exerts profound effects on the landscape of the Third Age and indeed on the actions and eventual outcomes of the War of the Ring itself.

The Alliance is an untold tale: a sprawling allusive web after the manner of the Baldor episode explored in chapter 1. In Hobbit parlance, it might be described as all "filling up the corners" and no main course (*FR,* I, i, 28). It is never delivered directly or fully, but rather told (but mostly untold) by a cast of characters as diverse as Samwise Gamgee, Elrond Half-elven, and a pair of bantering Orcs; whispered through snatches of dialogue, stanzas of verse, prose summaries, scroll fragments, scorched earth, poisonous marshes, ruined towers, and broken swords. It is Tolkien's crowning achievement of this literary technique, each crumb tantalizing and whetting the appetite for more, conjuring that potent sense of rooted antiquity and thick-webbed story that he so admired in works like *Beowulf* or *Sir Gawain and the Green Knight.* Yet like these poets of old, Tolkien draws on the Alliance as more than just window dressing; this is an untold tale essential to plot and theme.

In the invitation to untangle the Alliance yarns spun throughout *The Lord of the Rings,* we find not only a critical thematic parallel with Tolkien's own war experience and his efforts to come to terms with its legacy both of heroism and horror, but also a gateway into the very fabric of his fantasy, the text's commentary on memory, mythmaking, and narrative art.

THE DARK AGE OF MIDDLE-EARTH

Before delving into the nature of the few extant records of the Last Alliance and their influence on the events of the War of the Ring, it may be useful to clarify something of the textual history of Tolkien's writings on the Second Age in relation to *The Lord of the Rings*. While early readers of *The Lord of the Rings* would have no recourse to seek out more on the history of the Last Alliance beyond this text, posthumously published works edited by Tolkien's son Christopher (particularly in *Unfinished Tales* [1980] and in several volumes of *The History of Middle-earth*) do provide some additional information on this period in the evolving history of Middle-earth and its development in Tolkien's writing. Such availability might suggest to the casual reader that the "lore" of the Second Age (and the Last Alliance matter in particular) occupies a position similar to those First Age events alluded to in *The Lord of the Rings,* such as the story of Beren and Lúthien, or the Orcs' affectionate dubbing of the battering ram, which breaks down the Gates of Minis Tirith, "Grond . . . in memory of the Hammer of the Underworld of old" (*RK,* V, iv, 828). I have already noted Christopher's declaration that "the allusions in *The Lord of the Rings* are not illusory" (*BLT* I, 3). It has been taken for granted that, while Tolkien's imitators and journeyman fantasists often bluff about their backstories and sources, Tolkien stands apart in his ability to support them substantially.

But this is somewhat misleading, particularly of the Second Age, which develops for the most part alongside the creation of *The Lord of the Rings* (and in large part in subservience to it) and in many regards remains only "sketched," never assuming the same depth and breadth of the legends of the Elder Days. The Last Alliance does not date back to Lost Tales like *The Fall of Gondolin,* begun on hospital leave during World War I; what Christopher Tolkien calls the germ of the Alliance story—"How Amroth wrestled with Thû and drove him to the center of the Earth and the Iron-forest"—comes from a much later text (*LR,* 12).[4] This earliest glimpse of a Last Alliance is found at the tail end of an outline for *The Fall of Númenor,* which was to be part of Tolkien's time travel story, *The Lost Road,* started in the mid-1930s. The tale was soon abandoned; the closest we come to the Alliance in it is the "tantalizingly brief" note projecting "the Elendil and Gil-galad story of the assault on Thû" (*LR,* 77–78). Tolkien's work after *The Lord of the Rings* likewise demonstrates his continued interest in the legend and its legacies, but conspicuously skirts any direct account: "The Disaster of the Gladden Fields" begins, achingly, "After the fall of Sauron" (*UT,* 259)

Those "verifiable" allusions, like the ones to Beren or Grond mentioned above, are of undeniable merit. Still, to know—as the Orcs do, and as some of the more bookish defenders of Gondor might—that the battering ram Grond recalls Morgoth's weapon of choice in ages past and his devastating victory over King Fingolfin is to add a little to the terror and the thrill of battle already desperate. On the other hand, to know what came of the disaster of the Gladden Fields, to answer the riddle of Isildur's Bane, or see The-Sword-that-was-Broken reforged—this is a different sort of knowledge: the sort that could, and does, determine the fate of Middle-earth at the end of the Third Age.[5]

To put it another way, I would say that what allusions to a nebulous Second Age may lack (initially, at least) in "tradition" and backing—they begin like the "holes" Hemingway cautions against in his Iceberg Theory[6]—they often make up for in artful integration in the text. The author himself is in search of their source and import, which may help account for the kind of literary care with which untold tales like the Last Alliance are handled: these are no lazy intertextual nods but subtly woven gaps in the fabric of the text.

Not uncharacteristically, Tolkien offered a fictive explanation for the gaping lacunae in the Matter of Middle-earth between the First and Third Age: much of this period is likened to a "Dark Age," owing not just to the wide expanse of years but to the dominion of Sauron and the regression (of both Men and Elves east of the Sea) in this time. In response to the first of many queries regarding the Last Alliance, this one on the part of Frodo, Gandalf says that this "long story" begins in "the Black Years which only the loremasters now remember" (*FR*, I, ii, 51). "Black Years" seems to be the wizard's preferred descriptor (one of his scholarly/pedantic quirks, no doubt), as he later, at the Council of Elrond, recalls the ring verse's first haunting live performance: "Out of the Black Years come the words that the Smiths of Eregion heard" (*FR*, II, ii, 254). The narrator seems to favor "Dark Years," as in the case of his inability to fill in the blanks of Shelob's history, for "out of the Dark Years few tales have come" (*TT*, IV, ix, 723). Other characters cite "Dark Days" or even the dramatic "Accursed Years," but whatever the nomenclature, its significance—laden with the suggestion of untold tales obscured and out of sight—is largely unchanged.

Many of these references point to the forgotten works and deeds of Men during the Second Age. The Tale of Years again characterizes the Second Age as "the dark years for Men of Middle-earth. . . . the records are few and brief, and their dates are often uncertain" (*RK*, appendix B, 1082). Dunharrow, mountain refuge of the Rohirrim, is "the work of long-forgotten men" who "laboured in the Dark Years," though "for what purpose . . . none could say" (*RK*, V, iii, 795).

The delving of Dunharrow is marked by a layer of antiquity even deeper than the Alliance, which is at the heart of this chapter's inquiry. During the events of the War of the Ring, the Wild Men of the Woods lend a hand to the Rohirrim, perhaps out of "fear lest the Dark Years be returning" (*RK*, V, v, 831).

But Elves and Dwarves, too, look back to this period on occasion. On learning that a Dwarf is a member of the Company seeking entrance to Lórien, Haldir does not hide his concern: "We have not had dealings with the Dwarves since the Dark Days" (*FR*, II, vi, 343). Gimli himself invokes this shadowy period, lost for words on how to relate his harrowing experience on the Paths of the Dead: "like the echo of some forgotten battle in the Dark Years long ago" (*RK*, V, ix, 876). It is a strangely effective simile, but not one that draws on prior experience.

It is tempting to see in this a private joke on the part of a writer who was himself a scholar of our own Middle Ages. Tolkien was certainly grateful that from this "dark" period was rescued *Beowulf*. Would that we had more of the lost lore of the Dark Years of the Second Age of Middle-earth. Surely there were some cracking good tales in those days as well.

But let us return to the Alliance, and lend an ear for the "echo" of this particular "forgotten battle in the Dark Years." In beginning to explore the Alliance tradition and its reverberations, I should like to take a curious point of departure: to consider Gollum's keen ear for story, how it solidifies his role as a knowledgeable historian, and—from a certain point of view—a hero.[7]

GOLLUM THE GREAT

Ironically enough, it is the forthright and recently lettered Sam who first entertains the notion of Gollum as a hero. During a respite in the Gollum-led expedition to Mordor, he and Frodo engage in a reflective discussion on the nature of stories and their own brief cameos in what they call the "Great Tales." As if out of a grudging politeness, the Hobbits' talk shifts to include the third member of their unlikely trio, with Sam quipping, "'I wonder if he thinks he's the hero or the villain?' 'Gollum!' he called. 'Would you like to be the hero—'" (*TT*, IV, 8, 713). Jarred somewhat by their guide's disappearance, Sam's joke is interrupted, and this last invitation never receives formal response.

Scholars of Tolkien's work have often, and with good reason, mined the riches of this exchange before the Stairs of Cirith Ungol, finding in it the invitation to a number of readings. It is surely meta-Tolkien of some weight; the Hobbits' self-referential discourse is music to the postmodernist's ear, and, as

Verlyn Flieger argues in "A Post-Modern Medievalist," it seems to presage if not directly inspire works like John Gardner's *Grendel,* a retelling of *Beowulf* from that moor-stalker's perspective (2012b, 260). It is another opportunity to advance the elaborate conceit of the story's transmission, from the original Red Book of Westmarch, all the way to an Amazon fulfillment center near you;[8] a final tragic reminder of Gollum's agency in the upcoming betrayal of his companions;[9] or perhaps just a bit of Hobbit humor that Tolkien could not bring himself to excise—just a joke.

I should like to advance yet another reading: Like it or not, Gollum *is* the hero, his final act a tacit acceptance to Sam's invitation (he gave no other options, after all). But his accidental heroics are enabled by the old war stories; Gollum, too, is a reader, or a listener, interested in the storytelling art and the way his own tale interacts with others.[10] Foremost among these tales, not only in terms of Gollum's pet interest but for the fate of Middle-earth itself, is that of the Last Alliance. Gollum's last feat of arms (or rather teeth) and unwitting sacrifice bring the Quest to fruition, but the deed echoes and is modeled in the tradition of the shadowy old tales of the Alliance, in which Isildur cuts the Ring from Sauron's hand. If we can entertain the idea that Gollum is our hero, then Isildur is his role model, and the Alliance tradition in whatever form—be it the *Fall of Gil-galad* in its original language or the vague oral traditions of the Stoors—his inspiration. In beginning this inquiry into the overlooked debt owed the Alliance in the War of the Ring, I will first consider Gollum's aptitude for reading generally; then, his knowledge concerning Isildur and the great war of the Second Age specifically; and lastly, his final act at the Cracks of Doom.

While our own ignorance of the ways of Middle-earth is often shared with the more provincial Hobbit-kind, we have less in common with Gollum, who has been around the block (more than once) and is characterized by an extensive knowledge of lore. In this he functions more like an Elrond, Gandalf, or Aragorn; indeed, at times he is a kind of ironic surrogate for the latter two, taking over where they leave off in guiding Sam and Frodo to Mordor. The germ of this is present even in *The Hobbit,* where the narrator's introduction of the creature—"I don't know where he came from, nor who or what he was"—would seem to speak for Tolkien himself (*H,* 68). For though the ring was not yet the One Ring and Gollum not yet the withered old Hobbit-creature once called Sméagol, his mode of sizing up Bilbo is in proposing a riddle game: "riddles were all that he could think of" out of his distant memories of long ago (69). His reaction ("Sssss") to Bilbo's declaration that he wields a sword from Gondolin is likewise suggestive of familiarity with the old tales (69). While Gollum's regrettable intention to violate the sacred rules of the game demonstrates bad form, this does not deny his genuine enjoyment in the riddling itself, nor his plain knack for recitation and impressive storehouse of lore.

Gollum's reverence for riddling (if not for the rules) is further emphasized in *The Lord of the Rings,* placing him in company not only with Bilbo but with lore-masters like Gandalf as well (the wizard is more than once accused of speaking in riddles). In the journey through the Dead Marshes, he not only recalls his "Alive without breath" challenge but expands it, appending some ten extra lines of verse (*TT,* IV, ii, 621). Way back in Bag End, Gandalf cites the riddle challenge as the first piece of evidence for a common ancestral ground between Gollum and Hobbit-kind, a first attempt to soften Frodo's initial repulsion and indignation.

As we might expect of a philologist of Tolkien's caliber, some indication of Gollum's scholastic interests is present in the name Sméagol itself. While Tolkien has in appendix F emphasized its sense of "burrowing, worming in" as in OE *smygel* (*RK,* 1136), scholars have noted the likely derivation from OE *Sméagan* "to inquire, investigate, be curious about." Both senses harmonize beautifully in Gandalf's sketch of a backstory for Gollum in "The Shadow of the Past": The wizard's tale claims that Gollum "wormed his way . . . into the heart of the hills," seeking the cool and shade and "great secrets buried" under the Mountains (*FR,* I, ii, 54). Although largely consumed by his desire for the Ring, he recalls still the pleasure of exchanging stories: "tales from the South" in his youth—"O yes, we used to tell lots of tales . . . by the banks of the Great River" (*TT,* IV, iii, 641). Setting aside his loathing for an instant, Sam at least recognizes a shared affinity with his unlikely tour guide: "he used to like tales himself once, by his own account" (*TT,* IV, viii, 713). This much is reaffirmed by Gandalf, whose brief biography of Sméagol characterizes him as "inquisitive and curious minded"; his research interests are "in roots and beginnings" (*FR,* I, ii, 53). While he had no access to the libraries of Rivendell or Gondor, the matriarch of his community was "wise in old lore, such as they had" (53). Even if written lore is beyond his means, he can learn much from the hearing and telling of oral history. His healthy appetite for stories, coupled with advanced age and furtive travel, all help to account for his accumulation of lore.

Once in possession of the Ring, Gollum's inquiries turn almost exclusively toward mischievous ends, but his "sharp" ears and aptitude for "listening secretly and peering" remain well suited to gaining knowledge of all sorts (*FR,* I, ii, 57). He is no mere passive receiver and gatherer of knowledge either, but an important voice of transmission—a medium through which the stories live on. His knowledge is a prized commodity on both sides of the conflict, and he is handled ungently, if not tortured, by Gandalf and Strider as well as Sauron.

When Frodo subdues Gollum in the Emyn Muil, his threat and brandished blade harken back to a fairy tale they know all too well—*The Hobbit:* "This is Sting. You have seen it before once upon a time" (*TT*, IV, i, 614).

That Gollum is versed in both canon and apocrypha of the Last Alliance there can be little doubt. Most tellingly, Sauron himself only discovers "where Isildur fell" through torturing Gollum; this lowly creature possesses exclusive knowledge, and in many ways surpasses even the wisest in Ring-lore (*FR*, I, ii, 59). The breadth of his grandmother's knowledge is perhaps dubious, but the proximity of their ancestral Stoor community to the Gladden Fields, the site of Isildur's disappearance, strengthens the case. It is not then implausible that her area of expertise would concern the folklore surrounding this greatest of local legends. Gollum recalls fondly the "wonderful tales" of the South: "O yes, there were many tales about the Tower of the Moon" (*TT*, IV, iii, 641).

Like others of Hobbit-kind, he shows a particularly keen interest in the bloodier tales out of the past.[11] Guiding Frodo and Sam through the Dead Marshes, which have swallowed up one of the key battlegrounds of the old war, he reminisces on the memorable oral traditions of "a great battle long ago, yes. . . . Tall men with long swords, and terrible Elves, and Orcses shrieking. They fought on the plain for days and months at the Black Gates" (*TT*, IV, ii, 628). While these musings suggest beyond doubt a familiarity with stories of Isildur and accounts of the great war, they appear generic and sparse in detail.

However, Gollum's knowledge of more specific evidence, including the crucial detail of Isildur's stroke, is revealed in an exchange as the Hobbits draw near to Minas Morgul. "Yes," he says, confirming Frodo's recollection that it was Isildur who cut the Ring (and a finger) from Sauron's hand, "He has only four on the Black Hand, but they are enough" (*TT*, IV, iii, 641).[12] Of all the many epithets used to name (or avoid naming) Sauron, this one is employed seldom, and only by Gollum (*TT*, IV, iii, 638). Not only does he know the story, he has seen its outcome—seen Sauron, spoken to him, perhaps even felt the dread touch of the Black Hand. It must have been an audience rare and terrible indeed, and one that Tolkien is careful to keep largely offscreen. As for Gollum's use of the epithet, certainly his unrelenting lust for the Ring might go some way toward explaining this semiotic choice, equating Sauron with that part of him that wields the Ring. But it might also, in some corner of his mind, bring comfort and hope. It grounds Sauron to a more tangible form (more concrete than a Shadow, a Nameless fear, or an all-seeing Eye), and though it is an undoubtedly menacing Hand, its fingers can be cut, as history and legend teach.[13]

Elements of the Alliance narrative seem to be present in the uneasy bargain struck (presumably with much dissembling on both sides) between Gollum and Sauron after this interrogation. Gandalf reasons that Gollum is set free "on some errand of mischief," and Strider corroborates this, believing it to be "some evil errand" (*FR,* I, ii, 59; *FR,* II, ii, 255). This is later confirmed by the Orcs whom Sam overhears outside Cirith Ungol: "He's been here before. Came *out* of Lugbúrz . . . and we had word from High Up to let him pass" (*TT,* IV, x, 738). Gollum, having made his fateful promise by the precious, fears that Sauron will get wind of the vow, which runs plainly "against His orders" (*TT,* IV, ii, 633). It may be that a curious connection is formed between the two, and that Sauron seeks to exploit some strain of empathy and shared grievance in telling his "side" of the story; Gollum might like a story about getting revenge on a thief. Such a spin would certainly speak to his own enmity for the Baggins clan, and might presumably stir him to a frenzy, which may ultimately help Sauron recover his Ring in time. Gandalf suggests as much in recalling his own wearisome encounter with Gollum: "Some other fear was on him greater than mine. . . . People would see if he would stand being . . . *robbed.* Gollum had good friends now" (*FR,* I, ii, 57). Despite this animosity toward the Baggins family—and any "orders" he has been charged with—ultimately Gollum appears to reject association with Sauron, embracing more of the Alliance side of the story and the Isildur role in particular.

Indeed, in ancillary material like "The Hunt for the Ring," Gollum is charmingly said to view Sauron as "his greatest enemy and rival" (*UT,* 322). There is little indication to the contrary in *The Lord of the Rings:* he promises "not to let Him have it—never" (*TT,* IV, ii, 632–33). Engaged in one of his inner debates, he reckons that ownership of the Ring will make him "stronger than Wraiths. Lord Sméagol? Gollum the Great? *The* Gollum! Eat fish every day" (633). Fish dinners aside, Gollum's ring delusions do not differ greatly from those "wild fantasies" that Sam receives during his brief tenure as Ring-bearer: "striding with a flaming sword . . . as he marched to the overthrow of Barad-dûr" (*RK,* VI, I, 901). It does not take much to see the image of Boromir in this vision, and behind him, maybe, an Isildur.

The nebulous and generally unsatisfactory accounts of the last combat in the Alliance render direct comparison of the Second and Third Age Ring-reavings impossible; nevertheless, some compelling similarities can be teased out.[14] Perhaps the most reliable, if not the most detailed, account of "the last combat on the slopes of Orodruin" comes from Elrond, who describes the event from memory at his Council: "Gil-galad died, and Elendil fell, and Narsil broke beneath him; but Sauron himself was overthrown, and Isildur cut the Ring from his hand with the hilt-shard of his father's sword, and took it for his own" (*FR,* II, ii, 243).

A few yards and an age of history removed, it is Sam who bears witness to the decisive conflict of his time.[15] At the Cracks of Doom, he sees Gollum struggling with the invisible Frodo, before his "fangs gleamed, and then snapped as they bit" (*RK*, VI, iii, 946). The gleam here might suggest the flash of a blade. That Gollum's chompers in one age pale in comparison to Narsil, legendary sword from Telchar's forge in the other, would not be lost on the chroniclers who have spent much of their art in describing the long and slow, but inexorable decline of enchantment in Middle-earth.

Nor is this the only instance in Tolkien's work associating tooth and sword; recall Smaug's rather blunt boast: "my teeth are swords" (*H*, 213). The poetic bite of a blade is often favored by Tolkien. Farmer Giles wields a blade called Tailbiter; while "the bite of swords / is cruel and cold," remarks Tídwald, knowingly, in *The Homecoming of Beorhtnoth* (5). In *The Hobbit* the goblins recall Biter, a storied blade from Gondolin; while Gimli, musing on the efficacy of an army of the Dead, wonders if their swords "would still bite" (*RK*, VI, ix, 876). Whether Gollum's fangs broke or merely "snapped" shut, faint echoes of Narsil, broken under Elendil, its hilt-shard enough for Isildur to reap his *weregild*, may be heard.

That this moment is described from Sam's point of view (a lover of tales in his own right) certainly supports Gergely Nagy's theory of typological readings;[16] the storytellers and redactors, starting from the Hobbit authors of the Red Book, may have chosen to cast the scene with a nod to the older legends. Sam additionally gestures toward this idea as he prepares to jettison his gear for the final push up Mount Doom but fears lest certain items should fall into Gollum's hands: "he isn't going to add a sword to it. His hands are bad enough when empty" (*RK*, VI, iii, 938). But, at any rate, Gollum's own interests and background in lore encourage us also to consider the eerie historical echoes in his tactic as a borrowing from the secret annals of military history.[17]

Fittingly it is Frodo who offers the highest praise and most moving eulogy for Gollum: "But for him . . . The Quest would have been in vain, even at the bitter end" (*RK*, VI, iii, 947). Thus Gandalf's prediction that Gollum would yet have a part to play comes off. And, perhaps more importantly, his ambiguous assertion made in Bag End at the beginning of the story, that the Alliance is a "chapter of ancient history which it might be good to recall," proves truer than even he could have guessed (*FR*, I, ii, 52). And so, rather than waving a dismissive "goodbye to all that,"[18] Tolkien asserts that the shadow of the past is worth remembering.

THE FOG OF WAR

Although there is, as Gollum demonstrates, much to be gained by such remembrance, it does not come easy. Inquiry into what Gollum knows and how he acts on that information draws us inevitably to consider what others know (or think they know) and what happened in the first place—questions not readily addressed by Tolkien's web of allusions. That Tolkien's untold tales seem to find purest expression in the context of war may be worth further consideration.

There are a few explanations for this special association of war with unstory. For one, the war story needs a witness, a survivor, and this may, in the thick of battle, prove difficult.[19] To tell it "true," of course, the teller struggles with the polarized inclination to romanticize or deromanticize (dramatized in the voices of Totta and Tída in *The Homecoming of Beorhtnoth*, discussed in chapter 4), whether actually present (Elrond), not present (Totta and Tída again), or unconscious (Bilbo). Even eyewitnesses may find themselves tongue-tied, like those wanderers in Faërie described in "On Fairy-stories," unwilling or unable to tell the tale.[20] The overwhelming, the sublime, the ineffable experience of war is well suited to the ultimate understatement of an untold tale.

Given the practical constraints on the dissemination of old war stories, Gollum's knowledge of these events becomes all the more impressive. When measured against peers, elders, and betters, it is often they who come up wanting. Boromir, for instance, is said to care little for ordinary lore, though he does at least cultivate a taste for "the tales of old battles" (*RK*, appendix A, 1056).[21] This interest notwithstanding, the heir to the Steward of Gondor is shocked enough to interrupt Elrond's account. He breaks in: "So that is what became of the Ring! . . . If ever such a tale was told in the South, it has long been forgotten. . . . Isildur took it!" (*FR*, II, ii, 243). Faramir, the younger and more widely read brother, fares somewhat better. He recalls Gandalf's frequent questions about "the Great Battle . . . upon Dagorlad" and his eagerness "for stories of Isildur, though of him we had less to tell" (*TT*, IV, v, 671). In spite of the uncertainty, Faramir's hypothesis concerning Isildur's Bane is not far from the mark: "that Isildur took somewhat from the hand of the Unnamed" (671). Sam, meanwhile, studied lore under Bilbo, and heard snatches of his translation of *The Fall of Gil-galad*, but though there is "a lot more" to it, he can only clearly recall three short stanzas (*FR*, I, xi, 186).

It is, we might say, Tolkien's Ur-war story, a shadowy measuring stick against which the battles of the immediate narrative are sized. And, like many good war stories, much is left to our imaginations. While we are assured of the tale's importance at every turn, no one seems keen to spill the beans.

Gandalf sets a precedent for a lack of transparency and a preoccupation with the tale's implications. In effect he at once declares that he will not tell the story, but that it ought to be kept in mind anyway. Others follow his example, so that, were it not so deadly serious, it might be seen as a running joke. The wizard's cautious analysis precedes any actual account of the war; he deems it "good to recall; for there was sorrow then too, and gathering dark, but great valour, and great deeds that were not wholly vain" (*FR*, I, ii, 52). His hedging and equivocation suggest a reluctance to offer final judgment on the events. This hazy assertion of importance, taken together with his Virgilian excuse of it being such a "long" tale that, were he to attempt a full telling, "we should still be sitting here when Spring had passed into Winter" and his placating (but false) assurance—"One day, perhaps, I will tell you all the tale, or you shall hear it told in full by one who knows it best"—present a Middle-earth equivalent of the teacher including uncovered material on the final exam (*FR*, I, ii, 51–52). The few crumbs he does let slip grant stirring glimpses of a bygone heroic age: "It was Gil-galad, Elven-king and Elendil of Westernesse who overthrew Sauron, though they themselves perished in the deed; and Isildur Elendil's son cut the Ring from Sauron's hand and took it for his own. Then Sauron was vanquished" (52).[22] The value Gandalf places on the story here likely stems from its hints of inspiring heroism rather than any special tactical revelations. While frustrating to readers, it reflects an understanding of his audience within the text; Frodo is no general or politician who might benefit from lessons of diplomacy or battlefield movements. Realization of his predicament and burden overwhelm him, the shadow of the past towers over his once comfortable Hobbit hole. Gandalf, by his précis, seeks to encourage him, to remind him that there is historical precedent for Sauron's defeat.

We have the distinct feeling of missing a step, as the lore-masters continue to sidestep the tale itself, focusing instead on the lessons to be gleaned from it, or on secondary concerns of propriety and timeliness. While Gandalf at least regards the story as one to remember, others are more skeptical of its value, and it is in part for this reason that hope of a fuller account is repeatedly dashed. After the wizard's introduction, Strider takes up the desultory narrative on encountering the Hobbits at *The Prancing Pony*. The Ranger, too, is a respectable historian, his memory a repository of old tales—he strikes the Hobbits as learned in old lore and they wonder "how old he was, and where he had learned" it all (*FR*, I, xi, 191). Later he reminds them that Elendil's heirs "do not forget all things past," and we can well imagine that, along with the shards of Narsil, many lessons are handed down (*FR*, I, xii, 201). Like Gandalf, Strider is often tight-lipped, preferring laconic suggestion to elaboration:

Before hiring him on to join the expedition, Frodo asks him what he knows. His grim reply is telling: "Too much; too many dark things" (*FR*, I, x, 163).

Strider strikes a delicate balance in his storytelling practices while leading the Hobbits toward Rivendell. When pressed to reveal more of Gil-galad and the Alliance, he balks, arguing that the tale should not be told "with the servants of the Enemy at hand" (*FR*, I, xi, 191). He then takes Gandalf's dubious offer of a later telling one step further, dangling the tale as a reward for reaching Rivendell, should fortune and courage hold—"If we win through . . . you may hear it there, told in full" (191). Sam's visceral response to parts of the Gil-galad lay—"There was a lot more . . . all about Mordor. I didn't learn that part, it gave me the shivers"—suggests that Strider's taboo may be wholly justified (186). Yet both the Hobbits and their guide at least intuit a palliative (if not greater) potential in stories. Dreading the arrival of the Riders, Aragorn relies on his storehouse of tales to "keep their minds from fear," and they, in turn, "begged" for more (190). With even the name of Mordor off limits, he settles instead on another, even more ancient tale, that of Tinúviel.

Frustrated in his attempts to have *The Silmarillion* published alongside *The Lord of the Rings*, Tolkien thus manages to get a small fraction of his wider mythology into print. But it is not a mere egoistic digression: Strider's telling of the story takes on added poignance when set against his own ordeal to win the hand of an Elf King's daughter (Arwen). But there is this about it, too: Strider, perhaps knowingly, has chosen another tale of a man wresting from a Dark Lord's grasp a treasure he values above all else—and using Telchar-forged hardware to boot: Angrist, the dagger Beren uses to cut a Silmaril from Morgoth's crown, like Narsil, was forged by that legendary smith. These parallels would be lost neither on Strider nor on Tolkien.

At any rate, while Strider's "brief" treatment of Tinúviel is yet more thorough than any accounts of the Alliance, it, too, is preceded by a sort of prefatory assessment: "It is a fair tale, though it is sad . . . and yet it may lift up your hearts," a concise description indeed applicable to much of Tolkien's work (191). Strider's role as storyteller brings us no closer to a clear picture of the Alliance, but his provocative silence further complicates the questions of value and interpretation.

Though the Hobbits do ultimately win through to the Last Homely House, a thorough account is, unfortunately (but unsurprisingly), not forthcoming from Elrond. This is all the more frustrating as it becomes plain that the Elf lord is the referent in Gandalf's "one who knows it best." Elrond is no mere scholar dabbling in the archives—he was *there*, the last veteran of the Alliance. He reminisces before a captive audience and a dumbfounded Frodo:

"I remember well the splendour of their banners" (*FR*, II, ii, 243). His terse and disappointing recapitulation begins, like the others, with commentary on what to make of the Alliance. A veteran of many wars,[23] Elrond is initially dismissive, counting it one among the "many fruitless victories" he has witnessed (243). A brief overview then follows, with his own role as witness and testimony emphasized: "I was the herald of Gil-galad. . . . I was at the Battle of Dagorlad . . . where we had the mastery: for the Spear of Gil-galad and the Sword of Elendil, Aiglos and Narsil, none could withstand. I beheld the last combat . . . where Gil-galad died, and Elendil fell, and Narsil broke beneath him; but Sauron himself was overthrown, and Isildur cut the Ring from his hand with the hilt-shard of his father's sword" (243). These striking but brief reminiscences are immediately followed by a partially revised assessment, more in line with Gandalf's initial reading: it was "not wholly" fruitless, though "it did not achieve its end" (244). Though Elrond remains cautious in his review, the shift is nonetheless significant. But why the sudden change of heart? It could be that, as in Gandalf's place in Bag End, he feels that those attending the Council are in need of some encouragement, a glimmer of hope. Or perhaps his heart is stirred by calling to mind once more his firsthand recollection of "the mastery" of Gil-galad and Elendil, of the "Spear" and "Sword" that "none could withstand," and of "Sauron himself . . . overthrown" (243).

But as Gollum's interest has indicated, this tale does not belong exclusively to the traditional lore-masters of the West. Indeed, while we have only the faintest of glimpses to work with, it seems clear that a very different version of the story is told by the Orcs. In his later writing, Tolkien wrestled with questions moral and metaphysical regarding the origin and nature of the Orcs, whose status as cannon fodder became increasingly untenable in his sub-creation.[24] But even from early days they were storytellers, as in *The Lay of Leithian*, when they recall the single combat between Morgoth and Fingolfin: "Yet orcs would after laughing tell / of the duel at the gates of hell" (*LB*, 285–86). Something of that tradition remains in the Third Age, as they troll prisoners with stories of the good times to be had in the Dark Tower, or "lovely Lugbúrz" as they call it: "We can tell him a few stories at any rate" (*TT*, IV, x, 741). As in the case of Gollum, the Orcs' taste for story—while perhaps different in kind from our own—is one possible hallmark of their sentience, their humanity.

It also happens to engage with the Alliance matter in occasionally revelatory ways. When he and Merry are held captive by a motley band of Orcs with varying agendas, Pippin, in a moment of rash inspiration, baits their captor, Grishnákh, by alluding to what little he knows of the Ring's history. Once Pippin is sure that the Orc knows of—and may naturally covet—the Ring, he works to exploit this desire. A bizarre conversation unfolds, full of *gollum* noises and oblique assurances, but it is enough to get their captor's attention: "'Do I want it?' said Grishnákh, as if puzzled; but his arms were trembling" (*TT,* III, iii, 455). The Hobbits are saved more by a timely arrow than by Pippin's skill in spinning yarns about the One Ring, but the gamble serves to illustrate more than Tookish resourcefulness. We learn that Grishnákh is conniving and quite independent—with private dreams of his own—by his shared knowledge of the Ring's history and its former keeper.[25] The exchange demonstrates that Orcs are more than mindless automatons—and Middle-earth is richer and more alive because of it.

Much later, the exchange Sam overhears between Gorbag and Shagrat reveals a side of Orcs almost tender in its downtrodden pessimism—but it does so by calling on what appears to be an Orcish tradition of the War of the Alliance tales:

"No one has ever stuck a pin in Shelob before. . . . there's someone loose hereabouts as is more dangerous than any other damned rebel that ever walked since the bad old times, since the Great Siege. . . .

"Ah well, you always did take a gloomy view." (*TT,* IV, x, 739)

"Great Siege" here can only refer to the seven-year Siege of Barad-dûr, culminating in the last combat wherein Sauron is vanquished and his ring cut loose. There is a sense that the Orcs are singing the blues of the "bad old times," drawing on the "Great Siege" for their bogeymen, the monstrous Men and Elves of their nightmares.

A tale—untold or no—of such magnitude transcends a Free Folk vs. Orcs dichotomy. Other, older figures remark on the Alliance and its legacy. The two oldest sentient beings in Middle-earth, Treebeard and Tom Bombadil,[26] engage with the tale in surprising ways, ultimately suggesting that it is a story about more than just pitched battle.

Fittingly, Treebeard alludes to the Alliance tale almost casually, in the midst of another digression, one likely nearer his heart, on the separation of the Ents and Entwives—an untold tale worthy of its own chapter. The Ent recalls for Merry and Pippin his fruitless search for the shepherdesses: during "the war between Sauron and the Men of the Sea. . . . We crossed over Anduin and came to their land: but we found a desert: it was all burned and uprooted, for war had passed over it" (*TT,* III, iv, 476). Treebeard's reminiscence is intriguing for several reasons. Firstly, there is the implication that even Ents might make use of the wars of Men and Elves in their ordering of history. It is possible that the reference is offered as a courtesy—though likely of little use to Merry and none to Pippin—to the hasty folk with which he converses, but it is nonetheless noteworthy.

Furthermore, Treebeard's recollection of "the Men of the Sea" as the chief faction in the war is quite unusual. The epithet recalls something of the vast history (and Treebeard's knowledge thereof) behind the men of Westernesse: their forefather Eärendil the Mariner, their ancestral homeland and its eventual downfall, drowned in the Sea.[27] The absence of the named leaders (Elendil and Gil-galad) and the more typical "alliance of Elves and Men" or "Men of the West" is enough of a departure that many readers would be forgiven for assuming that Treebeard recalls not the Last Alliance here but merely some other war out of the distant past.

But it is indeed the Alliance that Treebeard recalls, though we can only confirm it by looking elsewhere:[28] first at the Company's journey down Anduin in "The Great River," where the environmental story of the Brown Lands—the former gardens of the Entwives—begins. The travelers can only guess what had caused the wasteland they see before them: "What pestilence or war or evil deed of the Enemy had so blasted all that region even Aragorn could not tell" (*FR*, II, ix, 380).[29] While this wanton degradation is associated with Sauron, Treebeard surely knows also that the Men of the Sea were historically great shipbuilders, and indeed it is hard to imagine that Treebeard would have sympathies for the Númenórean timber industry of the Second Age. Elsewhere, in *Unfinished Tales,* we learn that they "became ruthless in their fellings, giving no thought to husbandry or replanting"—not wholly dissimilar to the "orc-work, the wanton hewing" taking place at the time of our story (*UT,* 252; *TT,* III, iv, 485).

And so one wonders: Why does Treebeard single out the Men of the Sea as the chief antagonists in the war against Sauron? Might the devastation wrought on the peoples and lands of Middle-earth have been so great that Treebeard would, charitably, not wish to attribute any great role to the Elves who woke up the Ents long ago? Is this an uncharacteristically hasty slip of the tongue, eliding the equal role traditionally set for the Elves under Gil-galad? Does this phrasing somehow accentuate their role in the great deeds of those times, celebrating Isildur's decisive cut with the hilt-shard of his father's sword? Or might it in fact censure his subsequent taking of the Ring, the failure to make this victory last, to be a war to end all wars? Is it simply a quick and dirty version for two Hobbits unlikely to grasp the import of any such subtleties of history? Perhaps in his wisdom Treebeard already sees in the Last Alliance the first steps toward the world of Men without Elves.

Later, when the Ents have held their moot and decided to march on Isen-gard, Treebeard notes ancient precedent for the apparently mercurial change in temperament; it "has not happened in this Forest since the wars of Sauron and the Men of the Sea" (*TT*, III, iv, 485). No extant tale, it seems, tells more of this Second Age march of the Ents, but it may be that these brief reminis-cences on the Alliance tradition have helped spur them to their present course toward the flooding of Isengard and the downfall of Saruman.[30] Gandalf, too, recalls a distant precedent for their uprising: such an event "has not happened since the Elder Days" (*TT*, III, v, 500). And an almost fey Treebeard declares, "Now at least the last march of the Ents may be worth a song" (*TT*, III, iv, 486). As he does so, he seems to recall another aspect of the Alliance legacy, its spirit of shared sacrifice and unified purpose, recalling the days when "all living things were divided" in the struggle against Sauron—presumably the Ents, too (*S*, 294).

In this way, Treebeard's final comment to the Hobbits on his grief over the lost Entwives is especially telling: "But there, my friends, songs like trees bear fruit only in their own time and their own way: and sometimes they are withered untimely" (486). Of the Entwives' fate, nothing is known for cer-tain. But, as Treebeard, Gollum, and others have shown, the Alliance stories have nonetheless borne many curious fruits.

Not to be outdone, Middle-earth's other eldest denizen, Tom Bombadil, touches on the Alliance legacy while rescuing the Hobbits from the Barrows and guiding them on toward Bree. Tom's engagement with this untold story offers a unique blend of pathos and sense of a vanished past. Like Treebeard, Bombadil does not focus on the climactic contest on the slopes of Orodruin, nor even the Battle of Dagorlad. Instead, he provides context on the legacy of the war on the lands bordering his own small country,[31] offering one of the narrative's few windows into the long, slow decline of the realm of Arnor, Gondor's northern sister. It is a coda to the Alliance tale, and the first presag-ing of the returning king in Aragorn.

Tolkien himself called Bombadil an enigma, and as such it is unsurprising that this short episode leaves us with many tantalizing questions (*Letters*, 174). The clues and lessons gleaned from Bombadil are not prompted by queries from the Hobbits (who likely know nothing at all of this history, and, at this early juncture, may care even less), but from the environment they traverse and the artifacts they encounter.

The Hobbits learn of the Barrow downs and their relation to the North kingdom first through the mesmerizing tales told in Tom's house. Seemingly entranced by the spell of his words and the scope of his thought and memory, they glimpse as if in time-lapse photography: "Kings . . . and . . . their . . . greedy swords. . . . towers fell, fortresses were burned, and flames went up into the sky. Gold was piled on the biers . . . ; and mounds covered them . . . and the grass grew over all. Sheep walked for a while. . . . A shadow came . . . and the bones were stirred in the mounds. Barrow-wights walked in the hollow places. . . . Stone rings grinned out of the ground like broken teeth in the moonlight" (*FR*, I, vii, 130). With horror, the Hobbits are reminded of "the rumour" of the Wights, unwelcome even as "fireside" tales in the Shire. That fear is now heightened, as they find themselves in a house "nestled under the very shoulder" of the hills, and the Hobbits soon lose track of Tom's story.

Even for the lore-masters, the histories prove challenging, so it is unsurprising that the Hobbits soon forget what they have learned in Tom's house and become entangled in the Barrows after dark. Luckily, Frodo does not forget Tom's rescue rhyme, at least, and, once summoned, the old Master delivers them from the wight's spells. Tom's selections from the Barrow hoard prove to be of practical value, and the names and details he drops offer a bare-bones sketch of the decline of the Dúnedain in the North. He gives the Hobbits daggers of "marvellous workmanship." "Then he told them that these blades were forged many long years ago by Men of Westernesse: they were foes of the Dark Lord, but they were overcome by the evil king of Carn Dûm in the Land of Angmar" (*FR*, I, viii, 145–46). Tom is setting us up to see the pale king of Angmar unmasked atop Weathertop, for the first time filling in some sense of backstory to the hooded menace of the Black Riders. Later he again taps a balance between pathos in personal remembrance and a glimpse of the vanished past in guiding the Hobbits through historic landscapes. The "dark line" they see "had once been the boundary of a kingdom," about which Tom "seemed to remember something sad . . . and would not say much" (146–47).

In his foreshadowing of Aragorn's coming shortly before the Hobbits meet him in *The Prancing Pony,* Bombadil offers an enchanting glimpse of the "heart-wracking sense of the vanished past" so intimately tied to untold tales. The Hobbits do not fully grasp his murmurings of "sons of forgotten kings walking in loneliness," but as Tom speaks, they receive "a vision . . . of a great expanse of years behind them, like a vast shadowy plain over which there strode shapes of Men, tall and grim with bright swords, and last came one with a star on his brow" (146). This glimpse is the first gentle indication to the Hobbits that their safety and oblivious comfort is dearly bought by the tireless work of the Rangers and their allies.[32] They are waking from a dream; these untold tales begin to instruct them as to just how little they know.

The glimpses of the Alliance history and legacy afforded by Tom and Treebeard give us something different from martial heroics. Their brief allusions allow the reader to survey a vast expanse of time and to consider the wages of war on the land and its people. They become linked to other stories, other legends: of Entwives, Barrow-wights, and islands buried beneath the sea.

SCROLL, CHAPTER, AND VERSE

It seems clear that this variety in treatment detailed above does not come only from the subtleties of a speaker's style or small point of emphasis; these discrepancies point instead to wholly different traditions, different branches from a larger tree of tales—if not entirely different trees.[33] Tolkien further complicates the situation by muddying the textual waters of the Alliance tradition. Interpretation of history's successes and failures—separating great deeds from fruitless vanity—is evidently a challenge even for the Wise and naturally hinges on certain textual considerations. A difference of opinion between scholars on the war's takeaways would certainly be plausible in its own right, but when we consider the possibility that our heroes might be relying on different editions, another layer of complexity is added.

Indeed, this framework is developed even before Gandalf begins to offer the first crumbs of the tale to Frodo in "The Shadow of the Past." Elendil is mentioned twice in the prologue to the text. The first is in passing, offering a legendary measure of time in discussion of the provenance of pipe-weed, which traveled along the Greenway in the "centuries between the coming of Elendil and our own day" (*FR*, 9). The second reference is in regard to the Shire Records and the textual history of these legends, noting that at Great Smials could be found "copies or summaries of histories or legends relating to Elendil" and his descendants (15). Readers might be forgiven for overlooking such references, but I contend that they are nonetheless significant: they include and privilege the legends of the Last Alliance in the metafictional framework of the text, thus both asserting the importance of such legends and, achingly, foreshadowing their ultimate position being somewhere out of reach.

Returning to the question of Alliance textual history within the story proper, Gandalf, of course, alludes to the tale as a "chapter of ancient history" but does not specify author, title, or ISBN. Given his close relationship with Elrond, and the ways in which the language of their separate accounts is similar, we might assume that Gandalf's version is at least in part derived from Elrond's. On the other hand, the wizard's extensive research outside of Rivendell—his visits to Gondor's libraries and discovery of Isildur's scroll come to mind—suggests that Gandalf has other sources, perhaps then accounting for the variance in their views.

An additional branch of the tale's complex textual situation emerges during Strider's lectures to the Hobbits on the history of Weathertop.[34] The lay that Sam begins to chant is privileged with a proper italicized title, *The Fall of Gil-galad,* suggestive of a more formal, physical manuscript history. Sam, of course, is mistaken about the poem's origins; Strider assures him that, learned as Bilbo may be, "he did not make it up." Instead, he "must have translated" *The Fall* from its original, which Strider notes is in an "ancient tongue," though he does not specify which (*FR,* I, xi, 186). Thus we are led to consider also the vexing issue of translation and the potential excesses, errors, flourishes, and arbitrations on the part of the translator.[35] While we glimpse only three stanzas of Bilbo's effort, the title alone is telling; its apparent emphasis on Gil-galad's defeat over other more positive elements (the league between Men and Elves, the victory on Dagorlad, the Ring-winning, and so on) points toward a potentially epic but surely tragic poem, which, given the situation on Weathertop, it might in fact be better to forget than recall.[36] Strider offers little more to go on, but surely having been fostered in Rivendell he is likely to be familiar with Elrond's version of events. As the heir of Elendil and bearer of Narsil, the great heirloom of his house, he is personally invested in the story and its origins, and his service in Rohan and Gondor and legendary periods of errantry may have provided seasoning for his own bowl of Alliance soup, to borrow from Tolkien's Cauldron of Story metaphor in "On Fairy-stories."[37]

The subject of the story's written records is again raised at the Council, when (quoted and discussed in regard to Celebrimbor in the previous chapter) the narrator bizarrely cites these texts as rationale not to bore us with the whole of Elrond's story. Elrond's "clear voice" is undoubtedly a pleasure for those at the Council, but for readers it rings the death knell for our hope of hearing the fuller account of the tale promised us. We are pulled from the immediacy of recorded dialogue, and instead get something of the terse and remote summary characteristic of the published *Silmarillion.*[38] In spite of the story's apparently meticulous documentation, it remains out of reach.

All of this reflective talk of texts and traditions might naturally lead us to believe that, outside the covers of *The Lord of the Rings* at least, much more can be discovered of the heroic deeds that punctuate the Second Age. At this point I wish to reiterate a point of difference outlined in the early portion of this chapter. The Alliance material, despite its careful crafting and tremendous impact on the text, remains apart from the more "verifiable" untold tales. Of the tales of Túrin or Tinúviel, the 1977 *Silmarillion* gives at least a taste, while the *History of Middle-earth* offers a heartier portion; for more on Arwen and Aragorn, we have only to turn to the appendices. But there remains little such recourse for those readers eager for a robust account of the Battle of Dagorlad, the Siege of Barad-dûr, or the last combat on Orodruin.

Now, if posthumous publication by a literary executor is not a perfect measure of authorial intent and vision,[39] then, by the same token, the surprising dearth of resources on the Last Alliance is not a definitive statement of Tolkien's insistence on leaving the tale forever untold. Nevertheless, the scraps that we do have available seem to strengthen the case that Tolkien was content to write *around* these events and preserve the powerful aroma of untold tales at their center.

The appendices avail us little in an attempt to engage with the Alliance tale more deeply; the time line offered in "The Tale of Years" makes Elrond's account appear elaborate in comparison. The last three entries for the Second Age are barebones:

> 3434 Battle of Dagorlad and defeat of Sauron. Siege of Barad-dûr begins.
> 3440 Anárion slain.
> 3441 Sauron overthrown by Elendil and Gil-galad, who perish. Isildur takes the One Ring. Sauron passes away (*RK,* appendix B, 1084)

The revelation that the Siege of Barad-dûr took place over seven years seems only to exacerbate frustrations about knowing so little. Questions linger, even if we confine ourselves to the mysterious last combat: Why does the fighting shift to the slopes of Mount Doom? How does it become almost a duel between the Alliance leaders and Sauron? Why, if Gil-galad brings Elendil (and Elendil, Isildur), does Sauron have no second with him? What was the nature of Gil-galad's wound?[40] Does Isildur strike the decisive blow or merely despoil Sauron's body in the aftermath?

For this last query we may refer to Isildur's words in *The Silmarillion* for an indication: "This I will have as weregild for my father's death, and my brother's.[41] Was it not I that dealt the enemy his death-blow?" (295). Yet without a straightforward account of the battle to corroborate his statement, it remains somewhat suspect; we could certainly point to examples of bent truths, equivocations, and outright lies told in service of laying claim to the Ring (both Bilbo and Gollum are notably guilty of this). It would seem, anyway, that Aragorn is convinced of his feat, else why, under the doubtful gaze of Boromir at their first meeting, refer to himself as "but the heir of Isildur, not Isildur himself" (*FR*, II, ii, 248)?[42]

While I do not wish to stray too far from the focus on the Alliance's treatment, dissemination, and impact within the covers of *The Lord of the Rings*, "The Disaster of the Gladden Fields" material (mentioned above) casts further light on Tolkien's continued preoccupation with the great war of the Second Age, one that seems not to have diminished over time: Christopher Tolkien's introduction calls "Gladden Fields" a "'late' narrative . . . it belongs in the final period of my father's writing on Middle-earth" (*UT*, 11). The final section of this chapter is titled "The sources of the legend of Isildur's death," and it is chiefly concerned with the story's transmission: establishing "eye-witnesses," naming the "escaped" survivors, and weighing hearsay against "surmise . . . well-founded" (*UT*, 263–64). Its conclusion bears all the hallmarks of Tolkien's preferred literary device. On discovery of the Elendilmir in the treasure hoard of Orthanc, the narrator muses: "Why . . . were there no traces of his bones? Had Saruman found them, and scorned them—burned them with dishonour in one of his furnaces? If that were so, it was a shameful deed" (*UT*, 265). It seems fitting that the last word on Isildur would be one of ambiguity and mystery, his missing bones almost a reflection of the great lacunae that elide so much of the heroic chapter of the Alliance.

FRAGMENTS SHORED AGAINST RUIN

It is easy to become entangled in this web of half-stories and glimpsed traditions, dusty old manuscripts and firsthand accounts cut short; indeed, Tolkien fully acknowledges the powerful allure of such an endeavor in "On Fairy-stories," what he calls "the fascination of the desire to unravel the intricately knotted and ramified history of the branches on the Tree of Tales" (*MC*, 12). But Tolkien also recognized that this search for origins risked obscuring—or sterilizing—the stories themselves. The emphasis Tolkien places on present value in his essay goes for the Last Alliance as well; it is the story's use now that matters, more even than its definition or roots. The extant threads of the Alliance tale may ultimately be impossible to untangle—soup and bones inseparable—but its applications are unmistakable; Gollum is not the only character whose acts reflect the story's lasting relevance. Take Strider, for instance.

It is in a way fitting that Strider first encounters Gollum near the Dead Marshes, the haunting but fertile landscape of story that proves so important to them both. Not only does the Alliance tale assert its significance in

Strider's tactical decisions and travel plans during the War of the Ring, it also exerts a more fantastic influence in his ability to summon the very specters of characters on the fringes of the tale. In his haste to reach Gondor under siege, Strider treads a path and enlists the help of a people kept alive only in the old stories. The opportunity to travel "the swiftest way" east and muster such formidable support relies on Aragorn's application of Alliance lore (*RK,* V, ii, 779). It is Elrohir who jogs his memory, bringing counsel from Elrond: "*If thou art in haste, remember the Paths of the Dead*" (775). The advice is not to take, seek, tread, or walk—but first *remember.* Théoden's skepticism—"If there be in truth such paths," he doubts—likely speaks for many, but Aragorn can take solace in his education (779). He demonstrates this deep well of knowledge in reciting the words of Malbeth the Seer and then kindly quoting from Isildur's curse on the Oathbreakers for his friends: "this curse I lay upon thee and thy folk: to rest never until your oath is fulfilled. For this war will last through years uncounted, and you shall be summoned once again ere the end" (782). The summoning of the Dead emphatically asserts the relevance, the redemptive potential—even the real presence—of the past.

Elendil's sword, Narsil, or what is left of it, serves as another link to the past—a tangible reminder passed down with the same care as the stories themselves. If the songs have withered somewhat, as Totta would say in *Homecoming,* still the sword has been revered (5). We learn through Elrond at the Council that Isildur's squire, Ohtar, escaped the Orc ambush that killed the king, and delivered the shards to safety. This escape at all costs is recounted in "The Disaster of the Gladden Fields" as Isildur's last command to Ohtar, suggesting the significance he placed on the heirloom, in spite of its disrepair.

Aragorn honors this commitment even to the point of encumbrance, evidently carrying the broken sword with him on his many perilous journeys: "Not much use, is it Sam?" he asks, brandishing it before the Hobbits in Bree (*FR,* I, x, 171). Later, he claims that as a guide in the wild his "cuts, short or long, don't go wrong"—but the words might obliquely refer to the family pedigree in bladework (*FR,* I, xi, 181). Such reverence seems a just recognition of the blade's impact in the wars against Sauron. The fact that it merits mention in Elrond's account of the Alliance victory, where words are at a premium, is telling. Unlike most swords, its value is not wholly diminished when broken, as the hilt-shard alone is enough to strike the legendary blow.[43] Like the stories themselves, the broken sword represents a latent possibility.[44]

The sword's eventual reforging as Andúril brings this latent potential to fruition. Elrond's negative assessment of the Alliance legacy is based in part on a motif of unfinished business—the dark tower is broken but its foundation remains. Yet some of this business can also be set right: the broken sword can be salvaged, repaired, made whole, and perhaps even stronger than before. Hard lessons of history, inspiring lessons, these can be preserved, shared, learned from, and put to use. Aragorn demonstrates the same reverence for the restored heirloom, declaring it against his will to "put aside" the sword before entering the Golden Hall (*TT,* III, vi, 510).

The blade's long and secret safekeeping begins to pay dividends in its effect on both friends and foes. At the battle of Helm's Deep, the sight of the weapon serves as a morale boost and rallying cries proclaim its pedigree: "Andúril goes to war. The Blade that was Broken shines again!" (*TT,* III, vii, 534). Aragorn's swordsmanship aside, mere sight of it appears to have the opposite effect on his enemies—"the terror of the sword for a while held back the enemy" (537). Orcs and Uruks, as discussed above, are not wholly ignorant of heroic legend either: perhaps this very blade figures prominently in their horror stories of the Great Siege and the bad old days.[45]

Exploitation of the sword's legend indeed proves even more critical than manipulation of the weapon itself. Aragorn says as much when he judges his contest with Sauron via the *palantír* "grimmer . . . than the battle of the Hornburg" (*RK,* V, ii, 780).[46] Like the War of the Last Alliance, this episode, too, is narrated only afterwards, vaguely, and in brief, as Aragorn reflects on the experience to Gimli and Legolas: "It was a bitter struggle. . . . And he beheld me . . . but in other guise than you see me. . . . Sauron has not forgotten Isildur and the sword of Elendil. . . . I showed the blade re-forged to him. He is not so mighty yet that he is above fear; nay, doubt ever gnaws him" (780).

Aragorn relies on the suggestive power of the Isildur legend, knowing that the Enemy with whom he communicates would be intimidated by the sight of Elendil's heir and the "Sword that robbed him of his treasure re-made" (*RK,* V, ix, 879). It is a tactical feint, a bit of saber rattling, made to provoke a panicked response because, as Aragorn reasons, "the hasty stroke goes oft astray" (*RK,* V, ii, 780). While it is no guarantee of ultimate success, this gamble is largely dependent on the mystique of the Alliance story.

In "telling" his story via the seeing stone, Aragorn is channeling a kind of inner Norse poet. As Tolkien once declared in his lectures on Eddaic verse: "To hit you in the eye was the deliberate intention of the Norse poet" (*SG,* 17–18). It would seem an apt description of Narsil here, and of Strider's pointed use of the old story (and the old sword) slung like mud in Sauron's eye: "the Eye turned inward, pondering tidings of doubt and danger: a bright sword, and a stern and kingly face it saw, and for a while it gave little thought to other things" (*RK,* VI, ii, 923).

The Ranger's saber-rattling gamble pays off; as Frodo comes closer to his goal, the narrator reminds us that Sauron is distracted: "The Eye was not turned to them" but looked instead to the Captains of the West (*RK*, VI, iii, 942). Reputation—and story—precede them: In the words of the Mouth of Sauron to Gandalf, "Have we not heard of thee at whiles" (*RK*, V, x, 889)? Desperate—even absurd—as the Captains of the West and their play may be, Gandalf notes, "there are names among us that are worth more than a thousand mail-clad knights apiece" (*RK*, V, ix, 882).

Pippin is also among them. And in that last desperate stand before the Black Gate, even he, in his way, takes a moment to reflect on the links between past and present. Admiring "the flowing characters of Númenor" that glint on his sword, he feels that it is "made for just such an hour" (*RK*, V, x, 892). Just before passing out under the hulking body of a troll, he hears faintly the coming of the Eagles, and thinks of Bilbo. "But no! That came in his tale, long long ago" (893). Perhaps a more learned character would, with the blade of Westernesse and the Black Gate before him, note the similarities to a much older war, but Pippin feels only the echoes of Bilbo's story of the Battle of Five Armies. With Pippin's last thought we are brought full circle to Tolkien's gripe in the foreword about historical amnesia: "it seems now often forgotten that to be caught in youth by 1914 was no less hideous an experience than to be involved in 1939 and the following years" (xxii).

In 1944, long before there could be any hope of a second edition foreword in which to vent frustrations about short-term historical memory, Tolkien wrote to his son Christopher expressing his dismay over what "seems almost a world wide mental disease" (*Letters*, 88). Christopher was training in the Royal Air Force at the time, and the frustration was perhaps brought into focus by his son's involvement in this most recent installment of the "War of the Machines," as he called it. "Even if people have ever heard the legends (which is getting rarer)," he wrote, "they have no inkling of their portent" (88).

The Lord of the Rings is woven about with the threads of the Last Alliance web, the portents of which we only partially grasp. The whole truth, if there be any, is lost to the Dark Ages of Middle-earth, and much remains untold, uncaptured, beyond the reach of even a score of tales or tellers. Nevertheless, as Gollum, Strider, and others demonstrate, much depends on our attempts to remember, understand, and interpret the shadows of the past.

Chapter Three

"STRANGE LUMBER"
Faded Tradition in the Túrin Saga

Far more often it was by subtle transformation in stages, so that the growth of the
legends . . . can seem like . . . the product of many minds and generations.
—Christopher Tolkien, foreword, *The Book of Lost Tales Part I*

He fingered the carving on the chair, and sighed. "I wasted my time . . . though
the hours seemed pleasant. But all such things are short-lived; and the joy in the
making is their only true end, I guess."
—J. R. R. Tolkien, *The Children of Húrin*

We have seen how Tolkien in *The Lord of the Rings* could skillfully create and
draw on new imaginative spaces via allusive webs like that of the Alliance. But a
question remains in how a sense of untold tales might function, if at all, within
those "vast backcloths" of established legends that largely predate Tolkien's
work on the matter of the Third Age. This chapter seeks to answer the question by probing the possibilities and limitations of "the impression of depth" in
what could only be described as Tolkien's *most-told* tale. That is to say, "the tale
now turns to Túrin" Turambar, tragic hero and dragon-slayer, who wandered
Beleriand in an interbellum period near the end of the First Age and haunted
Tolkien's imagination longer than any other figure in or out of Middle-earth.[1]

Túrin makes two brief but noteworthy appearances in *The Lord of the Rings*.
In Rivendell, Elrond assures Frodo that his free acceptance of the Ring's bur-
den would place him in the company of "all the mighty Elf-friends of old,
Hador, and Húrin, and Túrin, and Beren himself" (*FR*, II, ii, 270).

Later, it is Sam who, in his struggle against Shelob, draws comparisons to the heroes of antiquity.[2] Here the narrator cautions against thoughts of impending victory, despite Sam's doughty stroke with a "bright elven-blade": "But Shelob was not as dragons are. . . . Knobbed and pitted with corruption was her age-old hide. . . . The blade scored it with a dreadful gash, but those hideous folds could not be pierced . . . , not though Elf or Dwarf should forge the steel or the hand of Beren or of Túrin wield it" (*TT*, IV, x, 728).

The basic thrust of these allusions is clear enough from context. In the first case, Frodo's sacrifice earns him a place among the heroes of the past; while in the second, even the mightiest and best-armed of these storied warriors would fail to pierce Shelob's hide. Beyond the basics, however, the reader could not possibly be expected to understand more about Túrin—not at least until the publication of *The Silmarillion* in 1977, four years after Tolkien's death.[3] Indeed, the more scrupulous reader, in mining appendix A, could discover little more, or might indeed be thrown further from the trail by confounding with their First Age namesake the two Stewards of Gondor (Túrin I and Túrin II) mentioned therein.[4]

And, in hindsight, this dearth of lore on Túrin within *The Lord of the Rings* seems odd.[5] With due respect to the tale of Beren and Lúthien, which Tolkien described to Milton Waldman as the "chief of the stories of the *Silmarillion*," and which provided a far more pleasant set of epitaphs for the Tolkien gravestones, it seems to me that the Túrin story instead deserves pride of place (*Letters*, 149). It was Tolkien's prosimetric 1914 "Story of Kullervo" (who soon became Túrin, walking out of the Finnish *Kalevala* and into Tolkien's legendarium) that "set the rocket off in story" (*Letters*, 214). In fact, the earliest *Silmarillion*-like text, a 1926 *Sketch of the Mythology*, was produced to supplement and provide context for his unfinished alliterative tale of Túrin— they were sent together to his former King Edward's teacher R. W. Reynolds. And when the matter of the Third Age began to cycle off with the completion of *The Lord of the Rings* in the early 1950s, it was again the Túrin saga that became, according to Christopher, the "dominant story of the end of the Elder Days" to which "for a long time he devoted all his thought" (*CH*, 281). In size and scope, intricacy and immediacy, Túrin's story is the closest rival to *The Lord of the Rings* in Tolkien's oeuvre. Yet, while the tales of Beren and Lúthien and of Eärendil find ample space among the many digressions in *The Lord of the Rings*, that of Túrin remains essentially untold within its pages.

THE TÚRIN TREE AND ITS BRANCHES

I say the Túrin story, but Christopher's labor as literary executor makes clear
that we are dealing with a robust nexus of stories, a one-man tradition that
evolved from "The Story of Kullervo" in 1914 to Tolkien's final years, brought
to light posthumously over a thirty-year period, from *The Silmarillion* (1977)
through *The Children of Húrin* (2007). Most readers, even those somewhat
conversant with the legends of the Elder Days, would likely be surprised by
just how much Túrin there is; Drout, Hitotsubashi, and Rachel Scavera, in
Tolkien Studies, count fourteen published variants of the story, not including its progenitor in *Kullervo* (181).[6] Most significant for the purposes of this
chapter are the prose *Tale of Turambar and the Foalókë* (in existence at least
as early as 1919), published in *The Book of Lost Tales Part II* ([1984] 2002b);
the unfinished alliterative verse *Lay of the Children of Húrin,* written in the
1920s and published in *The Lays of Beleriand* ([1985] 2002c); and the much
later prose *Narn i Chîn Húrin,* written in the 1950s and posthumously published in *Unfinished Tales* (2006g), which forms the basis of the stand-alone
novella, *The Children of Húrin* (2007)—the first of Christopher's swan-song
triptych, his editions of the three "Great Tales."

In *Beowulf: A Translation and Commentary,* Tolkien noted a "tendency
in tales that are popular and long re-told for them to be enlarged, until they
become 'cycles,' taking up or being linked to other stories with which they at
first had slender connexions, or none at all" (*B,* 291). As so often happens with
his scholarly remarks (particularly those concerning *Beowulf*), this proves an
apt description of his own legendarium's development, including the ways in
which Túrin and the other Great Tales become increasingly entwined.

While enlargements (and compressions) abound in the Túrin cycle, many
of the essential elements of the story fall into place quite early. Setting aside
the frequent changes in names of people and places, surprisingly little of the
early *Tale of Turambar* might be said to directly contradict the later renditions. For those engaging with Túrin for the first time or in need of a brief
refresher, I offer the following brief plot skeleton of *Turambar* as the earliest
extant and complete rendition.

Túrin's father is defiant in captivity after a disastrous battle (here called the
Battle of Lamentation), and for his resistance he earns the hatred of Morgoth,
who curses his family. Túrin, still a young boy, is sent away by his mother and
fostered in the court of an Elf king (here called Tinwelint). Separation from
his mother and sister makes Túrin gloomy, but he grows hardy and wins fa-

vor by his prowess in battle on the borders. On a return to the court, Túrin is provoked by a haughty courtier and retaliates too forcefully, slaying him by accident.

Believing himself outlawed, Túrin flees and lives on the margins, gathering a ragtag band, including Beleg, the great Elf hunter. Túrin is eventually captured by Orcs, but before he can be brought before Morgoth, Beleg, with the aid of an escaped Elf, Flinding, rescues him from an Orc encampment by night. Beleg's sword slips in cutting Túrin's bonds, pricking his foot. Roused suddenly, Túrin mistakes friend for enemy and kills Beleg with his own sword. Before he can be recaptured, Flinding leads a shellshocked Túrin away to a hidden Elf stronghold (here the home of the Rodothlim).

Túrin becomes known in the Rodothlim dialect as "the black sword" for his prowess with Gurtholfin, a blade made by the Elves. He also wins the favor of an Elf maiden (here Failivrin), but by his counsel and skill the Rodothlim abandon secrecy for open war. When Morgoth sends a force led by his great dragon (here Glórund), they are utterly defeated. Túrin is spellbound by Glórund and looks on helplessly as Failivrin is led away. At the dragon's suggestion, Túrin opts not to pursue her, embarking instead on a fruitless search for his mother in their old home of Hísilómë. He does not find her, as she has long since fled to Tinwelint's halls. In his rage, Túrin murders Brodda, lord of his old family land. Fleeing, he wanders in the wild and eventually takes up with a band of hunters.

Túrin begins a new life with these woodsmen, becoming their chief and taking a new name: Turambar, or "master of doom." He rescues a maiden in the woods under a spell of forgetfulness, naming her Níniel. Unbeknownst to him, she is his sister, Nienori, who with his mother left Tinwelint's court to seek news of him, and was spellbound by Glórund. Love grows between Níniel and Turambar, and they wed. But Glórund soon enters the woodsmen's realm seeking ever more destruction and plunder. Túrin and a few companions set out on a desperate quest to come at the dragon's unguarded belly from below as he crosses a ravine. Túrin's companions desert him but he manages to drive his blade into the worm's belly. Glórund, mortally wounded, pulls his bulk up onto the further bank, and Túrin follows to retrieve his sword. As he taunts Glórund and withdraws the sword, he is burned by gouts of dragon blood and faints. Níniel comes to the site and believes him dead. Glórund, with his last breath, lifts his spell from her and reveals their identities as brother and sister. Nienori casts herself into the river. When Túrin wakes, he seeks news of Níniel and becomes enraged at hearing the truth. He slays the messenger and runs wild through the woods. Finally, he asks his sword to slay him. It agrees to do so, and Túrin casts himself on the point.

Apart from the shifts in proper names characteristic of Tolkien's experiments in linguistic aesthetics, the essential story beats of *Turambar* should look on the whole quite familiar to a reader of *The Children of Húrin.* But each successive rendering of the Túrin story, each alternative compression and enlargement, each move from verse to prose and back again sheds new light and opens new avenues—or "new vistas" as Tolkien was wont to describe the depths in *The Lord of the Rings.*

In his scholarly writing, Tolkien cautions against the practice of "pondering a summarized plot"—at least for the purposes of literary criticism.[7] We could say the same of Túrin as Tolkien does of *Beowulf.* And if Tolkien is surprisingly forthcoming about the "sources" of Túrin—from Kullervo to Sigurd to Oedipus—it may be because he knew that Túrin also transcended them and became something new.[8]

Despite its demonstrable sources and frequent retellings,[9] the Túrin cycle also carves out space for untold tales. The invitation to explore and delve for the roots of the faded Túrin tradition makes for a challenging and rewarding study of the technique. The saga became a kind of lifelong playground for Tolkien and in its unfinished layers he creates—intentionally and accidentally—a depth and sense of untold stories that even *The Lord of the Rings* might envy. As we uncover all that has been forgotten of Túrin in the Third Age, we come to two impassible bookends: the Dírhavel lay, which launches the tradition on the one end, and the mysterious prophecy of Túrin's role in the Ragnarökian Great Wrack on the other. But the way is shut, and they are (mostly) irrevocably lost.

This chapter unfolds in three parts: the first considers the aesthetic effects imparted by intertextual connection and the conceit of faded tradition; the second, Tolkien's ability to open new unexplained vistas even as he expands the tale in later renditions; and the third, on that latter bookend and what may be the most mysterious untold tale of all, the prophecies of Túrin's shadowy role in an unwritten Last Battle at the world's end.

INTERTEXTUALITY, REFLEXIVITY, AND RUMOR

Everywhere in Tolkien's writing are suggestions of tradition. We learn that following the War of the Ring, Hobbits began to take "a more widespread interest in their history," writing down much of what was "up to that time still mainly oral" (*FR*, prologue, 14). Some of these oral traditions are hinted at within the narrative: Hobbit children hear "old bogey-stories" concerning the forest just outside their Shire (*FR*, I, vi, 109). The halflings hear of Mordor, too, "like a shadow on the borders of old stories" (*FR*, I, ii, 51). More apropos a study of Túrin is Bilbo's remark in *The Hobbit* (evidently a commonplace of the family if not of Hobbits at large): "'Every worm has his weak spot,' as my father used to say, though I am sure it was not from personal experience'" ([1937] 1994, 208).

Often damage is done to the stories enshrined in traditions—and not those of Hobbits alone. When Aragorn calls for *athelas* to revive those stricken by the Nazgûl after the siege of Gondor, the so-called herb-master dismisses the folk-rhyme concerning the herb as "doggrell . . . garbled in the memory of old wives. Its meaning I leave to your judgement, if indeed it has any" (*RK*, V, viii, 865). The joke, as it were, is on him. But nowhere else in Tolkien's legendarium is tradition so fully explored, realized, and felt as in the Túrin material.

Let us first consider the extant allusions to Túrin beyond the frame of his own story. Little enough seems to survive into the Third Age, as we see from the sparse references to Túrin in *The Lord of the Rings,* though with the benefit of familiarity with the cycle, we can acknowledge the fitness of Túrin's invocation during a comparison of the hides of dragons and of Shelob. As Gergely Nagy (2003) puts it in his illuminating study of the intertextual Túrin web, the narrator formulates a typological scheme in which Sam's fight with Shelob is set against a kind of archetype in its historical precedent: the case of Túrin versus Glaurung. To Túrin's faded legacy in the Third Age we might add another moment in *The Hobbit,* after Bilbo shares with the Dwarves news of the "bare patch" in Smaug's armor. The party embarks on a discussion of "dragon-slayings historical, dubious, and mythical, and the various sorts of stabs and jabs and undercuts, and the different arts devices and stratagems by which they had been accomplished" (215). While no names are mentioned, there can be no more likely candidate than Túrin, whose slaying of Glaurung had already (at *The Hobbit*'s publication in 1937) been a fixed event in the mythology for almost twenty years. By the end of the Third Age, the extant Túrin tradition is reduced to a few tattered and tantalizing fragments, through which the association of Túrin with dragon-slaying can be faintly glimpsed.

That association is revived in another unlikely place: the anthology of poems that Tolkien published as *The Adventures of Tom Bombadil and Other Verses from the Red Book* ([1962] 2014a). In the preface to this work, Tolkien assumes his role as editor and expands his conceit of a manuscript tradition linking the Primary and Secondary world via the Hobbits' Red Book of Westmarch.

Concerning "The Hoard," the fourteenth poem in the *Bombadil* collection, he has this to say: it "depends on the lore of Rivendell" and "seems to contain echoes of the Númenórean tale of Túrin and Mîm the Dwarf" (*ATB*, 32).

For readers of this collection in 1962, Túrin was hardly a household name—and Mîm completely unknown. But again, with the benefit of hindsight, we might recognize more than whimsy at work here. In the years following publication of *The Lord of the Rings,* Tolkien devoted a good deal of thought to lines of traditions and transmission; in *Morgoth's Ring,* for example, he declares that the "three Great Tales must be Númenórean," though there he suggests that they are compiled not out of the libraries of Rivendell but "from matter preserved in Gondor" (2002e, 373). Certainly, important elements of the Túrin story appear in the poem: the cursed treasure recalls the hoard of Nargothrond; the dragon slain in surprise by a young warrior with a bright sword, Glaurung and Túrin; the old man, Húrin the wanderer after his release from Angband; the Dwarf, Mîm. Thus "The Hoard" does indeed "seem to contain echoes" of Túrin's story. Though perhaps an "echo of an echo," as Tolkien describes our modern experience of reading *Beowulf,* would be more accurate.[10] If we take Tolkien's editorial stance seriously, the lesson must be that the lore concerning Túrin and Mîm has become so mangled in the Third Age of the Shire as to be largely incomprehensible.

Túrin also appears as a lost tale in *Tuor and the Fall of Gondolin.* Beyond the notion that the Great Tales would be derived from Númenórean tradition, we know little of Tolkien's specific plans for *Gondolin*'s development as a story within the fictional frame. But in any case, as Tuor's cousin and contemporary, Túrin's appearance on the margins here suggests historic plausibility. If we are to see *Gondolin* as a contemporary work begun shortly after the city's demise, Túrin would have been a recently deceased legend; news and knowledge of his feats and whereabouts might have been more readily available.[11] On the other hand, if *Gondolin* were conceived as a much later work, allusions to Túrin might yet be explained by the antiquarian poet's sensibility—it is a delicious "What if?" moment for the writer of historical fiction, an almost irresistible temptation to work a figure like Túrin in, or indeed to place these two kinsmen in contact, if only for a fleeting and strange moment. This is indeed what Tolkien does. After Tuor and his guide Voronwë come upon the old tracks of the "Great Worm of Angband," they also hear "a cry in the woods" and soon spy

> a tall Man, armed, clad in black, with a long sword drawn; and they wondered,
> for the blade of the sword also was black . . .

But they knew not that . . . this was Túrin son of Húrin, the Blacksword. Thus
only for a moment, and never again, did the paths of those kinsmen, Túrin and
Tuor, draw together. (*FG*, 179–80)

Christopher rightly singles this moment out for special attention in his recent and final publication, *The Fall of Gondolin*, last of the Great Tales; for a
moment Tuor and his companion touch "the greatest story of the Elder Days"
(2018b, 235).[12] Something in this brief digression recalls Tolkien's commentary on the *Beowulf* poet and his audience. We glimpse faded tradition here
through a kind of fan service for an audience long departed; and we can imagine the fireside scenes at which such chance meetings would be recounted.[13]
What listener could have refrained from goosebumps hearing that our heroes
had stumbled upon Glaurung's tracks, and who among the crowd would *not*
have heard of the fall of Nargothrond, or known at once that the black sword
belonged to Túrin?

The cousins do not cross paths again, but one further allusion to Túrin's
movements is woven into the later rendition of Tuor's tale. As Tuor makes
his stealthy way toward his fabled destination, we hear of the military movements of the Orcs in the vicinity: "Morgoth had set a guard on the highway,
not to ensnare Tuor and Voronwë (of whom as yet he knew nothing) . . . but
to watch for the Blacksword" (*FG*, 184). This peek at the Orcs' scouting report suggests some historical silver lining to Túrin's movements and deeds,
which is seldom, if at all, detected within the frame of his own story; there,
his actions seem more often to hurt rather than help the cause, and even the
dragon-slaying is hardly a cause for celebration. In the explanation of the
Orcs' movements, there is also, more subtle but still present, an echo of the
great gamble of the Captains of the West in *The Lord of the Rings*, and their
power not to defeat but to distract Sauron from the threat of the ringbearer.
The value of a deed or heroic gesture is one of the central questions posed by
Túrin's saga, and here, in this other text, we are offered a glimpse of a wide
(and weird) web of fate linking his story to a larger history.

Returning to Túrin's own story, the idea of tradition is foregrounded even
in its earliest rendition. *Tale of Turambar*, like the rest of the Lost Tales, is
transmitted orally by a teller on the Lonely Isle—in this case, one Eltas. Eltas
notes that his story is "a favourite," though: "In these days many such stories
do Men tell still, and more have they told in the past especially in those kingdoms of the North that once I knew. Maybe the deeds of other of their warriors have become mingled therein, and many matters beside that are not in
the most ancient tale—but now I will tell to you the true and lamentable tale,

and I knew it long ere I trod Olórë Mallë in the days before the fall of Gondolin" (*BLT II*, 70).

Eltas claims the authority to render truly a story already ancient. And
through him, Tolkien advances the conceit of his stories as antecedents of our
Primary World legends: those of Beowulf or Sigurd, for instance. The link becomes even more pronounced in Tolkien's own experiments with Norse poetry
(more on this below). Once it gets going, Eltas's *Tale* is studded throughout
with allusions to untold tales concerning Túrin's deeds: "Now in many adventures were those twain together, Beleg the Elf and Túrin the Man, which
are not now told or remembered but which once were sung in many a place"
(*BLT II*, 76).

Later variants of the story retain and even heighten this reflexive sensibility. Eltas claims that "all folk gathered" with him "know" the story of Turambar; his story, in other words, is an oldie but a goodie—and spoilers abound.
In our last rendition, *The Children of Húrin,* chapter headings do not leave
us in suspense:[14] we know well enough what is coming under titles like "The
Death of Beleg," "The Death of Glaurung," and finally, inevitably, "The Death
of Túrin." These titles suggest that the tale is one already weighted with age
and familiarity, that its pleasures come not from surprise twists but the slow
and inexorable buildup of tragedy: in the end, we, like Túrin, not only hear,
but also recognize "the feet of his doom overtaking him" (*CH*, 251).

Like the *Beowulf* poet who inspires him, Tolkien fills his alliterative verse
Lay with scenes of storytelling, verse-making, and the work befitting the Old
English *scop*. In Doriath are described scenes of feasting and minstrelsy. And,
even in his early years, Túrin's own deeds become part of the bards' repertoire
in Thingol's halls:

> and tales of Túrin were told in his halls,
>   and how Beleg the ageless was brother-in-arms
> to the black-haired boy from the beaten people. (*LB*, 17)

The scene is reminiscent of those in Hrothgar's halls in *Beowulf,* and it situates Túrin already within a developing storytelling tradition.

Most of these tales are viewed from a distance, tantalizing half-line allusions as in the catalog of old swords in Beleg's sharpening spell:

> the sword of Saithnar, and the silver blades
> of the enchanted children of chains forgéd

in their deep dungeon; the dirk of Nargil,
the knife of the North in Nogrod smithied (*LB,* 45)

There is also an experiment of a lengthy digression, wherein Túrin's boy-hood guide Halog tells him the tale of Beren and Lúthien (a clear precursor to Strider's campfire *Lay of Leithian*). We are, like Grendel, on the outside listening in, even if he would like to eat the singers and we would like to hear them more closely.

The long prose *Narn i Chîn Húrin* follows suit in its emphasis on meta-narrative and the transmission of story. Absent cell phone service, characters spend a great deal of time seeking one another out, and in so doing they rely primarily on the rumors and stories they gather. When, for instance, Beleg seeks to deliver the king's pardon to Túrin after his self-imposed exile from Doriath, the trail he picks up is just as much wonder tale as it is mud track: "There he heard a strange tale that went among them. A tall and lordly Man, or an Elf-warrior, some said, had appeared in the woods, and had slain one of the Gaurwaith, and rescued the daughter of Larnach whom they were pursuing" (*CH,* 108).

This rumor does more than provide explanation for the heroes' eventual reunion. It also offers an early indication of fringe traditions, divergent avenues for the Túrin cycle's development within the secondary world. For the grateful family of Larnach, Túrin must have seemed a guardian angel of sorts—a cloaked crusader—and the story of this daring rescue might spread, and grow, and be changed in the telling.

Throughout much of *The Children of Húrin,* Tolkien turns the creative writing adage "show—don't tell" on its head. He *tells*—again and again—of Túrin's unmatched prowess with sword and shield. When "scarcely out of his boyhood his strength and courage were proved" on the marches of Doriath, though we do not see up close his "deeds of daring" or the "many wounds" he receives (2007, 85). Once he takes up the Dragon-helm, the rumors that spread of Túrin's deeds are measured also against the legends of the past: "Then many wondered, saying: 'Can the spirit of any man return from death; or has Húrin of Hithlum escaped indeed from the pits of Hell?'" (85). When Beleg and Túrin renew their partnership in arms after his exile from Doriath, we are told that "far and wide . . . the whisper went" of the return of Bow and Helm (144).

The account of Túrin's meteoric rise to fame in Nargothrond—from shell-shocked refugee to high captain—opens not with a terrific scene of action on the battlefield but a change in moniker: he "became known in Nargothrond as Mormegil, the Black Sword, for the rumour of his deeds with that weapon" (160). Having found work after his heart, his legend spreads that "so valiant was Túrin, and so exceedingly skilled in arms, especially with sword and shield, that the Elves said that he could not be slain" (164). It is by "the prowess of the Blacksword" that the roads of Beleriand are made safe for a time; his "fame" goes "far and wide, even into the deeps of the wood" (188, 195). But we seldom see this prowess up close, even in this largely expanded and practically novel-istic form. The distance maintains an air of untold tales: the events themselves in their vivid immediacy are usually withheld—they are lost to the ruin and abyss of time; all that is left is the echo and rumor, the summary report. Or, as Christopher Tolkien puts it in his foreword to *The Book of Lost Tales I* (cited in chapter 1, but worth repeating here): "the compendious or epitomising form and manner of *The Silmarillion,* with its suggestion of ages of poetry and 'lore' behind it, strongly evokes a sense of 'untold tales,' even in the telling of them; 'distance' is never lost" (*BLT I,* 4).

This distance in the prose *Narn* is remarkably effective, believable. Readers inhabit the position of those around Túrin: they may be frustrated by Túrin's decision-making, but they do not doubt his courage or his skill; we occupy a space among the people of Brethil, drawn toward some strange spectacle in the dragon-fight: "indeed so great in their minds had the Black Sword become that few could believe that even Glaurung would conquer him" (*CH,* 232). The legend of Túrin's swordsmanship grows all the greater for being largely obscured from view.[15]

THE BEGINNINGS OF TRADITION AND DÍRHAVEL'S LOST *NARN*

Of course a single dragon-slaying—the first in history—would be more than enough to sustain a legendary reputation.[16] Christopher notes in his commen-tary on the developments of this scene that it was "an episode of great impor-tance: there are few 'monsters' to rival Glaurung, and my father strove to per-fect the tale of how Túrin earned the title of *Dagnir Glaurunga*" (*WJ,* 156). So, too, might the bards and tale-tellers of the invented world strive. Thus in *The Children of Húrin* we are given this one battle scene of rare immediacy, sus-pense, and horror. Glaurung is revealed from below in all his monstrosity—the growing menace of "the snarling of the Great Worm in his watchful sleep . . . the huge shadow of his head against the stars . . . his jaws gaped, and he had seven tongues of fire" (*CH,* 236). And, not to be outdone, the revolting sight

and smell of those "midmost parts of the Dragon. . . . Pale and wrinkled . . .
all dank with a grey slime, to which clung all manner of dropping filth" (237).
The struggle is as much internal as external, and our narrator pauses long
enough to imagine Túrin's curious nightmare during the wait for Glaurung
to cross the chasm; he has "a dream, in which all his will was given to cling-
ing, though a black tide sucked and gnawed at his limbs" (235).[17] Finally, the
moment comes: "Then Turambar drew the Black Sword of Beleg and stabbed
upwards with all the might of his arm, and of his hate,[18] and the deadly blade,
long and greedy, went into the belly even to its hilts" (237). The sentence—
like the sword—is long and well-crafted, punctuating this greatest of deeds
for which Túrin's name will be "praised for ever . . . among Elves and Men"
(254). In it are captured Túrin's great facility with a blade, the slow build of
his vendetta against the dragon and his Master (a power almost to contend
with Morgoth's curse), the horror of Beleg's slaying, and the ominous (and
nowhere explained) sentience of the sword called Gurthang. Can this scene
be anything but the invention of the poet, however? Túrin is alone, and would
soon lie dead, telling no more tales.[19] There were no witnesses save the worm's
body, rent by the sword.

That the text is suffused with half-remembered tradition can be seen even
on the sentence level in the use of parentheses.[20] Take, for instance, the description of Túrin's training with Beleg, who taught him "woodcraft and ar-
chery and (which he liked more) the handling of swords" (81). There is a nod
here, an understated wink, in this aside: Túrin's swordplay is the stuff of legends, and surely there were other tales of his training, of how, in the alliterative *Lay,* he "learned the lore of leaping blades" (*LB,* 30). When Túrin later
takes the name of Neithan, the Wronged, as an outlaw, he does not reveal his
past to his fellows, "though he claimed to have suffered injustice (and to any
who claimed the like he ever lent too ready an ear)" (101). The parenthetical comment again nods to a known character trait, a weakness of Túrin we
might imagine to be so ingrained in the stories about him as to be (almost)
not worth mentioning. Then, in the buildup to the final confrontation between Túrin and Glaurung, a parenthetical note of bardic pedantry is struck
in the interpretation of the properties of Morgoth's curse: whether the dragon
sniffed out Túrin's hiding place, or "(as some hold) he had indeed for that
time escaped from the eye of Evil that pursued him, is of little matter" (221).

Parentheticals were not the only editorial tool mustered here. C. S. Lewis's
quip that Tolkien was an "inspired speaker of footnotes" dovetails nicely with
the digressive sensibilities of his fantasy narratives, and it is worth noting that
footnotes themselves are in fact used on occasion in his fiction.[21] Only one

appears in *The Children of Húrin,* but its timing and content are both significant. Thus the narrator describes the betrayal of the House of Ransom: Mîm's
hatred for Beleg leads to an evil decision. He leaves the house under the guise
of foraging for winter food, but "his true purpose was to seek out the servants
of Morgoth, and to lead them to Túrin's hiding-place*" (148).

And with this asterisk we arrive at the lone footnote, which states that
"another tale is told, which has it that Mîm did not encounter the Orcs with
deliberate intent. It was the capture of his son and their threat to torture him
that led Mîm to his treachery" (148). Who is speaking through this footnote?[22]
Such a provocative note invites consideration of the constructed nature of
the text and its suggestion of tradition—or traditions. It reminds us that even
important elements and motives may be dubious, confused, or contradictory.
The author at any rate eschews a bibliographic entry, and if this other tale was
once in circulation, it appears to be no longer extant in Tolkien's writing.

Just as The Lost Tale of *Turambar,* the earliest extant version of Túrin's
story, opens with a keynote of tradition via Eltas's discourse on the min-
gling of tales, the latest prose telling closes on a similarly reflexive endnote as
Túrin is laid to rest: "the minstrels of Elves and Men . . . made lament," and
"the Elves carved in the Runes of Doriath: TÚRIN TURAMBAR DAGNIR
GLAURUNGA" (257). Already here are the beginnings of oral—Elvish and
Mannish—and written—at least runic—traditions. Whether or not these first
works in the Túrin tradition were heroic-elegiac in nature (as Tolkien classi-
fied *Beowulf*), we can only speculate.

In the previous chapter, I stressed the narrative and thematic significance
of Tolkien's untold tales, their function often transcending mere window
dressing or unspecified depth-making. And in Túrin's saga this is no different. The presence of untold tales here might be said to reflect and amplify a
central question posed of the parents of Túrin and Niënor. Reunited at last—
"too late"—at the Stone of the Hapless, Morwen asks Húrin, "'If you know,
tell me! How did she find him?' But Húrin did not answer" (260). Are some
tales better left untold? Is it more painful to know or not to know? The tragic
saga is framed by Húrin's piteous plight: cursed to sit and see all through a
glass darkly, while Morwen and their children grope about blind and bewil-
dered to tragic ends. Húrin's refusal to speak speaks volumes. His horror has
been unspeakable; but Morwen's has been no less.

In spite of his silence, Húrin himself will continue the story and the tradition, making a grave for Morwen at the same spot. In fact his misadven-
tures after release from Angband, described in the unfinished *Wanderings of
Húrin,* represent a broken link to the final tales of the Elder Days, and show

the unfinished potential of the Túrin saga's pride of place: a kind of linchpin in all the late history of Beleriand.

While these lands and much of their history will eventually be drowned, the Stone of the Hapless stands as a monument to this Great Tale: the tip of the iceberg in the Túrin legends: "It is told that a seer and harp-player of Brethil named Glirhuin made a song, saying that the Stone of the Hapless should not be . . . ever thrown down . . . and still Tol Morwen stands alone in the water" (*S*, 230). Whether or not touristic pilgrimages to Tol Morwen were ever attempted, the tales do not tell.

While the broad strokes of tradition remained ever an abiding interest for Tolkien, his scholarship (as I discussed in chapter 1) and fiction often focus on the unique voice of the individual poet whose works are rooted in that larger tradition. The Túrin story is certainly no exception in this regard, and the allusion to Glirhuin above is only an appetizer to the main course: the Mannish poet Dírhavel (or Dírhaval). While there are many singers and storytellers in Tolkien's legendarium, few receive the kind of attention that Tolkien lavishes on Dírhavel and his seminal lost work the *Narn i Chîn Húrin*.

Dírhavel is first mentioned in Christopher's introduction to *Unfinished Tales,* where he notes that his "father delighted in re-telling on different scales," though the "overlapping and interrelation between" works could sometimes be explained "at a different level," one within the fictional world: "Legends like that of Túrin Turambar had been given a particular poetic form long ago—in this case, the *Narn I Hîn Húrin* of the poet Dírhavel—and phrases, or even whole passages from it . . . would be preserved intact by those who afterwards made condensations of the history of the Elder Days" (7). More on Dírhavel is revealed in the notes following the prose *Narn* of *Unfinished Tales* and, at greater length, in *The War of the Jewels*. There, in drafts of an introductory note to accompany the long prose saga of Túrin, Tolkien presents Dírhavel's *Narn* (formerly the *Húrinien*) as a kind of ur-text—the prized source for all later renditions of the Túrin legend—and explores everything from its inspiration, sources, prosody, reception, and translation.

The poet, who "lived at the Havens in the days of Eärendel," in one version of the note, "came of the House of Hador, it is said, and the glory and sorrow of that House was nearest to his heart" (*WJ*, 311, 313). In the making of this famed text, he "gathered all the tidings and lore that he could of the House of Hador" (311). These notes afford special attention to questions of lacunae filled (at least partially) and the corruption and loss due to the challenges of translation, etc. An effort is made to clarify the poet's research and the links of transmission that shed light on the more obscure chapters in Túrin's life: "he found . . . the son of that Androg who . . . alone survived the battle on the summit of Amon Rûdh. Otherwise . . . Túrin's deeds in those days" would be forgotten (311).

The note goes on to name and characterize the verse form of Dírhavel's "prized" lay, and to trace the first steps of translation and redaction in a fictive manuscript history of the Túrin saga:

> His lay was composed in that mode of verse which was called *Minlamad thent / estent*.[23] Though this verse was not wholly unlike the verse known to Ælfwine, he translated the lay into prose (including in it, or adding in the margins as seemed fit to him, matter from the Elvish commentaries that he had heard or seen); for he was not himself skilled in the making of verse, and the transference of this long tale from Elvish into English was difficult enough. Indeed even as it was made, with the help of the Elves as it would seem from his notes and additions, in places his account is obscure. (*WJ*, 311–12)

Christopher has noted the temptation to see some link between the verse known to Ælfwine (i.e., Old English verse) and Tolkien's unfinished alliterative lay. The comparison is indeed tempting, and through it we might see another point of contact between the manuscripts of the Primary World and the heroic tradition within the secondary. The note's assessment of Ælfwine's work as "in places . . . obscure" is at least an eerily prescient view of Tolkien's own unfinished work on Túrin. The second draft of the Dírhavel note (B), tellingly written from Ælfwine's own perspective, denies any extraneous meddling with the Dírhavel original; he claims only that "on matters that seemed of interest, or that were become dark with the passing of the years, I have made notes, whether within the tale or upon its margins, according to such lore as I found in Eressëa" (313).

Tolkien thus offers up an elaborate ur-text—Dírhavel's *Narn i Chîn Húrin*, from which later retellings of Túrin can draw. But there are a few catches: Dírhavel is himself working from sources—"much Elvish lore"—and gathering or piecing together presumably quite disparate fragments and reports. Just as the abandoned alliterative lay tempts comparison to Ælfwine's verse forms, we might also see some parallels between Dírhavel and Tolkien's principal models—the *Beowulf* poet or Elias Lönnrot, compiler of the *Kalevala*, for instance.

The real catch is that we do not have Dírhavel's *Narn*. Thus the chief impression remains one of loss. Tolkien's (unfinished) modern English Túrin lay is plainly *not* Dírhavel's *Narn*. Nor is the long prose *Narn* of *The Children of Húrin*—in fact, it is no *narn* at all. It can hardly be said even to resemble Ælfwine's prose translation, for where are his notes, marginal and otherwise? Only one footnote—that which questions Mîm's treachery—remains, and its fictive editor is unknown. Dírhavel's masterpiece eludes our grasp; it is a lost tale that not even Ælfwine can recover.

The Túrin tradition that we do have is beautiful and varied, but its missing antecedent is felt deeply. Tolkien here achieves by design an elegiac effect that the old poems produce partly by accident—the ravages of time, or conflict, or consuming fire. As Tolkien said of translations—which our extant Túrin tales must certainly be accounted—"No translation that aims at being readable in itself can . . . indicate all the possibilities or hints afforded by the text" (*MC*, 50) Thus there must be much of Túrin lost in translation, as is indeed suggested in the opening moments of the Túrin chapter in the 1977 *Silmarillion,* with its reference to the *Narn i Hîn Húrin,* where this "longest of all the lays" is "full told" (*S,* 198). Tolkien is meticulous in building up an elaborate sense of rootedness behind the story, but we are barred—emphatically—from digging too deep.

THE SHADOW OF THE PAST

The intertextual development of the Túrin saga and its strong suggestion of tradition and roots out of reach render it unique among Tolkien's tales. But it should not be forgotten that the longest and most nearly complete retelling of the Túrin story comes close to replicating that enchanting sense of depth found in that "Frameless Picture . . . surrounded by the glimmer of limitless extensions in time and space" that is *The Lord of the Rings.* This next portion of the chapter takes up Tolkien's efforts to create depth via untold tales between the covers of the long-form prose *The Children of Húrin.*

I say replicate—in spite of the fact that plenty of Túrin long predates *The Lord of the Rings*—because the various unfinished attempts to expand upon the Great Tales in the 1950s likely owe a debt to Tolkien's mature experiments in depth during the development of *The Lord of the Rings,* where a core narrative in the foreground stands out from seemingly limitless extensions in the background. So it is in *The Children of Húrin:* Túrin's birth (like most) comes in medias res, and its narrative alludes with great frequency to events in the past and on the periphery. Most of these extensions need not be bluffed either as Túrin comes on the scene at the end of the Elder Days, and could draw from many of the same "verifiable" backcloths as *The Lord of the Rings.*

Looming most large is the disaster of the Nirnaeth Arnoediad, the Battle of Unnumbered Tears. It was a defeat with ramifications for all Beleriand, but of course for Túrin it marked his severance from his father whose heroic resistance brings down Morgoth's curse that will dog his family for the rest of their lives. The Nirnaeth is a proper digression, earning its own chapter heading and brutally truncating Túrin's already troubled childhood. In its presentation and placement it might be said to bear some of the important hallmarks of the *Beowulf* digressions. Tolkien does not simply copy and paste an account of the great battle from his other writings but develops one specifically for the Túrin story, to meet that tale's particular artistic needs and dramatic purposes.

So at once the Nirnaeth chapter of *The Children of Húrin* sets the table for Túrin's tale while reminding us that we glimpse only a small piece of a great history: "If all were now retold a man's life would not suffice for the hearing. Here then shall be recounted only those deeds which bear upon the fate of the House of Hador and the children of Húrin the Steadfast" (52).[24] It is here that we gain our first glimpse of Gwindor and the warriors of Nargothrond, "ever in the forefront of that battle," until, in the courts of Angband, "Gwindor was trapped there and taken alive and his folk slain" (56). Their furious charge, spurred by the desire to avenge the death of Gwindor's brother, sheds light on Nargothrond's later policy of secrecy and sets up a poignant contrast to the Gwindor whom Túrin encounters many years later in the wood of Taur-nu-Fuin: tortured, maimed, and broken by years of enslavement.

Before telling of the battle in the west and the deeds of Húrin, the narrator alludes to deeds unfolding elsewhere: "Of all that befell in the eastward battle: of the routing of Glaurung . . . ; of the treachery of the Easterlings . . . and the flight of the sons of Fëanor, no more is here said" (56). These details, too, are selected with care. Just as the Last Alliance casts a shadow over the War of the Ring, the story of Glaurung's wounds, though only mentioned briefly here, will return: Túrin will hear it from veterans of the Nirnaeth, he will retell it to his own men in Brethil, and he will interpret and act on its lessons to great effect when the dragon comes for him at last. Elsewhere, the historians of the *Grey Annals* will, with the benefit of hindsight, make note of the continuity between these two iconic encounters with Glaurung: "Azaghâl drove a knife into his belly. . . . Had Azaghâl but borne a sword great woe would have been spared to the Noldor that after befell [*added:*] but his knife went not deep enough" (*WJ*, 75). The allusion to Túrin's later encounter is plain, and may presumably have been derived from the tradition of Túrin's own words on the matter:

"For hear now this tale that I was told . . . when I and most that hear me were children. . . . Azaghâl of Belegost pricked him so deep that he fled back to Ang- band. But here is a thorn sharper and longer than the knife of Azaghâl."

And Turambar swept Gurthang from its sheath" (226)

Thus the entry from the *Grey Annals* might be viewed as a step in the devel- opment of a body of dragon-lore in Middle-earth—an early effort in a long chain echoed even in the discussions of dragon-slaying stratagems held be- tween Bilbo and his companions many thousands of years later in *The Hobbit*.

Whatever the differences between this account and other extant references to the Nirnaeth, the narrator of *The Children of Húrin* is quick to emphasize the battle's ultimately ineffable qualities: the sum of its sorrows "no tale can contain." In this way it shares something in common also with the Last Al- liance's presentation in *The Lord of the Rings*. We might say that Tolken's greatest stories shared a similar leaning in drawing on the shadowy backdrop of a legendary battle.[25]

The last words of this account of the battle, at any rate, are spent on Húrin's heroic gesture, which gains added emphasis against the sparse allusions to the other movements of the battle.

Húrin . . . cast aside his shield, and seized the axe of an orc-captain and . . . it is sung that . . . each time that he slew Húrin cried aloud: "*Aure entuluva!* Day shall come again!" Seventy times he uttered that cry; but they took him at last . . . and dragged him to Angband with mockery.

Thus ended the Nirnaeth Arnoediad. (59–60)

Húrin's failed stand strikes the endnote for the whole terrible battle as well as the keynote for his son Túrin's saga. Surrounded by Orcs, Húrin throws cau- tion (and his shield) to the wind and goes down swinging. Defeat, for Túrin's father, is no refutation, as Tolkien describes the heroic ethos in "*Beowulf*: The Monsters and the Critics." Indeed, this last stand reads something like Tolkien's attempt to rival Byrhtwold's renowned summation of the code in *The Battle of Maldon*. The account of Húrin's deeds in the Nirnaeth helps to clarify how difficult it will be for Túrin to find/cleave his own path under the hopes and expectations laid on the Heir of the House of Hador. A good deal of the story's force comes from its examination of fate and free will; Húrin's shadow—while not so obviously influential as Morgoth's curse—adds one more layer of complexity. Of course the stories of the Nirnaeth cannot be contained to a single chapter either. Wherever Turin's story takes him, to the hidden Elf-kingdoms or the wilds of Beleriand, these shadows of the recent past are always creeping in.

While the Nirnaeth is the chief digression and the principal touchstone for a wider world of story beyond Túrin's own, it is by no means the only one against which the threads of the prose *Narn* are woven. Allusions abound to other legends of the Elder Days, many of them well-documented elsewhere. There are links to the other two Great Tales, of course; indeed the essential nature of these three stories becomes clearer for the links Tolkien weaves between them. The Great Tales are Tolkienian fairy stories, of course; they treat with "the *aventures* of men in the Perilous Realm" (*MC*, 113). But they are different in kind: Beren and Lúthien dance through a fairy-tale romance, Tuor marches to and from Gondolin in an epic—but poor Túrin wanders his way into Tolkien's darkest tragedy. At first he seems to follow in Beren's footsteps, finding favor in Doriath.[26] Later, Gwindor contrasts these two heroes of Men in warning Finduilas that her love for Túrin will not yield a happy ever after: "But this man is not Beren. . . . A doom lies on him; a dark doom. Enter not into it!" (168). Gondolin and its impending fall—just a few years out from Túrin's death, are frequently cited. Both bit and key players of the Gondolin story enter and exit the stage: Gelmir and Arminas bring news of their meeting with Tuor; in the Nirnaeth chapter, Maeglin overhears Huor's promise to Turgon of "a new star" rising from their houses, foreshadowing not only the fall of Gondolin but a fourth Great Tale, that of Eärendil and his voyage (58).

There are nods to the legendary duel between Fingolfin and Morgoth, which Húrin and his son seem to treat as a model for heroic conduct. Such allusions to the single combat at the gates of Angband are especially appropriate considering Túrin's role in the prophecy of a cosmic duel to come at the world's ending, discussed in the final portion of this chapter. At the death of his daughter Urwen, a distraught Húrin declares his desire to see Morgoth "face to face," and "mar" him as king "Fingolfin did" (40). The first part of his wish will soon be granted—but the marring will have to wait. Húrin's language is echoed in the narrator's later speculation on Morgoth's triumph in the Nirnaeth: Turgon's escape "troubled him deeply and marred his victory with unquiet" (60). Morgoth's frustration is attributed to several factors, not least of which are "the wounds that Fingolfin gave him in battle" (60).

More subtle is the allusion made later by Túrin in conversation with Finduilas. He claims to have it from Melian that Morgoth will "never again" leave the comforts of Angband, and must rely only on his minions, "the fingers of his hands" (166). Túrin's argument, that Nargothrond abandon its secrecy and openly engage those fingers—"smite them, and cut them off, till" Morgoth draws back—relies on a reading of the Fingolfin duel as purely heroic and admirable: he takes not only inspiration from the High King's courage in defeat but sees in it some fruits of success: the wounds inflicted on Morgoth remove him from the playing field (166). It is intriguing to note Túrin's source—a lesson from Melian—and, without any other record of this exchange, to speculate on the details. It may be that Melian's lore, like Beleg's gesture in delivering to Túrin the Helm of Hador, "had wrought otherwise with Túrin than" was hoped (146). Indeed, it might be that the stirring tale of this duel, like the stories of Húrin's indomitable resistance, formed the blueprint, for better or worse, for much that Túrin attempts after his exile from Doriath. Beleg later cautions that the Land of Bow and Helm is not a viable long-term community: "We have burned the fingertips of the Black Hand—no more. It will not withdraw." Túrin's earnest response is only to ask: "But is not the wrath of Angband our purpose and delight?" (146). He knows no other form of resistance—no other way to be—than to lop off the fingers and arms of the enemy until he is finally buried under them. If Fingolfin's deeds have taken Morgoth off the board, Túrin will play for pieces.[27]

Perhaps more subtle still is the allusion in Túrin's response to Mablung near the end of the tragedy. Mablung, finding Túrin at last, notes the obvious, that by his appearance "the years have been heavy on" him. Túrin's reply—"'Heavy! . . . Yes, as the feet of Morgoth.'"—recalls Fingolfin's end, pinned to the canvas outside the gates of Angband: "and Morgoth set his left foot upon his neck, and the weight of it was like a fallen hill" (*CH*, 253; *S*, 154).

A STORE OF STRANGE LUMBER

In addition to the digressions and the network of allusions to tales existing outside the frame of Túrin's saga, it is useful to remember that several noteworthy puzzles, cruxes, and dubious allusions to lost tales are embedded therein. As far back as his undergraduate days, Tolkien perceived the "thick dust of a no longer understood tradition" blanketing the Welsh and other old tales of the primary world (*SK*, 107). This mysterious baggage—what he calls "strange lumber"—was a lifelong fascination for him (108). In his undergraduate appreciation of the *Kalevala,* he goes so far as to suggest that misunderstanding of this baggage may not be exclusive to a modern audience; these obscure "names and allusions" may have been "already nonsense for the bards who related them." Surely we glimpse this in Beleg's catalog of swords quoted above from the alliterative lay of the 1920s. But even in the most nearly "complete" and seamless treatment we have of Túrin, a substantial stock of strange lumber remains.

Mîm's intrusion in the tale, and all the secret lives of the Petty-dwarves ("long out of mind, for Mîm was the last"), may be viewed as one such example in the Túrin saga (121). Mîm occupies a place in the tale not unlike that of Gollum in Frodo's story: an ancient, pitiable creature from a forgotten people, Mîm is at turns kind—he takes a shine to Túrin—and wicked—he eventually betrays their camp to Morgoth's spies. Without Mîm, Túrin's band of outlaws would have had no shelter through the winter, would have known none of the secret ways of going about the hill of Amon Rûdh. In the end, Mîm the dispossessed inherits the whole of the treasure hoard of Nargothrond—but only for a fleeting moment, meeting his death at the hand of Húrin.

The curious matter of Mîm's sack and its contents is one enduring piece of "strange lumber"—an accretion to the tale first taken up in the expanded prose *Narn* published in *Unfinished Tales*.[28] It is never quite rightly explained or fully integrated with the larger narrative, yet it adds just the kind of color and intrigue of the old tales that Tolkien so hoped to emulate in his own work. Mîm's sack is one example of Tolkien's continued efforts to open up "new vistas"—even if the view is the bottom of an old bag—all while greatly expanding one of the earliest tales of his legendarium.

The sacks carried by Mîm and his sons are a defining feature of their first appearance to Túrin and his band: "they saw three hooded shapes, grey-clad . . . burdened each with a great sack" (123). Mîm promises to return in the morning light and guide Túrin's men to his secret dwelling. But when Túrin asks him to leave "some pledge" as collateral—"Shall we keep your sack and its load, Mîm?"—the Dwarf refuses to be parted from it, falling "on his knees again in great trouble," though he dismisses the "old sack of roots" as immaterial (125). At this Túrin "marked, and others also, that Mîm set more store by the sack and his load than it seemed worth to the eye" (125).

Nothing more is said of sacks until Túrin and his company have begun to settle in Mîm's House of Ransom atop Amon Rûdh. There the hungry Men receive a lesson in foraging and cookery from their host:

Three great cooking-pots he lent . . . and he brought out a sack.
"Rubbish. . . . Only wild roots."
But . . . they were good to eat (134)

When asked the name of these roots, Mîm clams up, refusing to teach the secrets of his mother tongue—or to teach Men ("greedy and thriftless") to forage them (134). Still, he goes on to expound their virtue—they are worth "more than gold in the hungry winter"—while denying again any attachment to the contents of the sack, calling the men "fools" to think he "would not be parted" from them to save himself. Yet Ulrad, who had gotten a glimpse of the sack, is unconvinced, observing that the Dwarf's defense makes him "wonder the more," for he plainly "would not be parted" (135). Mîm angrily denies once more any special value to his sack, and Ulrad retorts:

> "Nonetheless the old rogue had other things in his sack. . . . Maybe there are other things beside earth-bread in the wild which Elves have not found and
> · Men must not know!"
> "That may be," said Túrin. (136)

And these words of doubtful possibility would seem to be the last on the matter.

Perhaps Túrin would go on to learn more of the mystery sack. We are told that as his friendship with the Dwarf grew, he "listened more and more to his counsels," and he was admitted to Mîm's private "smithy at times, and there they would talk softly together" (138). But on these "long hours" spent "listening to his lore and the tales of his life," the reader, like the men of Túrin's band, is left out in the cold (138). Christopher's note 19 in the *Narn* of *Unfinished Tales* follows up one final lead from a "hastily scribbled note": "which suggests that there were ingots of gold disguised as roots, and refers to Mîm seeking 'for old treasures of a dwarf-house.' . . . But there is nowhere any indication of what part this treasure was to play in the story of Bar-en-Danwedh" (143). If the secrets have died with the last of the Petty-dwarves, the reader's temptation to speculate remains very much alive.[29]

One further piece of strange lumber tucked away in *The Children of Húrin* is the lore surrounding the swords Anglachel and Anguirel, its lesser-known forge-mate. Anguirel is in fact mentioned only in this one context in all of Tolkien's published writings. The passage, describing Beleg's selection of a sword from Thingol's hoard, is a tour de force, reveling in the evocation of untold tales even as it appears to reveal the history of perhaps the most legendary weapon in the legendarium. It is

> a sword of great fame, . . . so named because it was made of iron that fell from heaven as a blazing star; it would cleave all earth-dolven iron. One other sword only in Middle-earth was like to it. That sword does not enter into this tale, though it was made of the same ore by the same smith; and that smith was Eöl the Dark Elf, who took Aredhel Turgon's sister to wife. He gave Anglachel to

Thingol as fee, which he begrudged, for leave to dwell in Nan Elmoth; but the
other sword, Anguirel, its mate, he kept, until it was stolen from him by Maeglin, his son. (96)

The passage is written as if in response to the eager chorus of questions
from listeners seated at the Tale-fire: Why was the sword called Anglachel?
What distinguishes heavenly iron from plain old iron? Was there any other
sword like it? Could you tell us more about it? Who made it? Other questions
go unanswered: Why, for example, was Anglachel already "of great fame" if it
sat idly in Thingol's armory? There is a sense here that we glimpse a narrator
accommodating an audience far removed from ourselves as modern readers,
one who is still conversant in these intricacies of Middle-earth's history and
linguistics. Consider the naming question: the narrator's explanation of the
name Anglachel is glib in its assumption that the reader will have detected in
the sword's Sindarin name the elements *ang-* for iron and *–el* for star.[30]

It is tempting to see this episode as an example of Tolkien "drawing on . . .
long works that already existed in prose and verse" for an effect summed up by
Christopher quite movingly: "that characteristic tone, melodious, grave, elegiac, burdened with a sense of loss and distance in time, which resides partly
. . . in the literary fact that he was drawing down into a brief compendious history what he could also see in far more detailed, immediate, and dramatic form"
(*WJ*, 245). Yet in no other published material—on Eöl or on his son Maeglin—
does Anguirel receive mention. Was this to be another story, one in which this
twin blade might play a role in the fall of Gondolin and beyond? Regardless, it
stands in the Túrin saga as a memorable lost tale, a reminder that for all the woe
and heroism of Túrin's story, he is only a little fellow in a wide world. Túrin's
black sword was from the start one of the most iconic elements of the tale; as
Richard West argues, it "spoke powerfully to Tolkien's imagination," and he
"devoted much care to develop the weapon" (*TL*, 239). In this way, the tease
of a twin blade is of obvious interest—a delicious bit in the *scop*'s repertoire.[31]

Still more strange lumber is cut away from *The Children of Húrin* at Christopher's discretion.[32] Perhaps the most notable reduction concerns the heirloom Dragon-helm. In the text's appendix, Christopher clarifies his decision:
"I have omitted from the text . . . the history of how the Dragon-helm came
into the possession of Hador of Dor-lómin" (287). Though this passage was
included in *Unfinished Tales,* it was here deemed "parenthetical to the narrative." It must be said that, for those keen to hear snatches of untold tales,
the excision of the Dragon-helm's title search is a loss.[33] The omitted passage sketches the helm's lofty history and helps to explain, maybe, Thingol's

reverence for it—he "handled the Helm of Hador as though his hoard were scanty" (79). It also touched again on the Nirnaeth, on the adventures of the sons of Fëanor, and on Azaghâl and Fingon, the two principal heroes to have tangled with Glaurung in the past.

It is evident from Christopher's commentary that Tolkien had bigger, unfinished plans for the Dragon-helm, "to extend the history . . . into the period of Túrin's sojourn in Nargothrond and even beyond" (*UT*, 149). According to "an isolated scrap," the helm would be worn at the Battle of Tumhalac and figure prominently in the exchange between Túrin and the dragon thereafter (149). Túrin strikes a nerve in boldly proclaiming that "while there is one to bear" the helm, "doubt shall ever assail" the dragon, "lest the bearer deal" his "doom" (149). Glaurung, "desiring to rid Túrin of its aid and protection (since he himself feared it)," counters then that the helm "must await a master of another name" (149). The dragon's effrontery in declaring that Túrin "has not the hardihood to look me in the face, openly" is finally too much, provoking him "in pride and rashness" to "thrust up the visor" and meet the baleful eye (149). Christopher's commentary provides one final, tantalizing glimpse of his father's unfinished plans for the helm: that "Túrin was to wear the Helm when he slew Glaurung," taunting the dragon with his own words ("a master of another name") (149–50). Such plans had potentially serious implications; we can see that Tolkien was experimenting with the helm as a place to explore some of the cycle's thematic veins: (hidden) identity, pride and *ofermod*, combat ethics, and so on.[34]

The strange lumber, which is the result of an unfinished tangle of plotlines, developments, and movements, calls to mind once more Tolkien's professional interests in the legends of the Primary World. We know that Tolkien was deeply engaged with the stories of Sigurd and Fáfnir,[35] and that the shabby—or ruined—state of this story cycle both pained him and inspired him to rework the stories into his own form, published in *The Legend of Sigurd & Gudrun* (2009).[36] Tolkien had explicitly identified Sigurd (most clearly in the dragon-slaying episode) as a source for Turin, yet it may be that he took inspiration also from its convoluted tradition. He seems to revel in the sheer confusion—"Truly complicated!"—of the Völsunga material and the Sigurd-Brynhild-Gunnar triangle, a betrothal broken "both by fate and by magic." Not to be forgotten: "Behind all hangs Odin, and his doom. . . . Inextricably interwoven is the curse on the gold" (*SG*, 245).

While the unfinished incorporation of the Dragon-helm was probably not an intentional move on Tolkien's part, its imperfect handling—like the "product of accident . . . retained" in the Völsunga saga—does reflect what happens to stories over a great expanse of time (245). If here his powers failed him—if he never came even close to Dírhavel's celebrated text—it only strengthened the impression of antiquity and lost tales.[37]

Even in the long form prose *Narn,* Tolkien often moves from vivid immediacy to terse, fragmentary summary, suggesting a vast and fertile story land forever out of reach.[38] Sometimes a bona fide source is revealed in Tolkien's other writing. Such is the case of Túrin and Gwindor's journey to Nargothrond, described at length in verse in the alliterative lay but reduced to little more than a measly "Thus did Túrin come to Nargothrond" in *The Children of Húrin* (158).[39] We feel—even *know* (by the fragment of the alliterative lay)—that the later compression is but a summary of a much bigger story.

The feeling, if not the knowledge, lingers in other cases. The adventures of Túrin and Beleg, "companions in every peril" as "three years passed," are glossed in three paragraphs (86). The rise and fall of Túrin in Nargothrond and the doomed love triangle of Túrin, Finduilas, and Gwindor are the stuff of an epic, but Túrin's five years there are summarized in a single chapter. While the Nirnaeth Arnoediad earns its own chapter in the text, the host of Nargothrond is swept away in the disastrous Battle of Tumhalad over the course of a scant two paragraphs. Over the ruins of Nargothrond, Glaurung "ruled as a dragon-king," though of course no chronicle of his reign is here offered (221). At Glaurung's death, we are told that "true proved the words spoken" when Gurthang was forged: "that nothing, great or small, should live that once it had bitten," yet no prior record of such a prophecy is mentioned; the sword is merely "forged anew . . . by the cunning smiths of Nargothrond" (238, 160). Tolkien's terse summaries open up imaginative spaces for all manner of Túrin cycles: *Túrin in Love, Túrin Enraged, Túrin the Outlaw Swashbuckler, Túrin and Beleg: The Buddy Comedy.*

In light of these instances, we can see that Tolkien has the means to create an impression of depth even in going deeper down the well—he needed to discover new unattainable vistas, and he often did. With the benefit of much more than the 1977 *Silmarillion* to go on, we might recognize that Tom Shippey's suggestion that the inset stories would lack depth in themselves is not, at least in Túrin's case, accurate.[40]

TÚRIN, THE END TIMES, AND THE SEAMLESS WEB OF STORY

In Turin's case, Tolkien sought to create depth not only in looking back to a lost poetic masterwork but also forward to the unfulfilled prophecies of the world's end.[41] We might say that a kind of apotheosis is reached—in the developments of a Túrin story cycle particularly and in Tolkien's engagement with untold tales more generally—when we read of the mysterious destiny foretold for Túrin in *The History of Middle-earth*. Like most of the other major beats in the Túrin story, a *eucatastrophic* prophecy of The End is present from the early *Tale of Turambar*, at least as a kind of coda or epilogue.[42] Having recounted Túrin's earthly demise, the tale-teller Eltas concludes with an astonishing account of this far distant fate in a Ragnarökian finale:

> "the Gods had mercy on their unhappy fate, so that those twain Túrin and Nienori . . . dwelt as shining Valar among the blessed ones . . . but Turambar indeed shall stand beside Fiönwë in the Great Wrack, and Melko and his drakes shall curse the sword of Mormakil."
>
> And so saying Eltas made an end, and none asked further. (*BLT II,* 115–16)

Though it does not appear in any completed works published during Tolkien's lifetime, this special function of Túrin and his sword in the End Times is a concept that developed nearly as long as the legendarium itself, and I give below a brief overview of its chief movements as traced through the twelve volumes of *The History of Middle-earth*.

In *The Sketch of the Mythology* of 1926, the so-called Earliest Silmarillion, Túrin's role in this final struggle takes a further step from *The Book of Lost Tales,* moving from vague menace to Morgoth's executioner: "When the world is much older, and the Gods weary, Morgoth will come back through the Door, and the last battle of all will be fought. . . . it shall be Túrin who with his black sword will slay Morgoth, and thus the children of Húrin shall be avenged" (*Shaping,* 40).

Then, in the *Quenta Noldorinwa* (around 1930), this notion is attached to the prophesies of Mandos, where also Túrin's familiar nom de guerre, Conqueror of Fate (Turambar), is mentioned and his galactic vendetta is achieved not as redress for his family alone but for the race of Men more broadly: "Then shall the last battle be gathered. . . . Tulkas shall strive with Melko . . . and on his left Túrin . . . Conqueror of Fate . . . it shall be the black sword of Túrin that deals unto Melko his death and final end; and so shall the children of Húrin and all Men be avenged" (*Shaping,* 165).

The prophecy again appears in nearly identical fashion in the *Quenta Silmarillion* abandoned in 1937, with the added clarification that Túrin would join the battle after "coming from the halls of Mandos" (*LR,* 333). When Tolkien returned to the *Quenta* in the years following the completion of *The Lord of the Rings,* Christopher notes only "cursory corrections" made to the passage; Túrin returns not from the Halls of Mandos but "from the Doom of Men at the ending of the world" (*Peoples,* 375; *WJ,* 247).

The last we hear of this prophecy comes from a footnote to the linguistic essay, "The Problem of Ros." That this last word on one of the most mysterious and fantastic elements in Tolkien's legendarium would come in this manner, in a treatise on the suffix *-ros* in the Elvish languages is, I suppose, further proof of Lewis's claim that Tolkien was an inspired speaker of footnotes.[43] The essay is found in *The Peoples of Middle-earth,* the last volume of *The History,* and is grouped among other "late writings" that represent Tolkien's final work on the legendarium from the late 1960s on. The passage declares that the language of the people of Haleth would not "be heard again" "unless the prophecy of Andreth . . . should prove true, that Túrin in the Last Battle should return . . . , and before he left the Circles of the World . . . challenge . . . Ancalagon . . . and deal him the death-stroke" (374). In this last iteration we have also some of the first substantial changes to consider. While the core idea of Túrin returning from the dead to deliver a doughty stroke remains intact, the prophecy comes not from Mandos but from the woman Andreth, and the target is not Morgoth but Ancalagon.

One more dubious alteration concerns the battle itself: Christopher claims that Andreth's prophecy deals with "the Last Battle at the end of the Elder Days" rather than that which ends the world, the Dagor Dagorath (Battle of All Battles) (375). The claim is not at all unreasonable—it would be congruent with another usage of "Last Battle" in the essay, and it would presumably explain Ancalagon's appearance, though Túrin had never before been associated with the black dragon's defeat. Yet "Last Battle" frequently refers to both the War of Wrath at the end of the First Age and the Dagor Dagorath to end the world, and thus it is not impossible that it might be used in both senses over the course of a wide-ranging and unpolished/unpublished essay in Tolkien's lifetime. Furthermore, the note on Andreth's prophecy obviously alludes to another text or pseudotext, and thus the paraphrase of her words would need not be made consistent with the essayist's voice. In fact, Ancalagon's defeat in a Ragnarökian battle nicely echoes the earliest extant pronouncement of Túrin's destiny: that "Melko and his drakes shall curse the sword of Mormakil" (*BLT II,* 116). Indeed, I speculate that Andreth's prophecy is more consistent with the earlier versions and does in fact refer to the End Times, where presumably the spirit of Ancalagon could be present just as Túrin's is.

But such speculation is probably in vain. For this Last Battle remains the ultimate untold tale in Tolkien's legendarium. What seems most significant is that we are in any case dealing with prophecy, speculative glimpses of a far-off future. And, of course, we have only this footnote: no other mention is made of Andreth's prophecy, not even in the "Athrabeth Finrod ah Andreth."[44] Whatever Andreth's meaning, we might recognize in her rendition a kind of cynic's hope, setting the sights of her prophecy a smidge lower, whether in target or in distance of time.

This special function of Túrin must be one of the greatest surprises to readers encountering *The History of Middle-earth* for the first time.[45] The bombast of this image—Túrin returning from death to strike the world-ending coup de grâce with his trusty black sword—so far beyond Húrin's comparatively humble desire to "mar" Morgoth as Fingolfin did, seems a flourish not unlike that which Tolkien found so intoxicating in his youthful encounters with the *Kalevala*: "the deeds . . . are all splashed onto a clean bare canvas by a sudden hand: even the legends . . . of the most ancient things seem to come fresh from the singer's hot imagination of the moment" (*SK*, 109).

While many of the developments in Tolkien's legends since *The Book of Lost Tales* led to a purging "of the gross," a clearing away of the strange undergrowth and a subtle shading of tradition akin to the Welsh tales to which he contrasts *Kalevala,* this work of a sudden hand and a hot imagination remained. Or did it? Quite apart from the niceties of difference between Andreth and Mandos, the question of the canonicity of Túrin's return is a perplexing one.

Certainly no inkling of such a destiny is present in *The Silmarillion,* which ends without any mention of a Dagor Dagorath or of Túrin's part therein.[46] It notes only that "if any change shall come . . . it is not declared in the dooms of Mandos" (255). Douglas Charles Kane in *Arda Reconstructed* observes the difficult decisions on display in the contrast between this closing passage and Tolkien's own description of the legendarium's conclusion in his 1951 letter to Milton Waldman, given in a preface to the text's second edition. Here Tolkien writes that his legendarium's vision of the world's end comes "after a final battle which owes . . . more to the Norse . . . Ragnarök than to anything else (*Letters,* 149). The decision to abandon such an ending must remain one of the most controversial editorial moves made in presenting *The Silmarillion* for publication. Christopher's chosen end is derived from a passage out of another text, the *Valaquenta.* Based on this passage's reference to the dooms of Mandos, Christopher concluded in *Morgoth's Ring* that Mandos's Second Prophecy, including Túrin's return, "had . . . definitively disappeared" (204).

I would agree with Kane's assessment that this seems a hasty dismissal, and with the publication of *The Fall of Gondolin,* it would seem that Christopher does, too.[47] As he says after closing accounts of the *Sketch of the Mythology* and the *Quenta Noldorinwa*, "My history of a history thus ends with a prophecy, the prophecy of Mandos" (*FG*, 264). And so Túrin's mystery role makes a return in Christopher's final work of literary excavation. The question of canonicity is exceedingly complex, and Christopher's efforts following *The Silmarillion* show a dedication to presenting his father's unfinished and evolving work as authentically as possible. But the publication of *The Fall of Gondolin* may suggest a kind of turning point in the stock of the second prophecy.[48]

Reticence has characterized Christopher's commentary on this phenomenon, further contributing to its untold mystique. On the conclusion of Eltas's narrative in *Turambar*, he only notes "that nowhere is there any explanation given" (*BLT II*, 137–38). Christopher's response to the first bombshell description of The End in the *Sketch of the Mythology* might even be called evasive: "Into this final resolution . . . it would prove unprofitable, I think, to enquire too closely" (*Shaping*, 73). Later, in his commentary on the Prophecy of the *Quenta Noldorinwa*, Christopher notes that Túrin's appearance here "remains profoundly mysterious" (205). As to the question of his place among the Gods or time in the Halls of Mandos, Christopher "can say no more than that" Túrin's fate was not that of the race of Men (205). While interpretation is not Christopher's goal, his reluctance to engage with or attempt any explanation of these developments does contribute to their air of arresting strangeness.

Given Tolkien's treatment of battles like that of Tumhalad, or the Last Alliance, it will come as no surprise that the Dagorath is largely untold. It does, however, receive a few scattered references outside of the prophesies concerning Túrin. In the essay on the Istari from *Unfinished Tales* we read that "Manwë will not descend from the Mountain until the Dagor Dagorath and the coming of the End" (379). Christopher here anticipates his later cagey analyses, noting that "elucidation" of this allusion to the Second Prophecy "cannot be attempted here" (*UT*, 385). An untitled alliterative verse on the Five Wizards follows the essay, again alluding to The End with the line "until Dagor Dagorath and the Doom cometh" (379). These snatches of verse—tattered fragments of lore—whet the appetite but do little to satisfy our questions about the projected end of Tolkien's legendarium.

It may say something of the simmering of the Cauldron of Story that the scant but striking detail offered in the fragments of the Túrin prophecy echoes somewhat those accounts of historical battles in Middle-earth. The principals Túrin, Fiönwë, and Tulkas *en garde* against Morgoth find some corollary in the pitched battle between Sauron and the allies Elendil and Gil-galad—and, by extension, the standoff between Frodo, Sam, and Gollum. Tradition and typology draw on the past but are here projected into the future.

One of the central theses of this study has been that Tolkien's untold tales matter; they are integral to the author's total vision. As such, I would be remiss if I did not attempt at least some interpretation of this marvelous and largely untold offshoot of the Túrin tradition, even if "elucidation" of the subject, as Christopher puts it, may be beyond my reach.

One element, quite apart from Tolkien's draconian "soft-spot" for Túrin,[49] is that he is a Man, one of that race of Children of Ilúvatar whose Fall takes place offstage, whose Hopes are seldom whispered, and whose Doom (or Gift?) of death is a mystery even to the Valar. As some consolation, Men are given in Tolkien's mythology a special virtue of free will: "to shape their life . . . beyond the Music of the Ainur, which is as fate to all" else (S, 41). And it is their agency through which "everything should be, in form and deed, completed, and the world fulfilled" (41). Thus, almost at their first awakening, Men—Hobbits included—become the primary movers and shakers of the legendarium—great (Tuor, Aragorn) and small (Frodo and Sam), for good and ill (on both counts: Isildur, Gollum). Men are to take part in the mysterious "Second Music . . . after the World's end," so it may be fitting that a Man should help bring about that end (S, 29).

Túrin, we can imagine, is chosen not for his prowess alone. What better man than Túrin to make good on Eru's warning to Melkor after his discordant jam session threatens the Music of the Ainur? As Eru claims, "nor can any alter the music in my despite. For he that attempteth this shall prove but mine instrument in the devising of things more wonderful, which he himself hath not imagined" (S, 17). In this sense, the tragedy of Túrin's failed resistance in Beleriand is but a proving ground for the plains of Valinor, priming him for the Last Battle of all, and layering even this "most evil" work of Morgoth into Ilúvatar's all-encompassing theme.

The aftermath of the first of Mandos's prophecies, in which he foretells the doom of the Noldor after their kin-slaying and oath-taking, may also shed light on the second. Manwë's reaction references Eru's earlier words, noting that the immortal songs of the Noldor's deeds will be both "dear-bought" and "well-bought": "For the price could be no other, Thus even as Eru spoke to us shall beauty not before conceived be brought into Eä, and evil yet be good to have been" (S, 98). Túrin's pride of place in the second prophecy thus riffs on the first: his hopeless battle against Morgoth at least will make for a good tale, and, in some far-off melody of Ilúvatar, it may do more.

The prophecy seems to offer Túrin, in recognition for his services, a kind of mythological payday. The measure of a deed—its intrinsic value, utility, or futility—is in fact a central concern in the Túrin cycle. In the alliterative lay it is Flinding (later Gwindor) who anticipates Túrin's later rousing rhetoric in support of an open-war policy in Nargothrond, entreating him to remember the inherent worth of resistance against Morgoth and the Orcs: "less would like them thy living hatred / and vows of vengeance; nor vain is courage, / Though victory seldom be valour's ending" (*LB*, 57). Túrin, in *The Children of Húrin,* argues likewise: "if in the end we cannot overcome him, at least we can hurt him and hinder him. For victory is victory, however small, nor is its worth only from what follows from it" (161). He adds, with reference to his father, and perhaps, with an eye to his own legacy, that though a Man's life is short, he "would rather spend it in battle than fly or submit. The defiance of Húrin Thalion is a great deed; and though Morgoth slay the doer he cannot make the deed not to have been. . . . is it not written into the history of Arda, which neither Morgoth nor Manwë can unwrite?" (161).

Another text, the late prose Gondolin, casts some light on this concern about a deed's value and its connection to the Túrin prophecy. In Ulmo's revelation to Tuor we catch an echo of Túrin's rhetoric, and a promise of hope that may be applicable to others besides Tuor:

> in the armour of Fate . . . there is ever a rift, and in the walls of Doom a breach, until . . . the End. . . .
>
> believe not that thy one sword is not worth the sending. For the valour of the Edain the Elves shall ever remember . . . , marveling that they gave life so freely of which they had on earth so little. But it is not for thy valour only . . . but to bring into the world a hope beyond thy sight. (*FG*, 165–66)

In life, Túrin's "one sword" sought the rift in Fate's armor; but in the Prophecy he may find it. There is bitter irony in Túrin's inability to enjoy the earthly accolades ("I care not" is his response to the praise of the Elves after slaying the dragon) he receives (254). Even so, the prophecy suggests that "hope beyond . . . sight" may be his in the end.

Indeed, that Túrin gets—and even makes good on—his title shot against Morgoth might be viewed as one of the most striking exemplars of *eucatastrophe* in the legendarium. While we most often think of the coming of the Eagles or the One Ring's fortuitous destruction as chief examples of *eucatastrophe,* it seems to me a distinct possibility that, while revising "On Fairy-stories" in the early 1940s, Tolkien has in mind the glimpse of Túrin's victory in the Great Wrack.[50] *Eucata-*

strophe, he explains, is "a sudden and miraculous grace: never to be counted on to recur. It does not deny ... dyscatastrophe ... ; it denies ... universal final defeat ... giving a fleeting glimpse of Joy ... beyond the walls of the world" (*MC,* 153). Such a description certainly rings true of Túrin's tale: its atmosphere is almost oppressively one of "sorrow and failure"; it offers an abundance of "evidence" against the utility of the Northern heroic code and its doctrine of doomed resistance. Yet Túrin's prophetic turn does in the end deny "final defeat." When Túrin stands triumphant over Morgoth, "we get a piercing glimpse of joy, and heart's desire, that for a moment passes outside the frame, rends indeed the very web of story, and lets a gleam come through." Thus the Túrin story's mystery coda comes to satisfy Tolkien's own essential criteria for "true" fairy story: for not only is it a tale about the "*aventures* of men in the perilous realm," it has the *eucatastrophic* turn that is "the mark of the true fairy story" (*MC,* 155).

Perhaps, though, Túrin's upward turn is more accurately experimental than exemplary, coming as it does long after the story is over. It is a fairy-tale ending deferred and detached and by it, Tolkien tries to have it both ways: to preserve the absolute tragedy of Túrin's life yet still gesture toward a distant and magnificent redemption.

That this mysterious prophecy loops back to the notion of tradition is best illustrated by a strange irony: perhaps the most illuminating text for a study of Turin's place in eschatology is in the Norse poems of *The Legend of Sigurd & Gudrun.* Eltas had warned us, back in the 1919 *Turambar,* that Turin had been "put into the Pot," had become one of those ingredients simmering in the Cauldron of Story: "Maybe the deeds of other of their warriors have become mingled therein, and many matters beside that are not in the most ancient tale," he cautions, before launching into the proper tale (*MC,* 126; *BLT II,* 70). If Tolkien hesitated in his letter to Waldman to attribute too much influence to Ragnarök, it may be because by the time that the letter was written in 1951, his own retellings of the Norse legend owed something to the prophecies of Túrin in the Dagor Dagorath.

Tolkien's Sigurd seems to come right out of the Halls of Mandos: "If in day of Doom / one deathless stands, / who death hath tasted / and dies no more, / the serpent-slayer, / seed of Ódin, / then all shall not end, nor earth perish" (*SG,* 63). "Brynhild shall arm him / with belt and sword," and the reader might be forgiven for asking whether it is Gram or Gurthang that he wields (179). For Sigurd at least there is no confusion about headgear—"On his head the Helm" (180). Tolkien's Ódin, too, "seems more like Manwë of his own mythology," concludes Christopher (186).

The one-eyed god's strategy and Sigurd's Túrin-like role are explained in Tolkien's own commentary accompanying his *New Lay of Sigurd*. Chief of those Óðin gathers for the Last Battle is Sigurd:

> for Óðin hopes that by his hand the Serpent shall in the end be slain. . . .
> None of the Gods can accomplish this, but only one who has lived on Earth
> . . . and died. (This motive of the special function of Sigurd is an invention of
> the present poet, or an interpretation of the Norse sources in which it is not
> explicit) (*SG*, 53–54)

Later in his commentary, Tolkien clarifies the redemptive possibilities in his vision of the heroes gathered for Ragnarök: tragic and untimely deaths "only make them of greater worth for their ultimate purpose in the Last Battle" (54).

A weird feedback loop develops, whereby the Sigurd legend of the Primary World explicitly influences the subcreated Túrin Turambar, who in turn exerts an influence on Sigurd in Tolkien's *New Lay*. Christopher notes the "extremely probable" association between Túrin and Sigurd here, though, as is characteristic of his commentary on the Túrin prophecy, he is reluctant to speculate overmuch "in the absence (so far as I know) of any other writing of my father's bearing on his enigmatic conception of Sigurd" (*SG*, 184–85). And with so few crumbs to go on, Tolkien's Norse lays are in truth some of the most illuminating when faced with the untold story of the Dagor Dagorath.

If the prophecy provides a link to other worlds like that of the Norse, it also marks a next stage of the tradition, the strange fruits of story. We see Túrin develop from tragic history, to legend, to fairy story and mythology. According to the *Annals of Aman*, Varda goes about redecorating the night sky with constellations: "The greatest of these was Menelmakar, the Swordsman of the Sky. This, it is said, was a sign of Túrin Turambar, who should come into the world, and a foreshowing of the Last Battle that shall be at the end of Days" (*MR*, 71). Menelmakar is elsewhere identified explicitly with Orion.[51] If in life Túrin was the equivalent of the Japanese sword saint (*kensei*), his legend ultimately earns a place among the stars.

While he was quick to point out the challenges in pulling off a *eucatastrophe*, Tolkien noted that "even modern fairy-stories can produce this effect sometimes. It is not an easy thing to do; it depends on the whole story which is the setting of the turn, and yet it reflects a glory backwards" (*TOFS*, 154). Given the apparent disjunction between the self-contained tragedy of *The Children of Húrin* and its apocalyptic coda, such a backward reflection is not easily recognized. While we know that some version of the Túrin prophecy was still viably simmering in Tolkien's imagination in the late 1960s, the great developments of *The Children of Húrin* do not explicitly reference any such prophecy But might the special mythological function of Túrin, like that of Sigurd, be interpreted from "sources in which it is not explicit"? Certain elements—call them strange lumber, or dormant allusions—may be worth a closer look.

In *The Children of Húrin,* discussion of fate and doom abound, and these remarks take on an added edge in light of the prophecy looming outside the frame. "What is fate?" is the key question Túrin puts to Sador as he grieves for his sister Urwen (42). Melian suspects that Túrin's fate will not match Beren's, but it is only a guess: "Not so high is your destiny, I think" (85). The question—"Can the spirit of any man return from death?"—put in response to Túrin's prowess with the Helm of Hador may begin to look less rhetorical in this light (85).

Even Morgoth, we are told, fears "that Túrin would grow to such a power" that his curse would "become void" and his doom might be escaped (147). As the narrative closes with Túrin's suicide, his fears would seem to be misplaced— yet not so, in the long run. Finduilas shows uncanny foresight in her belief that Túrin "is mighty in the tale of the World, and his stature shall reach yet to Morgoth in some far day to come" (169). Arminas admonishes Túrin in the buildup to Nargothrond's ruin for taking counsel with his "sword only," warning that his doom might be "other" than expected of the noble houses of Men (175). The criticism is just, and yet, in light of the prophecy Túrin's "other" doom, with his "sword only," it can take on a distinctive coloring, far removed from what the Elf has in mind.

Subtle notes also of the star-lore of Menelmakar might be found in *The Children of Húrin.* The discourse between Húrin and Morgoth is full of cosmology. Húrin's final rebuke comes "not from the lore of the Eldar"—just as the Túrin prophecy and the *Annals of Aman* come to be filtered through Mannish lore (65). The discussion turns even to *Menel* and echoes Andreth in its reference to the Circles of the World. The reader eager for more on Túrin's link to the night sky might note the curious provenance of Túrin's famed sword, of ore "that fell from heaven as a blazing star" (96). Even Tolkien's most well-worn tales invite readers to delve deeper, speculate, and imagine new possibilities.

In the buildup to the carpenter Sador's lament for wasted time and the fleeting joys of making, which serves as the last epigraph to this chapter, a young Túrin—not yet bowed by the unbearable weight of his grief, his rash choices, and his cursed fate—urges his old friend not to abandon his craft. Sador

looked at the great chair of Húrin, which had been thrust unfinished in a corner. "It must go," he said, "for only bare needs can be served in these days."

"Do not break it yet," said Túrin. "Maybe he will come home, and then it
will please him to see what you have done for him while he was away." (72)

We never hear what becomes of the chair, but we can be grateful for the care
that Christopher Tolkien has lavished in preserving his father's unfinished
works—all this strange lumber—from the fire.

"Don't the great tales never end?" Sam asks, in that evergreen passage on
the Stairs of Cirith Ungol. Only "when the world is much older and the Gods
weary." Tucked away above the quiet of the Shire, we find an elusive third reference to Túrin and his strange prophecy within the pages of *The Lord of the
Rings:* "there leaned up, as he climbed over the rim of the world, the Swordsman of the Sky, Menelvagor with his shining belt. The Elves all burst into song"
(*FR,* I, iii, 81).

Chapter Four

A PORTRAIT OF THE POET
AS A YOUNG MAN
Omission in *The Homecoming of Beorhtnoth*

Possibly he was a member of Byrhtnoð's well-born heorðwerod, who
missed the battle and happened to be a practised poet.
—E. V. Gordon, introduction, on the identity of the
anonymous author of *The Battle of Maldon*

~~For the purpose of this modern poem, it is suggested that~~
~~Torhthelm (Totta) afterwards, when the duke's body has been brought~~
~~to its long home at Ely, composes the poem, *The Battle of Maldon*.~~
—J. R. R. Tolkien, Bodleian Library, MS. Tolkien 5

In the preceding chapters, we have traced Tolkien's success in sketching an
illusion of a Last Alliance tradition within the pages of *The Lord of the Rings*,
and single-handedly crafting one across the Túrin cycle. The empty spaces in
these traditions invoke a sense of wonder and loss, they comment on the nature of storytelling, and they help shape our interpretation of the texts themselves. This chapter aims to pick up some of the thematic threads of chapters 2 and 3—the interpretation of old wars and the fraught legacies of their
heroes—while exploring Tolkien's use of omission, which we might regard
as the epitome of untold tales. In doing so, we must once more step out of
Middle-earth and back into the realm of Tolkien's academic work, specifically
his scholarly and creative engagement with the Old English *Battle of Maldon*.

THE BATTLE OF MALDON AND THE
HOMECOMING OF BEORHTNOTH

The Battle of Maldon, a fragment of Old English verse commemorating the last stand and defeat of Byrhtnoth (hereafter following Tolkien's spelling, Beorhtnoth) and his English warriors at the hands of Viking invaders in 991, was a touchstone for Tolkien throughout his career. Excepting *Beowulf,* John R. Holmes has suggested that *Maldon* was "the Old English poem that most influenced Tolkien's fiction" (2007, 52) His engagement with the poem stretches back at least as far as his undergraduate study at Exeter College. It later became a standard text throughout his teaching career; the Tolkien archive at the Bodleian Library contains reams of his lecture notes and commentary, as well as a prose translation of the poem. Tolkien receives acknowledgment in the 1937 edition of *Maldon* edited by his former Leeds University colleague, E. V. Gordon. Finally, or most notably—for there is little reason to believe that Tolkien's interest in the poem had been exhausted—Tolkien's *The Homecoming of Beorhtnoth Beorhthelm's Son,* a response to *Maldon* in dramatic verse (with accompanying essays), was published in a 1953 volume of the journal *Essays and Studies.*

Tolkien's attraction to *The Battle of Maldon* would likely be clear to most readers of his fiction: it is a poem seemingly all about what Tolkien calls in his famous *Beowulf* lecture "the great contribution of early Northern literature": its "theory of courage" and of doomed—but unflagging—resistance (*MC,* 20). The poem's emphasis on the brave words and last stand of Beorhtnoth's faithful retainers earns it the title of "last surviving fragment of ancient English heroic minstrelsy" in the introductory portion to Tolkien's *Homecoming* (3).

That it was incomplete, too, must account for a measure of Tolkien's scholarly and creative fascination. As Tolkien describes it, the poem we call *The Battle of Maldon* is a 325-line fragment with "no end and no beginning, and no title." We are reminded in *The Notion Club Papers* that "the charm of the fragment is often largely in being unfinished" (*SD,* 189). And this sort of charm, this trigger for untold tales, is explored and exploited throughout Tolkien's work. Tom Shippey has observed that the "gaps and even the errors of ancient literature" were a great stimulus to Tolkien's imagination: "that the thing which attracted Tolkien most was darkness: the blank spaces, much bigger than most people realise, on the literary and historical map" (2001, 82; 2003, 38). Tolkien's engagement with the *Maldon* fragment is a useful reminder, however, that his creative response was not simply to fill the gap—he needed to make space still for untold tales. And so Tolkien's *Homecoming* is partly inspired by the tantalizing missing pieces of *Maldon,* but it makes no effort to fill those gaps by reconstructing the poem's beginning or end. Instead, it is something quite different.

Before we go on to consider what that something might be, and how omission plays into it, I must acknowledge that *Homecoming* may be something of an obscure text for those readers not accustomed to bingeing on old editions of *Essays and Studies*—or *The Tolkien Reader* and *Tree & Leaf,* where the verse drama has been reprinted in the years since its first publication. As such I offer a brief sketch of the text.

The Homecoming of Beorhtnoth Beorhthelm's Son is divided in three parts. At its center is a dramatic dialogue in alliterative verse (*The Homecoming* proper) that recounts the fictional journey of two of the duke's servants, Torhthelm (Totta) and Tídwald (Tída), sent by the Abbot of Ely to recover their lord's body on the night after the battle near Maldon commemorated in the Old English poem. Totta "is a youth, son of a minstrel; his head is full of old lays" about the old heroes of the North; Tída, on the other hand, is an old "farmer who had seen much fighting," though neither of the two fought in the previous day's battle (2).

As this odd couple wanders through the muck and gore of the battlefield, searching for the headless body of Beorhtnoth, their dialogue in alliterative verse explores the tensions between youth and age, romance and realism, pagan and Christian worldview. After much toil, and a scuffle with desperate battlefield scavengers that leaves one more needlessly dead, the two men succeed in loading the duke's body onto their wagon and then head for Ely Abbey. Totta, asleep in the cart, has a dream vision in which he mutters the most famous lines of the (as yet unwritten) *Battle of Maldon,* suggesting that he may in fact go on to compose that poem. His dream is interrupted by a jolt from the bumpy road, and the curtain falls with the monks of Ely chanting the Latin Office for the Dead. Their chant, briefly interrupted by a mysterious voice in the dark, closes out the verse drama.

This dramatic-poetic core is bracketed on the front end by "Beorhtnoth's Death," a prefatory historical note on the battle, and on the back end by "Ofermod," a critical endnote exploring the treatment of heroism in the Old English poem, arguing (with aplomb and against the grain) that the anonymous poet expressed severe criticism of Beorhtnoth's gallant blunder in allowing the much greater Viking force to cross to the mainland via a strategic causeway and join in a "fair" fight.

Initially published just a year before the first volumes of *The Lord of the Rings* appeared in print, *Homecoming* is often overlooked or viewed as an oddity in

Tolkien's oeuvre: it is increasingly of interest to scholars,[1] with special attention paid to the essay "Ofermod," but still obscure or elusive to most readers. Yet the author himself described it as "very germane to the general division of sympathy exhibited in *The Lord of the Rings*" (Hammond and Scull 2017b, 548). While it is not part of Tolkien's legendarium, *Homecoming* is an important work: in addition to being a rare completed and published example of Tolkien's mastery of alliterative poetry and a demonstration of the intersection of his scholarly and creative pursuits, it "echoes strikingly" with *The Lord of the Rings* (Honegger 2007).[2]

Some of the critical attention garnered by *Homecoming* has, I think, unfortunately obscured what makes the text so special. In what we might call a light case of what ailed *Beowulfiana* circa 1936, critics have, in viewing the text primarily as a vehicle for the argument set out in its endnote, "Ofermod," tended to overlook the fact that *Homecoming*, for all its scholarly baggage, is first and foremost a poem—a work of art.

Thus Tom Shippey's (2007) perspective on the poem in the influential "Tolkien and *The Homecoming of Beorhtnoth*" is that it is a kind of "Ofermod" essay writ large. In Shippey's view, the dramatic dialogue is a one-sided affair in favor of Totta's elder counterpart, Tída. He labels the work Tolkien's "act of parricide" against his own sources and their heathen heroic code, in *Homecoming* represented by the young poet, Totta (337). Totta, for Shippey, is a coward and a murderer—"simply a stooge" for Tolkien to deliver this critical message (329). Understandably, no mention of the possible ascription of Totta as the future *Maldon* poet is made in this essay.

Such a reading seems to me wide of the mark, for it misses the twofold purpose of Tolkien's verse drama: to present a balanced dialogue that probes the tensions between illusion and disillusion, and to draw up an imaginative genesis of the *Maldon* fragment and its poet. *Homecoming*, in fact, manages at once to be both coda and prequel to *Maldon*.

The kind of scholarly reaction to *Homecoming* characterized by Shippey's essay is partly Tolkien's fault, both for the novel force of his argument in "Ofermod"—whether one agrees or disagrees with its conclusions—and for the text's awkwardly placed initial publication in the pages of an academic journal. Tolkien's sheepish apology, which opens "Ofermod," can be taken at face value: *Homecoming* is "composed primarily as verse, to be condemned or approved as such" (13). While it seems hard to believe that Tolkien would simply scrape together a last-minute essay so that *Homecoming* could "merit a place" in a volume of *Essays and Studies,* it is also undeniable that the verse drama long precedes the scholarly apparatus that brackets it (13). As Thomas

Honegger observes from his study of *Homecoming*'s manuscript in *Tolkien Studies 4*, its poetic core makes it "one of the rare (known) instances where Tolkien's literary muse ostensibly inspired his scholarly genius" (2007, 195).

A NOTEWORTHY OMISSION

But another factor in this unfortunate scholarly reaction may be the challenge posed by an omission, an untold tale. The omission in question, cited in one form in the last of this chapter's epigraphs, is Tolkien's decision to leave out of the published text any *explicit* reference that would identify his fictional character of Totta as the poet who would go on to compose the Old English poem. What may at first glance seem like a throw(n)away detail is actually the unseen hinge on which swings much of our interpretation of *Homecoming*. The verse drama is, in the end, about more than putting to the sword the old heroic code and the literature in which it is enshrined—and Totta's *implicit* journey toward the *Maldon* poet is key to understanding Tolkien's technique and unlocking the text's buried treasures.

I argue that Tolkien purposefully omits the explicit identification of Totta as the poet not out of doubt but of confidence in his future role as the maker of *The Battle of Maldon*. Like the linked stories of Tolkien's legendarium, *The Homecoming* draws depth and splendor when read alongside the Old English fragment that inspired it. Tolkien's omission thus rewards attentive readers of *Homecoming* with more than a mere setup for the "Ofermod" essay on heroic excess; it tells by implication a moving origin story of *The Battle of Maldon* and its forgotten poet.

Thomas Honegger is the first to engage with the *Homecoming* manuscripts held in the Bodleian Library and to discover evidence of the crucial omission under examination. This discovery, of little relevance to the main thrust of Honegger's article, is relegated to a footnote, where it is tellingly explained away following Shippey's reading of Totta. As Honegger reckons, "This ascription is crossed out diagonally with black ink and did not make it into the final typescript because it would make Totta, who is presented in the poem as cowardly, boastful, murderous (cf. Shippey . . .), and naïve, into a poet who is subtly critical of misplaced heroism" (197).

Stuart Lee's wide-ranging "*Lagustreamas:* The Changing Waters Surrounding J. R. R. Tolkien and *The Battle of Maldon*" picks up on this omission as well. Lee notes that "the question of authorship and the identity of the poet" was of interest to Tolkien, and in one version "he even toyed with the idea of making" Totta "the eventual poet" (2020, 166). Lee's reading here is not nearly as dismissive as that of Shippey and Honegger, though it does still seem to suggest that Tolkien had dropped the idea as well as the line of text. In any case, that Tolkien once made explicit the identification of Totta as future *Maldon* poet is a major discovery and a move deserving of greater attention, having again dramatic implications for the interpretation of this text.

In fact, a closer inspection of Tolkien MS 5 in the Bodleian Library demonstrates that the identification of Totta as the future poet was not sui generis to the draft passage cited above. I count at least two other references to the idea in the manuscripts. The first comes far earlier than that discussed by Honegger and Lee, in a penciled marginal note, difficult to make out, at the top left of the first page of one early version of the dramatic dialogue: "Totta is of course imagined later to have made the extant poem, from hear-say" (fol. 16). It is worth noting also that the crossed-out passage Honegger cites from folio 63v continues on to consider not only Totta's place as author, but his sources of inspiration as well: the poem is "made up from his own knowledge, from survivors' reports, and from imagination and epic tradition—the last surviving fragment of ancient English heroic minstrelsy."

In a marginal addition to a draft of "Beorhtnoth's Death," the subject is again broached:[3] "It is here supposed that Totta afterwards becomes the author of the poem the fragment of which survives. It is based (on this theory) partly on survivors' reports, partly on imagination and epic tradition" (fol. 65v). These marginal lines and the main text on the page are all crossed out.

Such instances do complicate the case of the omission. Three drafted attributions (instead of one) certainly suggest a more established train of thought—not a one-off misstep or slip of the pen—and that train carried Tolkien even further into fascinating questions of tradition, poetic inspiration, and the meeting places of history and legend—always fertile ground for his scholarly and mythopoeic writing.

The question then is how to interpret Tolkien's cross out. Does he utterly reject the notion that Totta would become the poet, or is there another motive? In the famous letter to Milton Waldman, Tolkien noted in one breath that "the simple 'rustic' love of Sam and his Rosie" is in *The Lord of the Rings* "nowhere elaborated" and "*absolutely essential*" (*Letters,* 131). Other, perhaps more relevant examples can be taken from Tolkien's works in progress charted in *The History of Middle-earth*. In commentary on the *Lay of the Children of Húrin*, Christopher notes that "the line (1537) giving the meaning of *Narog* (Gnomish, 'torrent') was struck out, but this (I think) was because my father felt that it was intrusive, not that the etymology was rejected" (*LB*, 103). An editorial strike out can be excused in a number of ways.

Take for instance Christopher's footnote in *The Return of the Shadow* on the question of distance and the experience of travel in early drafts of the Hobbits' journey toward Rivendell. A drafted passage has Trotter (the mysterious Hobbit and early progenitor of Strider) tallying up approximate mileage for various stages of the journey. The passage was bracketed by Tolkien with a note: "Cut out—as this . . . is too cut and dried and spoils the feeling" (*RS*, 170). The excision leads eventually to the published text, where "cut and dried" pony mileage and wagon train timetables give way to Strider's vague and subjective but deeply lyrical "feeling" of the distance to be covered: "Some say it is so far, and some say otherwise. It is a strange road, and folk are glad to reach their journey's end, whether the time is long or short" (*FR*, I, xi, 187). The excision and revision are made not because the author has rejected the geo-temporal details of his world (on the contrary, Tolkien's note suggests that he may have kept the original passage close to hand as a "narrative time guide"), but for quite different artistic reasons. As in these cases, Tolkien's omission from *Homecoming* is an objection to the intrusiveness of such a clarification, not a rejection of the premise of Totta as *Maldon* poet itself.

No authorial move would seem more plainly at odds with the popular view of Tolkien as pure world-builder—or (somewhat relatedly) the dismissive view of him as a writer of bloated, overwrought prose or laundry lists—than that of omission by excision. Chapter 1 explored some of the tensions between elaboration and economy in Tolkien's writing; like most of us, he was at times reluctant to "murder his darlings." Yet omit he did, and often to great effect.

In Tolkien's letters, the subject is broached on occasion, particularly in regard to the exigencies of narrative pacing. On the links between *The Hobbit* and *The Lord of the Rings,* he noted that many of these were "cut out to lighten the boat" (*Letters*, 334). A measure of this cutting-room material finds its way into the appendices in *The Lord of the Rings,* to be sure, but even there Tolkien implies that narrative economy was a matter of some concern. Where, for instance, Tolkien chronicles the buildup to Bilbo's admission to the Dwarf party to the Lonely Mountain, differences between Thorin and Gandalf "are omitted" (334).

He was also famously keen to characterize his role in the creation of the text "as a 'recorder' only," and, in this role, to raise an important distinction between omission on the one hand, and error or untruth on the other. Whatever faults found in his narratives are not caused by error but by "omissions, and incompleteness of information, mostly due to the necessity of compression" (*Letters,* 289). Such remarks recall Tolkien's defense of the *Beowulf* poet against charges of discrepancies, discussed in chapter 1. While undoubtedly frustrating to certain readers, omissions are not, in Tolkien's view, to be seen as narrative flaws or authorial blunders. On the contrary, in this mode of recorder or chronicler, he goes so far as to prescribe omission, quite apart from its benefit to pacing and narrative buoyancy, for its virtue of lending an added air of realism to literary works: "it is better not to state everything (and . . . more realistic, since in . . . 'real' history, many facts that some enquirer would like to know are omitted, and the truth has to be discovered or guessed from such evidence as there is)" (*Letters,* 354). In placing such an emphasis on the role of omission in his texts, Tolkien seems almost to take a page from the manual of another twentieth-century writer scarred by experiences in the Great War: Ernest Hemingway.

HEMINGWAY'S ICEBERG

In the opening chapter of this book, I touched briefly on Hemingway as a notable contemporary and a proponent of an idiosyncratic theory of omission, but here I offer a more robust overview of the key features of Hemingway's Iceberg Theory and its development over the course of his career, followed by some preliminary considerations of its applicability to the study of Tolkien's works.

The story goes that Hemingway experienced something of an epiphany during the writing of his 1923 short story "Out of Season," which he produced some months after receiving a crushing blow from the loss of his manuscripts, stolen from his wife's suitcase in a Paris train station. Hemingway wrote about this turning point in his craft in the posthumously published memoir of life as an American expatriate in Paris, *A Moveable Feast.* As published, the awkward tale—in which a young American couple sets out with an old Italian drunkard, Peduzzi, on a trout-fishing expedition doomed to fail—ends with the young man noncommittal about regrouping for another outing on the river in the morning. In *A Moveable Feast,* however, Hemingway explains that he omitted the story's proper ending, a tragic one, in which Peduzzi commits suicide by hanging.

Such an omission was not meant to change or deny the tragic outcome of the story; rather it followed Hemingway's developing theory that details known to the writer to be true could be excised from the story. Thus in revision much explicit information is replaced by gaps in the text through which the reader may only vaguely glimpse the omitted material, and must work to intuit a backstory, outcome, or subtext. According to Hemingway, an artful omission actually strengthens a story, more than making up in feeling what may be lost in understanding (2003b, 75).

Hemingway's ideas about omission are first expressed in glacial terms in the author's 1932 study of bullfighting, *Death in the Afternoon,* where he likens the reader's engagement with a story's omissions to an appreciation of the movements of an iceberg, most of which is of course unseen (192). The text on the page is equivalent to the small portion of the iceberg visible on the water's surface, yet it is only the tip, and the whole substructure, in Hemingway's thinking, should be felt but not seen. When done according to Hemingway's specifications, a story's sparing detail is the result of purposeful revision by an author full of confidence and knowledge. He contrasts this with a vision of a kind of counterfeit theory, whereby hollow, unseemly, and ungainly passages result from the writer omitting in order to cover for gaps in his own knowledge (192).

In a 1958 *Paris Review* interview with George Plimpton, the iceberg principle is again discussed. Its formulation in the interview would be easily recognizable to a reader of *Death in the Afternoon,* save only that it seems to call for ever more omission, with Hemingway suggesting that just about anything a writer knows can be omitted in order to strengthen the iceberg. According to Hemingway scholar Paul Smith (1983), the theory of omission is finally "written into law" in Hemingway's rejected preface to a proposed school text anthology of his stories in 1959. Here Hemingway claims that the ultimate test of a story's strength is the quality of the material its author opts to remove (276). Alongside this dogmatic formulation of his theory is a self-assessment of several stories, according to the sole criterion of omission, apparently in ascending order.[4] In his Nick Adams stories, "Big Two-Hearted River" and "The Killers," he omits all reference to World War I and to the criminal underbelly of Chicago, respectively; while in "A Clean Well-Lighted Place," evidently the crowning achievement of his craft, he omits just about everything.

Whatever its tortuous development, the iceberg holds a steady position in the mythology of Hemingway. And while it may not be a wholly original contribution to literature, the iceberg remains an effective metaphor, with some valuable application to the study of Tolkien's untold tales as well. The snatches of story from Orcs, Elves, and Men in *The Lord of the Rings* weave the illusion of a massive substructure of Last Alliance lore beneath the surface, even if, in the end, these prove to be more like the "hollow places" that

Hemingway cautions against. In the case of Túrin, on the other hand, seven-eighths beneath the surface does not even begin to do justice to the material behind those sparse references made to him in the Third Age. More generally, I can think of no better description of the relationship between *The Lord of the Rings* and the body of legends behind it.[5] The first-time reader of *The Lord of the Rings* may sense that vague but powerful "impression of depth," of much at work beneath the surface of the text, and this is only enhanced by later familiarity with the legends of the Elder Day; the submerged mass of the iceberg is like those "vast backcloths" from which Tolkien draws. The unseen depths of Tolkien's mythology have been known to inspire some legends of their own; according to John D. Rateliff (2020), "Dr. Humphrey Havard, fellow Inkling and family friend . . . thought Tolkien had *only ten percent of his legendarium written down*. All the rest was in his head."[6] It's a ratio even Hemingway might admire.

While Tolkien's statements on omission offer little indication that he ever intended to codify (let alone subscribe to) a definitive theory à la Hemingway, his remarks in the *Smith* essay and elsewhere (see introduction and chapter 1)—on the importance of the edges of the canvas, and the symbiotic dialogue between story and untold story—suggest, at least, an affinity of technique. This is on full display in *Homecoming,* where, in spite of the omission, we "have a feeling" Totta is our poet "as strongly as though the writer had stated" it. And *because* of the omission, we "feel something more than" we understand.

THE CASE FOR TOTTA

Setting aside the omission for a moment, a major roadblock to this Hemingway-esque reading of *Homecoming* must be the Totta character assassination that Shippey ascribes to Tolkien. Given the esteem Tolkien shows for the *Maldon* poet, the two readings—Totta the *Maldon* poet/Totta the murderous coward—become wholly incompatible.

The charges of cowardice and murder are, I would argue, unduly harsh. Totta is young, naive, and impetuous, surely, but Tolkien drops him in a setting where he has ample reason to be afraid. Surely he speaks for us when he says that "more men than I find the mirk gruesome / among the dead unshrouded" (4). His well-intentioned if sometimes misguided pluck recalls more of Tolkien's Hobbits than it does a cowardly rogue. That his counterpart Tída can maintain his cool while trudging in the dark through a battlefield bathed in the gore of their countrymen in search of the headless corpse of their lord says more of Tída's grim experience and demeanor than it does of Totta's so-called cowardice. Likewise, his use of Beorhtnoth's sword is ironic and tragic, but a tussle with desperate corpse-stripping outlaws in the dark (incited in part by Tída's own threat of a fight) does not make Totta a cold-blooded murderer. Totta has a lot to learn, but this is why Tolkien places him here alongside Tída. At the time of *Homecoming* he has not written the poem, but he will eventually go on to do so. If the omissions of an explicit attribution may seem at first glance a blow to this reading, we might keep in mind Tolkien's remark on the need for some detective work: "the truth has to be discovered or guessed from such evidence as there is" (*Letters,* 354). Like the rash vows of Baldor, the search for Second Age Ring-lore, or the hurt for Túrin and the Second Prophecy, following the clues in *Homecoming* leads us toward a consideration of Totta as the poet-to-be.

Chief among these comes near the end of the drama, when, in the midst of a dream, Totta mutters a translation of the most unmistakably famous lines of *Maldon:* "Heart shall be bolder, harder be purpose, more proud the spirit as our power lessens!"[7] Knowing as we do that Totta is an aspiring poet and, in the fictional time of *Homecoming,* these lines have yet to be enshrined in the unwritten poem of *The Battle of Maldon,* we might for a moment feel that Tolkien has given up on subtle hints and chosen instead to make Totta's role as poet-to-be blatantly obvious.[8] But as Honegger's manuscript discovery reveals, he does not go quite so far. He does not, like a soil scientist, analyze the "leaf-mould" of the poet's experiences or, like a tidy biopic director, show us in paint-by-numbers the steps that shape a poet's great work. Ultimately, it is left to the reader to ponder how a thoughtful young artist could learn from a harrowing night with Tída, and from the horror of battle, but not wave a wholly dismissive good-bye to alliterative verse and heroic sentiment.[9]

To understand some more subtle elements of the text that link Totta to the *Maldon* poet, a brief sketch of what was surmised about the poet in Tolkien's day will serve. In this, the two scholarly portions of *Homecoming,* Tolkien's lecture notes on *Maldon* and E. V. Gordon's 1937 edition of the poem, should suffice. That these sources are largely in agreement is not particularly surprising. Gordon, in the preface to his edition, thanks Tolkien for his "many corrections and contributions," and notes that Tolkien, "with characteristic generosity, gave [him] the solution to many of the textual and philological problems discussed in the following pages" (vi).

Gordon paints a picture of a trained poet, "well versed in the old heroic and aristocratic traditions of poetry" (22). He is not looking back on some half-remembered legend but writing "soon after the battle: memory of all that happened was still fresh, and the heroism of individual deeds and speeches still seemed of primary importance, their glory undimmed by the defeat" (21). Indeed, he claims that "the poem impresses all readers as coming not long after the event" (22). On the poet's closeness to his subject, and the possibility of a role in the deeds recounted, Gordon asserts, "though the poet was not in the battle, it is not unlikely that he knew the heroes of his poem personally. . . . He tells the whole story from the retainers' point of view, as is especially noticeable when the poem is compared with the later accounts" (22).

Finally, Gordon emphasizes the kinship between *Maldon* and *Beowulf*. "*Maldon* is of the same school as *Beowulf* and nearer to *Beowulf* in heroic art and social feeling than any other Old English poem" (23). Whether or not he imitated or even knew of *Beowulf* itself (Gordon thinks it unlikely), the *Maldon* poet certainly "knew poetry of that kind" (24).

Tolkien's own notes sketch a similar picture of the poem and its author. He seems to agree with Gordon's time line; the poem is an example of the kind of "verse that was made to celebrate events while the news of them was still hot" (MS. Tolkien A 30/2, fol. 38v). Unlike other "long poems that have survived from an earlier age," which seem like "works of the minstrel turned scholar (or the scholar turned minstrel)," *Maldon* reads like the work of "the gleeman of a noble lord" (MS. Tolkien A 30/2, fol. 35). Tolkien seems to agree also on the kinship with *Beowulf*, placing *Maldon* in conversation with it in the "Ofermod" essay, and even suggesting that the *Maldon* poet might have invoked a line spoken by Wiglaf as an epigraph to his own poem (18).

Totta matches the profile remarkably well. The character sketch in the prefatory note identifies him in nearly identical terms. And, like Gordon's poet, neither of our two actors participated in the battle. Totta's presence, however, at the aftermath does help him fit into Gordon's scheme of a poem "composed soon after the battle" by a poet who knew the men he enshrined in verse—we need only look to Totta's reactions to the fallen warriors strewn about the field. Judging by his allusion to Grendel's eyes, the canon in Totta's day appears to have included *Beowulf* as well. In a game of intertextual ret-conning, the fallen bodies of Wulfmær and Ælfwine, the gold-hilted sword, all the details of their grim mission become refashioned in the poet's reenactment of the battle. To give an example, when Totta, wielding Beorhtnoth's famous sword, overcomes one of the corpse-strippers in the scuffle, he cries out

Take your trove then! Ho! Tída there!
I've slain this one. He'll slink no more.

If swords he was seeking, he soon found one,
  by the biting end. (8)

Though the stakes here are more tragicomic, the echoes of *The Battle of Maldon* are plain. In Tolkien's own unpublished translation of the poem, Beorhtnoth responds to the Viking offer of peace for tribute thus:

Do you hear, pirate, what this people says? They will for tribute
Give you spears, the venomed point, swords forged of old—
Such war gear as will be of little good to you in battle. (MS. Tolkien A 30/2, fol. 126)

The playful suggestion is that *Maldon*'s tight poetic movements might very well spring from the memories of Totta's night journey.[10]

Christopher de Hamel has characterized the scholar's dream as one "to reach back as nearly as possible to the primeval moment when the words left the pen of the author" (from *Meetings with Remarkable Manuscripts,* qtd. in Bowers 2019). By way of the omission at the poetic core of *Homecoming,* Tolkien invites us to reach still further back. *Maldon* is only beginning to come to a boil in Totta's cauldron of story during the action of *Homecoming.*

In fact, the case of Totta has more in common with the famously omitted epilogue to *The Lord of the Rings* than first meets the eye. By excising the scene of Sam's Q&A session held right out of the Red Book of Westmarch, Tolkien does not abandon his manuscript conceit or deny Sam's role in transmitting the stories. But he does acknowledge and preserve something of what he called in a 1956 letter "the 'mystery' of literary creation" (*Letters,* 231).[11] Totta in this sense shares much in common with the many authors who loom over Tolkien's legendarium: not only Bilbo, Frodo, and Sam, but Dírhavel and his *Narn,* Ælfwine and his *Book of Lost Tales.*

Homecoming is a work of poetry more than it is one of scholarly precision, and Tolkien's dramatic verse dialogue, not unlike his great works of fantasy, allows room for his readers to piece together suggestions and draw their own conclusions; as Hemingway would say, to make them feel something more than they understand. Tolkien did not learn the technique of omission from Hemingway but from those old anonymous poets he studied, and he sorely wished he had more of the *Maldon* poet's work to learn from. Apropos the *Beowulf* poet, at least, he once noted that myth is most powerful when "presented by a poet who feels rather than makes explicit what his theme portends" (*MC,* 15).[12]

VOICES IN THE DARK

Homecoming is also an immensely rich and complex text. It is not about one thing only, whatever that thing may be—the search for the *Maldon* poet, the duke's *ofermod,* or something else entirely. Like the mythopoeic stories of the legendarium, *Homecoming* resists dissection, squirms free from the point just when we think we have it pinned down. At the tail end of the verse drama, the dialogue between Tída and Totta is concluded, "*the rumbling of the cart dies away,*" and the monks of Ely Abbey chant the *dirige* for Beorhtnoth's somber homecoming. Only this, and nothing more, would seem a perfectly appropriate conclusion.[13] Yet the monks' chant is interrupted, not by Tída or Totta, but by an entity credited only as "*a Voice in the dark,*" which says, "Sadly they sing, the monks of Ely isle! / Row men, row! Let us listen here a while!" (13). The monk's chanting promptly resumes, but the reader is left with an indelible impression of mystery—another untold tale.

Those thorough enough to read "Beorhtnoth's Death" do receive a few choice comments on the mysterious voice. Tolkien suggests that its jarring use of rhyme presages the "fading end of the old heroic alliterative measure" (3). He also provides a source of sorts: the rhyme echoes "verses . . . referring to King Canute" in the Liber Eliensis (3). But the voice is surely not King Canute's within the context of *Homecoming,* for he may not have even been born at the time of the Battle of Maldon in 991.

So the questions remain: Who is this voice in the dark? What does Tolkien intend by its interjection? The source citation does at least imply a Viking connection. And such a perspective certainly suits the ironic tone of much of *Homecoming,* suggesting as it does that the Vikings might be moved by a dirge sung for the duke they have just slaughtered, or that the victory over Beorhtnoth is also the death knell for "the old heroic" verses—their own included. Ultimately one part, at least, of Tolkien's intent is clear: we are not supposed to know exactly who this is or what is going on.

In tuning an ear to the Latin chants "sadly" sung, the voice in the dark echoes not only the Liber Eliensis but also the broader problems of interpretation that so intrigued Tolkien about *The Battle of Maldon,* about history more generally, and about the great deeds and heroes of his invented world as well. What was the *Maldon* poet trying to tell us about battle? About Beorhtnoth? Perhaps, with a lot of effort and a little imagination, it's just as Tída says of the old songs: "you can hear the tears through the harp's twanging" (7).

Chapter Five

DESTROYING MAGIC, KINDLING FIRE

Untold Tales and Tolkien's Legacy

I jokingly referred to it, before I came up with the title, as the *GRRMarillion*.
—George R. R. Martin, on his book, *Fire and Blood*

It's as if *The Lord of the Rings* had only been published in Tolkein's [*sic*]
own Elvish, unreadable without long hours of gruelling study.
—*Guardian* review of *Sekiro*

With all this talk in the last three chapters of the challenges of interpretation posed by Tolkien's untold tales—of great battles, complex heroes, and lost poets both legendary and historical—we may well wonder how to read the author's own legacy nearly fifty years after his death in 1973. More specifically, if I have been in any way successful in arguing for the importance of untold tales in his literary project, how does this aspect of his work live on in popular culture, including his own "afterlives," the growing number of multimedia adaptations?

THE 1977 *SILMARILLION* AND THE RISE OF THE PREQUEL

After Tolkien's death on September 2, 1973,[1] the monumental task of preparing the long-expected *Silmarillion* fell to Christopher as literary executor. An audience, whose appetite for adult fairy stories could now never be wholly satisfied, eagerly awaited its 1977 publication, the result of Christopher's first effort to work the mass of manuscripts left him into publishable form. Fans expecting heroic romance like *The Lord of the Rings* were baffled and disappointed by this text on its arrival. The critical reception was no better.[2] Even today, *The Silmarillion* retains the popular reputation of a challenging curiosity not for the faint of heart.

In spite of its failure to reach the commercial and critical heights of Tolkien's other major works, *The Silmarillion*'s mystique—its legend of the untold stories (unfinished in its author's lifetime) behind one of the great literary phenomena of the twentieth century—remains potent. To call Tolkien the father of modern fantasy may feel like a slight to earlier writers like Morris, Dunsany, and Eddison, yet his influence in this arena is plainly great; his works have been adopted as a blueprint for those who followed.

That often superficial blueprint taken up by publishers and writers eager for success began with a quest, a company of mixed race and ability, a map, and a trilogy, but by 1977 at the latest, this blueprint would also include the great invented world, an ever-expanding universe where one might reap the promises of spin-offs and prequels, to explore the vast commercial opportunity of untold tales.[3]

Tolkien himself was not a genre fantasy writer, nor a particularly commercial one in the sense of his artistic ambitions being driven by dreams of profit. When his publishers Allen & Unwin called for a sequel to *The Hobbit,* Tolkien was famously resistant to the idea, having, as he thought, nothing more to say of Hobbits, and hoping instead to see parts of his preexisting mythology into print. Though he caved in the end, his "sequel" (*The Lord of the Rings*) took seventeen years to arrive, clocked in at over a thousand pages, and was written in a different style for a different audience.

Only after the success of *The Lord of the Rings* could Tolkien find a market for his legends and for adult fantasy in general. In the 1960s, he began a sequel to *The Lord of the Rings* set early in the Fourth Age, focusing on an occult revolutionary plot in Gondor. The draft did not go beyond thirteen pages, and in his letters he noted that it might have been a "'thriller' . . .—but it would have been just that. Not worth doing" (*Letters,* 344). And *The Silmarillion* could hardly be read as a marketable prequel to *The Lord of the Rings.* The gulf between the events of the First Age and the end of the Third is one that a brief chapter like "Of the Rings of Power and the Third Age" could hardly fill. As we have seen, the great events of the Second and early Third Ages are hardly sketched.

The Lord of the Rings alone seals Tolkien's reputation, but a part of his peculiar magic has something to do with the unfinished *Silmarillion*: the enchanting flicker of hope for more stories. That spark's lasting heat can be seen in the success of works like *The Children of Húrin.* This mostly complete prose tale from Tolkien, built on a story already mildly familiar to readers of *The Silmarillion,* was still, in 2007, a major literary event. Such hope—what else might Christopher have in his pocketses?—I suppose has only died out very recently, with the swan song *Fall of Gondolin* in 2018, and the passing of Christopher Tolkien in January 2020.

Posthumous publications curated by Christopher since the 1977 *Silmarillion* offer readers a window into Tolkien's creative life and process. But they have also given rise to cynical cries of commercial exploitation and reinforced certain mistaken assumptions about the role played by untold tales in his stories.[4] A good deal of what we get in *The History of Middle-earth* was very likely not intended for publication—even after heavy revision—at all. We glimpse here the bulk of the iceberg beneath the waves, but we can only guess at how, if at all, it would pierce the surface of the narratives he never finished. Indeed, some of the more beautiful and bizarre late writings on metaphysics and geography— reflecting some subconscious inability to finish the darn stories—are in a sense further evidence of the centrality of untold tales. Tolkien would have known that this was not what readers sought.

STARING EYES: TOLKIEN'S UNTOLD TALES IN MODERN FANTASY

In "The Staring Eye," a brief tribute essay following Tolkien's death, Ursula K. Le Guin counts herself lucky for not having "read Tolkien before I was twenty-five. Because I really wonder if I could have handled it" (1979, 172). While Le Guin is one of those notable writers to forge her own path in Tolkien's wake, we can note connections between their depth-craft. The early story of Earthsea, "The Rule of Names" (1975), is plainly an homage to Tolkien's work. This shows not only in the playful surface details, like the mysterious Mr. Underhill living in a hole in the ground, but also in its approach to world-building. The heroic world on the periphery comes to life through the stories of the mysterious wizard Blackbeard, who offers glimpses of long ago—"old days of war before the League"—and far away—"the West Reach, where dragons breed on the lava isles." But, in the climactic confrontation between Underhill and Blackbeard, this lore also reminds us of the dubious challenge of— and utmost importance in—interpreting the old stories.

Le Guin strikes a balance between telling and untelling in her celebrated Hainish Cycle as well. When asked in a 2008 interview about her apparently exhaustive universe-building for these books, her explanation recalled Tolkien's celebration of the *Beowulf* poet in "The Monsters and the Critics": "What I did was give the illusion of there being all those different worlds. That's called art, or fiction, or something. The rule is, you only invent what you have to. And that's pretty much what's right in front of the reader" (2008). More specifically, on the "invention" of the ansible, a device capable of faster-than-light communication, she explains: "But all I really invented was a) the idea of an instantaneous trans-mitter and b) a name for it. The reader does the rest. If you give them enough background/context, they can fill in the gaps. It isn't just smoke and mirrors. There has to be a coherent vision of how things hang together. . . . the details have to fit together and be thought through. . . . But, well . . . it's *mostly* smoke and mirrors" (2008). Le Guin, like Tolkien, suggests that the most spellbinding and enduring fictional worlds are not those in which all is spelled out.

Consciously and unconsciously, Tolkien exhibits an extraordinary influ-ence on the writers of fantasy who followed him. To trace this influence thor-oughly is far beyond the scope of this chapter, but, as regards untold tales, I would venture to say that many of these writers take to heart the importance of world-building, now considered the cornerstone of the genre, yet they also fall prey to those temptations explored in the first part of this book: "the ten-dency to treat the whole thing as a kind of vast game" (*Letters,* 210).[5] Or, like Tolkien's readers of *Beowulf,* these writers are overcome by the glamour of Poesis; they chase untold tales (destroying the magic in the process) so far that they cannot find their way back to the story that needed telling in the first place. This is the impression given by George R. R. Martin's *A Song of Ice and Fire* (2013), the latest volumes of which seem to introduce near book-length digressions and unforeseen claimants to the Iron Throne.[6]

Yet in some regards, Martin does draw from a Tolkienian playbook. As *The Lord of the Rings* and *The Children of Húrin* draw both historical depth and mystery from the backdrop of a great war only alluded to in the texts, so too does *A Song of Ice and Fire.* The sociopolitical background of the series as well as its central mysteries derive from Robert's Rebellion, in which Baratheons and Starks upend the rival Targaryen dynasty. In terms of distance in time, it is more reminiscent of the Nirnaeth to Túrin than the Alliance to Frodo and company; only about fifteen years separate the end of Robert's Rebellion from the first events narrated in *A Game of Thrones.* Yet in this short period the stories have already grown, and the fame or infamy of its heroes and villains, their motivations, and secrets are already the stuff of legends to be pieced to-gether as the series unfolds.

It remains to be seen whether any of this backdrop will yet be untold by the end of the series. Discussing the potential prequel avenues for the hit HBO adaptation of his work, Martin acknowledged the strong fan interest in seeing this war explored on-screen, but rejected the project on these grounds: "By the time I finish writing *A Song of Ice and Fire,* you will know every important thing that happened in Robert's Rebellion. There would be no surprises or revelations left in such a show, just the acting out of conflicts whose resolutions you already know. That's not a story I want to tell just now; it would feel too much like a twice-told tale" (Martin 2017).

Whatever the result, we can note that Martin has found the prequel form to be an attractive one. In 2018, with two volumes still outstanding in *Song of Ice and Fire,* Martin published *Fire and Blood,* the first of a proposed two-volume history of the Targaryen family long before the events covered in the main series. Martin's decision to frame the text as the work of a scholarly archmaester within the world is a Tolkienian touch. In an interview, he emphasizes the significance of the work's frame, cautioning that "you have to realize that you're reading the voice of a character, even as you're reading about other characters who existed hundreds of years before him" (2018a). When asked in the same interview whether he had taken any inspiration from the appendices to *The Lord of the Rings* or *The Silmarillion,* he notes, "Yes, definitely. I jokingly referred to it, before I came up with the title, as the *GRRMarillion*" (2018a).

Another noteworthy practitioner of untold tales is Patricia A. McKillip, most notably in her 1974 novel *The Forgotten Beasts of Eld.* John D. Rateliff includes the text in his series on classics of fantasy, observing in particular its Tolkienian sense of depth: "The sense of untold stories haunts this book: echoes of other tales that are mentioned only in passing. . . . These elusive allusions give McKillip's world a sense of depth—a very Tolkienesque feeling that it has existed long before the story began" (2002). I would add that it is not only the resultant sense of depth but the fragments and "elusive allusions" themselves that are Tolkienian.

Stephen King's *Dark Tower* series proudly displays its Tolkienian influence, though it does so alongside a great many other things as well, most notably the western, an American equivalent of sorts to a legend cycle.[7] King writes in his foreword to its first volume, *The Gunslinger,* that apart from Tolkien, the work of spaghetti western maestro Sergio Leone was his chief inspiration. King's series has its own artistic goals (he notes that the quest mode was a key borrowing from Tolkien, and the majestic backdrop from Leone—superficially at least), of course, but it is intriguing that he would here mash up Leone and

Tolkien in his own epic of modern fantasy. For Leone, too, was a great myth-maker, one who explored untold tales on the screen. Some further discussion of Leone follows below.

THE EDGES OF THE BIG SCREEN

From a production standpoint, Hemingway's image of the iceberg is again useful: what the viewer sees for two hours in a theater is a miniscule fraction of the total effort—filmed and unfilmed—that does not make the final cut. Extended editions of films raise destabilizing questions about canon and "authorial" intent, but on the whole most viewers can likely appreciate how a film is often improved by its deletion of scenes. Describing the challenges of writing a screenplay for *The Third Man,* the novelist Graham Greene declared that "one must have the sense of more material than one need to draw on" (1950). We do not grasp fully the ins and outs of the criminal drug trade in postwar Vienna from the film—"Reality, in fact, was only a background to a fairy tale," according to Greene, sounding rather like Tolkien—yet the film's affordances (the zither score, gorgeous noir cinematography, and snappy writing) come together to leave an indelible impression. To channel Hemingway again, they make us feel something more than we understand.

One important cinematic cousin to the untold tale might be the MacGuffin. The term, popularized by Alfred Hitchcock,[8] refers to that category of shadowy plot devices (often artifacts of value, or secrets of sinister and nebulous import) used to motivate characters and set a story in motion, though they often fade or disappear completely once said story takes off. Seldom captured on screen, the MacGuffin nonetheless exerts an influence over the actors in the drama and, in the more successful cases, the viewers as well. Though it is sometimes dismissed as cheap, lazy, or shabby filmmaking, the MacGuffin, like the untold tale, speaks to the imaginative power of suggestion. Notable MacGuffins include the titular Maltese Falcon,[9] the glowing briefcase of *Pulp Fiction,* or the Dude's favored rug of *The Big Lebowski.*

There is some likeness between the MacGuffin and the coveted treasures of Tolkien's fantasies: the Arkenstone, the Silmarils, and the One Ring. Tolkien falls short of the M word, but comes quite close to describing its function in a discussion of the Ring and the "springs of the story" in Lee's reconstructed 1968 BBC interview: "Power in a narrative is very . . . is only the thing that starts the wheels working isn't it? What you want is a story. . . . It's a mechanism which starts a story" (2018, 155).

The best MacGuffins, like the best untold tales, carry with them an air of mystery, but they also actually matter to their respective stories, and in these regards the One Ring is certainly a fine example. Characters and readers alike take the Ring seriously.[10] Yet part of its charm and power is in its elusive nature. Even today, we may find ourselves deep in conversation with other readers about the precise nature of the Ring: What does it really do? To whom? How? "You cannot press the One Ring too hard," Tolkien cautioned Rhona Beare, because it is a "mythical feature," though he might have said a Mac-Guffinal one (*Letters,* 279).

MacGuffins figure prominently in the spaghetti westerns of Sergio Leone, the other half of King's *Dark Tower* muse. In *The Good, the Bad, and the Ugly* (1966), whispers of a buried cache of Confederate gold are all that is needed to spur the three titular antihero gunslingers on a three-hour zigzagging, double-crossing adventure. Of course it is not gold that interests Leone, but the retelling of myth (and fairy story) on the fringes of history in the American West. His films are epic in scope, "mythic or Homeric, having to do with 'a simple world of adventure and of uncomplicated men'" haunted by their past and facing extinction in the future, full of staggering vistas and the heart-rending elegiac scores of Ennio Morricone (Fawell 2005, 76). His engagement with untold tales goes far beyond the MacGuffin, too; *The Man with No Name* (which made a name for its titular actor, Clint Eastwood, who portrayed him) is a master class in minimalist suggestion (incidentally, quite reminiscent of Strider sitting in the corner of *The Prancing Pony*) and still influential to this day. The fairy tales beneath the western facade of Leone's work are clear from the titles alone—we need look no further than his 1968 genre swan song (almost a *Smith of Wootton Major* moment): *Once Upon a Time . . . in the West.*

Tolkien, of course, believed fervently that fantasy and fairy story were most suited to the written word, and in "On Fairy-stories" he is particularly skeptical of drama and the visual arts in this realm. "Drama," he declares, "is naturally hostile to Fantasy. . . . Men dressed up as talking animals may achieve buffoonery or mimicry, but they do not achieve Fantasy" (*MC,* 140). In Tolkien's view, the visible form of fantasy on stage pales in comparison to the reader's freedom to imagine from the page. He is likewise critical of illustration as a constraint on the imagination: "the illustrator may catch . . . his own vision of such a scene; but every hearer of the words will have his own picture" (159). The written word for Tolkien was, in short, "more progenitive," and its fertile possibility becomes indeed infinite in the contemplation of untold stories. Tolkien was at pains to protect the openness of his own texts—recall his emphasis on "applicability" over "allegory" in the foreword to *The Lord of the Rings*—the former celebrates the "freedom of the reader"; the latter the "purposed domination of the author" (*FR,* xxii).

Those conflicts between applicability and the imposition of a single form may offer some additional clarity to the long-held view that *The Lord of the Rings* was "unfilmable."[11] This verdict is traditionally read in terms of the technical and budgetary exigencies of bringing to life on screen Middle-earth and its fantastic denizens. Some would have it that the grand New Zealand spectacle of Peter Jackson's trilogy (2001–3) has put to rest once and for all such doubts; others see in these films further proof to the contrary.

In a statement during the buildup to the first film's release, Christopher quietly suggested once more "that *The Lord of The Rings* is peculiarly unsuitable to transformation into visual dramatic form." A decade later, in an interview with *Le Monde* in 2012, on the eve of *The Hobbit* film cycle, his tone shifted from dispassion to disdain: "They have gutted the book, making an action film for 15–25 year olds. And it seems that *The Hobbit* will be of the same ilk" (2012).

A certain degree of cutting—if not gutting—is to be expected in any screen adaptation, let alone one of a work so long and complex. Whatever the Jackson films' strengths and weaknesses (and my consideration of them here is limited to their engagement with untold tales), most viewers would agree that they could not have been much longer. In the 1950s, Tolkien himself noted, in response to overtures from American filmmakers, a preference for "abridgement" over "compression" in a film treatment, the latter resulting in "over-crowding and confusion, blurring of climaxes, and general degradation" (*Letters,* 261). Some cuts—Bombadil, for instance—are grievous but perhaps excusable. Others, like the absence of "The Scouring of the Shire," radically change plot and theme.

The films' emphasis on spectacle over storytelling also necessitates the excision of most of the memorable untold tales of Tolkien's book. Gone are the bones of Baldor on the Paths of the Dead (though there are plenty of other bones). Gone are the allusions to Húrin and Túrin, the readings in the Hall of Fire and the campfire stories of Strider.[12] Individually, such omissions may appear inconsequential, but taken together, they amount to a flattening, a loss of that depth which Tolkien so carefully cultivates on the page.

We do see the Last Alliance, that great allusive web of an untold tale, discussed at length in chapter 2 of this book. In fact, the very first scene of Jackson's *Fellowship* ("Prologue: One Ring to Rule Them All . . .") offers a primer on the Ring's history, from its forging on Mount Doom all the way to its chance discovery by Bilbo. A montage of critical moments rolls by: the forging of the Rings of Power, the heroic resistance of the Last Alliance, the death of Elendil, Sauron's fall, and Isildur's ill-fated possession of the Ring. The images are striking, and voice-over narration by Cate Blanchett (whom we later discover to be Galadriel in the films) effectively digests this multimillennial backstory and sets the table for Frodo's tale.

The climactic struggle with Sauron is particularly interesting visually, nodding to the stark clues of Tolkien's text while interpreting a distinctly heroic role for Isildur, whose desperate cut with the hilt-shard of Narsil single-handedly vanquishes Sauron and delivers the Alliance forces from utter ruin.

But in Tolkien's story the past is more than prologue, and for all its style and production value, the scene in the film strikes a blow to the spirit of untold tales. Seeing these events unfold at all—imposing on them a single visual form—robs the viewer of the sense of mystery about that conflict, the strange nature of the duel between these titanic combatants of the Second Age and its dubious outcome. "History became legend, and legend became myth," declares the voice-over of Galadriel, but there is little sense of a story told here within the world of the film—no question about reliability, no *Rashomon* effect—despite the use of Galadriel's voice, it remains the now-obligatory info dump for the good of the viewer's introduction to this fantasy world.[13]

The extended visual presence of Sauron and the Ring also diminishes their power. Tolkien's warning about pressing the Ring too hard goes unheeded, and its intrigue as a MacGuffin and an artifact of mystery are reduced: we see the Ring in all its power and glory on Sauron's gauntleted finger. Sauron, such a menace offscreen in the books, here looks very metal indeed, sweeping aside the Alliance forces like rag dolls. Yet maybe his presence could have grown in the viewers' minds had he not been pictured, or been glimpsed only in the "artist's interpretation" in Rivendell (a nice touch), where an Alan Lee rendition of Isildur versus Sauron can be seen hanging across from the shards of Narsil later in the film.

Perhaps the most profound change in the Alliance from book to film comes back to the Shakespearean "past is prologue." Tolkien's book begins, as it were, in medias res, even if preparations for a birthday celebration in the Shire are not now seen as the standard opening move in genre fantasy. There are moments in which substantial history lessons come through, but these are paced, spread out. We receive them (or they go over our heads) alongside the Hobbits; they come as snippets of larger tales or lessons that are promised but seldom delivered later. And so the nature of the bird's-eye prologue dashes the sense of untold tales more even than the fixed visual forms themselves: we lose the slow drip, the breadcrumbs, the way that the Alliance is slowly and subtly woven into the landscapes and stories and ruins met along the journey.

PREQUELS: MARGARINE OVER TOO MUCH BREAD

Christopher's prediction that *The Hobbit* films (2012–14) would be "of the same ilk" as the earlier trilogy was in certain respects right on the money. The messy departure of Guillermo del Toro from the project opened the door for Peter Jackson and his team's apparently reluctant and rushed return to Middle-earth/New Zealand. Despite grossing nearly $3 billion worldwide, the critical response to this prequel trilogy was largely one of disappointment and disillusion. For the relatively small but vocal audience already wearied of Jackson's vivisection of *The Lord of the Rings,* the CGI spectacle of the prequels came as no surprise. Yet many critics who earnestly enjoyed the first trilogy appeared nonplussed by *The Hobbit* films' inability to recapture the old magic.

A few plausible theories have been advanced to account for *The Hobbit*'s shortcomings, but most relevant for our present purposes must go back to Tolkien's comments on the frustrations of publishing backwards. Here he fires off a warning that should be awfully familiar to anyone who has ever been disappointed by a highly anticipated prequel film: "To go there is to destroy the magic, unless new unattainable vistas are again revealed" (*Letters,* 333).

The *Star Wars* universe offers a useful analogue in this regard.[14] It all begins in medias res; the famous opening crawl (after its trademark take on the "once-upon-a-time" formula) declares, "it is a period of civil war." Once George Lucas knew he would make sequels, an episode number was retroactively stamped on the 1977 original—not with the Roman numeral I but IV. And into that empty space sketched out for I, II, and III, viewers could imagine all manner of galactic wonder tales.

The quirky and charming world-building of these films suggested untold tales at every turn: What went on in Han Solo's checkered smuggling past? Where have all the Jedi gone? Why do Obi Wan and Yoda hole up as hermits? And, of course, who is Darth Vader? We have our answer in the shocking revelation of *The Empire Strikes Back,* but the ghost of (spoilers) Anakin Skywalker remained a powerful presence in the original film trilogy. And so for the *Star Wars* prequels (1999–2005) we returned dutifully to the darkness of the theater, like Gollum and his fruitless search for the secrets under the mountain's roots. We wanted to know who Anakin really was, and we wanted to see Yoda in his prime. But the mechanical breathing and hideous mask of Darth Vader ("more machine now than man") was worth a hundred of the prequels' pod races and sulky teenage tantrums. The immeasurably old, tired Yoda, wrapped in his tattered blankets, was more moving than a thousand CGI lightsaber duels and gymnastics routines.

Even with the established reputation of their source material in Tolkien's 1937 classic (which was not, in fact, a prequel at all), Peter Jackson and his team found themselves facing challenges similar to those of George Lucas in his own prequel trilogy. In an effort to transform one short novel into three long films, *The Hobbit* filmmakers also fell into the same traps. They "went there" (and everywhere), plumbing the depths of untold tales, and came up with well-lined pockets but little magic.

When, in July 2012, just a few months prior to the December release of the first film installment of *The Hobbit,* it was announced that the story would be split into three films (two had long been projected), many cried foul, suspecting crass commercial motives from Warner Bros., and wondering how exactly Tolkien's children's story of no more than three hundred pages would be stretched to fill up three lengthy holiday blockbuster films. One sage commentator online noted that teachers would soon catch students looking for a shortcut by checking the book out of the library rather than sitting through nine hours of film.

Tolkien's book does possess that air of untold tales in abundance, and it is precisely this sense of depth that drew the first readers into Middle-earth and its author on to new discoveries (and new unexplained vistas) in its masterful sequel: "That, of course, is the dangerous part about caves: you don't know how far they go back, sometimes, or where a passage behind may lead to, or what is waiting for you inside" (*H,* 56). Jackson certainly recognized this quality, but he saw it as an opportunity to exploit rather than an imaginative space to preserve.[15] It was indeed built into the rationale for the move to three films, as he noted in a Facebook announcement of 2012:

> We know how much of the story of Bilbo Baggins, the Wizard Gandalf, the Dwarves of Erebor, the rise of the Necromancer, and the Battle of Dol Guldur will remain untold if we do not take this chance. The richness of the story of *The Hobbit,* as well as some of the related material in the appendices of *The Lord of the Rings,* allows us to tell the full story of the adventures of Bilbo Baggins and the part he played in the sometimes dangerous, but at all times exciting, history of Middle-earth. (2012b)

True to his word, these are all developed at length in the films, along with a hearty helping of fan service that is the currency of the prequel (a prominent role for Legolas, a bizarre allusion to Aragorn, etc.). Perhaps the most Tolkienian touch in all of this comes in the first film, when Bilbo asks Gandalf whether there are any other wizards. After naming Saruman, he recalls "the two blue wizards," though he has "quite forgotten their names." Whether this represents a moment of rare and moving restraint, or merely the cautious sidestepping of a legal dispute—Warner Bros. does not have the rights to draw from *Unfinished Tales*—this chapter cannot tell.

How the forthcoming Amazon production of *The Lord of the Rings* distinguishes itself from Jackson's trilogies remains to be seen. What is clear, however, is the studio's interest in tapping into the appeal of Tolkien's untold tales. Early rumors suggested that the series would open by exploring Aragorn's past in the decades before the War of the Ring—adventures hinted at mostly in the appendices. It was later announced that instead the series would take place at least a few thousand years earlier, during the Second Age of Middle-earth, that very "Dark Age" that was explored in chapter 2.

PROFESSOR TOLKIEN, DUNGEON MASTER

The great gulf between *The Hobbit* films and their source material shows also in one of the most widespread criticisms circulating in the days following the first film's release: that it felt like a video game.[16] It is in many ways an apt comparison to today's big-budget video games, and not only for the films' visual aesthetic but its approach to storytelling as well: three is better than two, heard melodies are sweeter (and could be turned "to 11" à la *Spinal Tap*), etc. The irony of course is that Tolkien's prints are all over gaming as well.

It would be difficult to overestimate Tolkien's influence on the development of role-playing games (RPGs): from the tabletop *Dungeons and Dragons* of the 1970s to the major computer and console franchises of recent years (*The Elder Scrolls*, *Warcraft*, *Diablo*, etc.), not to mention officially licensed works like *The Lord of the Rings Online* and *Shadow of Mordor*. When reviewers drew comparisons between *The Hobbit* films and video games, they did so in a pejorative sense, highlighting some of the least artistic and most cynically commercial tendencies of today's games, which are produced in an industry not so dissimilar to the Hollywood studios; it is a business where mass-market appeal and profitability are often at odds with more lofty artistic aims.

At its roots—on the tabletop, the rudimentary Multi-user dungeons, and text-based RPGs—gaming depended on imaginative engagement from players, and in some ways more readily revealed its Tolkienian roots. The theories of fantasy and sub-creation outlined in "On Fairy-stories" and explored in the *Smith of Wootton Major* essay prove flexible in their application beyond literature. Recent work by Peter Kristof Makai considers the ways in which Tolkien's theories "interface" with video game design principles. In "Faërian Cyberdrama: When Fantasy Becomes Virtual Reality," Makai (2010) takes up this question of interface, focusing in particular on Tolkien's curious notion of Faërian Drama—to be "in a dream that some other mind is weaving"—and its anticipation of virtual reality simulation and gaming (*MC*, 142). Makai suggests "that Tolkien's idea of an enchantingly coherent fictional world can be grasped best in theory by the discipline of ludology/game studies" (2010, 36). It is therefore to be hoped that the present exploration might likewise bear fruit in Tolkien and game studies alike.

But if there is a mode of or approach to gaming in which these Tolkienian elements, including untold tales, flourish, it is what I might call "slow-gaming,"[17] with a nod to the slow food movement founded in Italy over the outrage of a McDonald's opening in the historic center of Rome.

Let me offer a brief case study in slow-gaming using Blizzard Entertainment's *Diablo* series. *Diablo* (1997) nails Tolkienian slow-gaming—as one might hope from a project inspired in part by an earlier game called *Moria*.[18] The playable world of *Diablo* is small and tightly contained: a single town and its Gothic church-turned-dungeon. *Diablo*'s dark fantasy aesthetic recognizes an untold tale's ability to convey horror. Frodo sums this up quite nicely in his exasperated exchange with Gildor about the Black Riders who pursue him: "I cannot imagine what information could be more terrifying than your hints and warnings" (*FR*, I, iii, 83). The story of *Diablo*'s ghost town of Tristram, and the wider world around it, develops slowly and elliptically, as the player interacts with its townsfolk and delves into the labyrinth beneath its church, uncovering secrets and descending, level by level, into the pits of hell. This simple structure—descent and exploration below the surface—conveys in the most basic sense narrative *depth*.

Other elements of *Diablo*'s design enhance this sense of depth. Apart from a few set pieces (the town of Tristram and certain chambers within the dungeon), the levels are randomly generated so that no visit to the catacombs is ever quite the same. The player might stumble upon (but cannot count on it— these, too, are randomly selected from a larger pool for each game) a number

of scripted side-quests, which—like Beowulfian digressions, or Tolkienian untold tales—hint at a larger and living world. Fragmentary tomes of lore (recalling, of course, the Book of Mazarbul) are scattered sparingly across the dungeons you explore. Increasingly powerful treasures (swords, helms, rings, etc.)
are found as you descend the labyrinth. If a player has the luck to find a gold-
lettered "unique" item, it may awaken what Tolkien calls the "desire of the
hearts of dwarves" (*H*, 15).

Such features stand out in part because of the game's slow pacing. The
dungeons are dark and claustrophobic, and once foes are encountered, the
player can seldom outpace them. The return to town is a breath of fresh air, a
chance to hear some suggestive gossip from the locals while mending equip-
ment or healing wounds. Soundtrack, voice acting, gameplay, and artwork
all contribute to the atmosphere, a sense of a world alive and terrible—a perilous realm that the player only partially grasps.

The game's sequels, *Diablo II* (2000) and *Diablo III* (2012), reached new
commercial heights but shed their predecessor's atmosphere in favor of so-
called quality-of-life improvements. None may be more significant than the
player's ability to run in the *Diablo* sequels. This convenience speeds the
frequent trips to the town's blacksmith for repairs, but also fundamentally
changes the experience of the game world. Gone is the claustrophobia and
creeping dread of the first game and its Moria-like environments. Most threats
can simply be outrun—even without breaking a sweat once the player dons
a pair of magic boots, which offer increased run speed. The situation recalls
Tolkien's biting critique in "On Fairy-stories"; the player engages "in the soon-
cloying game of moving at high speed" (*MC*, 151).

A need for speed also reduces the games' immersive qualities. The care that
goes into crafting this world—its evocative art design and environmental storytelling—fly past us as we run. The game worlds of *Diablo*'s sequels are far more
vast and varied, yet in running through them—or, better still, teleporting about
via a system of waypoints—they inevitably feel flatter and smaller. Their emphasis is squarely on the metagame of loot-hunting: the third game in the series
went so far as to include an in-game auction house that allowed (via PayPal)
the exchange of primary world currency for secondary world loot. The auction house was eventually dropped more than a year after the game's release,
but its legacy lives on.[19] Terms like the "item-grind" and the "slot machine,"
frequently attributed to the *Diablo* franchise, are telling indications of a series
that has not learned, in Thorin Oakenshield's words, to value "food and cheer
and song above hoarded gold" (*H*, 274).

Peter Jackson's hit films also brought about a renewed salvo of officially licensed games set in Middle-earth. Some of these games have gone to the Mathom-house of Tolkien's untold tales in developing their game concepts. *The Lord of the Rings: War in the North* (2011) from Snowblind Studios, is one such example. The game's intentions are openly declared in introductory narration: "Of the great War of the Ring many songs have been sung and many tales told. . . . Yet Sauron's grasp stretched much further than the lands of Gondor and Rohan alone, and his forces might have done great evil in the North of Middle-earth had a handful of heroes not stood in his path. Their stories too, deserve to be told." *War in the North,* of course, promises to explore at least one such story.

During the buildup to the game's release, the developers stressed something of the imaginative potential untapped in Tolkien's world-building and sought to establish ethos as seasoned readers. A journalist for *Gamefront* noted in a promotional write-up of the game previewed at the Game Developers' Conference that its "entire concept is derived from a speech of Gandalf's, in which he points out that the efforts of the Fellowship on the war's southern front would be fruitless if not for the contributions of 'a few heroes in the North'" (Richardson 2011). This is a bit of a misquote, actually. But the sentiment is close enough. As Gandalf declares in appendix A, "'do not forget the battles in Dale and the valour of Durin's Folk. Think of what might have been. Dragon-fire and savage swords in Eriador, night in Rivendell. There might be no Queen in Gondor'" (*RK,* 1080). This is vintage appendix material, gesturing to untold tales and, as in the *Smith* essay, reminding us that the things not seen can still affect the picture.

Marketing for *War in the North* was eager to cash in on nostalgia for *The Lord of the Rings* while promising new adventure. The promotional gameplay video was aptly titled "*War in the North:* Untold Story Trailer," detailing the game's emphasis on this parallel action. Not all were keen to explore these unexplained vistas, however. Joel Gregory, in *PlayStation Magazine,* was unimpressed: "Remember all the stuff from those films and books you love so much? Here's some other really crucial stuff that happened at the same time . . . only it wasn't important enough for anyone to mention during those 1,500 pages" (2011).

Monolith's *Middle-earth: Shadow of Mordor* (2014) and its sequel, a more generically titled *Middle-earth: Shadow of War* (2017), represent another effort to come at *The Lord of the Rings* from an angle and explore untold stories. Perhaps, rather than turning first to the appendices for inspiration, the developers at Monolith sought instead no. 96 in *The Collected Letters,* which opens chapter 1 of this book. "I think you are moved by *Celebrimbor* because it conveys a sudden sense of endless *untold* stories," Tolkien wrote to his son in connection to his literary dilemma. *Shadow of Mordor* is a revenge tale set in the gap between *The Hobbit* and *The Lord of the Rings.* The player takes on the hybrid role of a Ranger named Talion, who was murdered by Sauron's goons but is, for dubious purposes, kept in a state of undeath by the timely haunting of—yes—Celebrimbor, that legendary Second Age ring smith.

One writer for *Polygon* found the premise to be a raw demonstration of the developers' legendarium street cred: "With this one character addition, this one plot point, Monolith Productions has proven the lengths to which they are willing to go to make *Middle-earth: Shadow of Mordor* true to Tolkien's world, even though its story wasn't written by Tolkien himself" (Corriea 2014). For this commentator at least, *Shadow of Mordor* compares favorably to other gaming experiments in Middle-earth, including the abovementioned *War in the North:* "These games used Tolkien's world at the surface level, but didn't delve very deep into the nearly endless lore.".

That may be true, yet Monolith here comes to play the part of the Dwarves of Moria, delving, maybe, "too greedily and too deep" as Gandalf puts it (*FR,* II, iv, 317). This is particularly evident in the sequel, which falls into a rhythm of dutifully filling in blanks. To see the Nazgûl unmasked, and to count Helm Hammerhand and Isildur among them does not only stretch plausibility or offend lore-masters. Such fan service, no matter how steeped in the appendices, has the unintended effect of shrinking Tolkien's world rather than making it grow.

This concern is exacerbated by the gameplay itself,[20] which has little of that Tolkienian slow-gaming touch. The game plays out in the "open-world," but this world is bloated with things, which come to seem like menial tasks, to be accomplished. A lone Ranger in Mordor sounds like a recipe for furtive and exciting exploration and struggle, but in these games the player is never for a moment lost: a mini-map and compass come just short of GPS, guiding the player toward objectives and points of interest. There is little tension to the game's combat; the godlike powers of Celebrimbor/Talion make most encounters with even hordes of Orcs trivial. Indeed, most can be sprinted past en route to the next objective.

Of the games described above, it seems to me that *Diablo* interfaces most clearly and most successfully with Tolkien's craft. I close this chapter with one additional case study, the *Dark Souls* series (2011–16), from Japanese studio From Software. Like *Diablo,* it has no direct ties to Middle Earth Enterprises or the WETA workshop. Nevertheless, it bears the marks of Faërie, and represents something of the possibilities of a Tolkienian touch in modern gaming.

A BROOCH AND A PENDANT

When in *The Lord of the Rings* Tom Bombadil rescues the Hobbits from the clutches of a barrow-wight and piles the contents of the hoard out in the sunlight, he makes some practical selections for the Shire-folk, handing them short blades of Westernesse with which they will, many chapters later, go on to smite some high-profile targets, including the Lord of the Nazgûl himself, Witch-King of Angmar, who once harried the lands about. But Tom also selects a "brooch set with blue stones": "He looked long at it, as if stirred by some memory, shaking his head, and saying at last: "'Fair was she who long ago wore this on her shoulder. Goldberry shall wear it now, and we will not forget her!'" (*FR*, I, viii, 145).

It is a puzzlingly poignant moment for readers willing to pause as Tom does. It invites speculation about this fair she of long-ago days—we can well imagine being joined in the endeavor by the author himself. Was the mysterious she some princess of the ruined realm of Cardolan? Or, Bombadil's memory stretching as it does to the Beginning, could this brooch be some more ancient relic of the First Age? Many readers are by this point in the narrative enchanted by Tolkien's craft in weaving the threads of his world into a coherent, consistent, and vivid picture. We believe that Tolkien has a plan, that his Middle-earth possesses the "inner consistency of reality," that perhaps the answer to the riddle is to be revealed later, at least in the appendices (*MC*, 139).

But in this case such speculation proves futile and perhaps misses the point, which seems to be that we *cannot* know what Tom knows. This is yet another example of Tolkien working through that "fundamental literary dilemma," which defined his literary project. The lost identity of the brooch-wearer stands in for the ruin of a whole kingdom or kingdoms. For Tom, maybe, this was only a little while, but for the Hobbits it is a glimpse of the heartrending sense of the vanished past. But it is also a moment of pathos, a strange grave tenderness from Tom, who speaks as if she were a friend, thus the two emotions—the one lofty, the other earthy—Tolkien sets at odds in his letter on untold stories coalesce in this brief reflection.

When a player launches a new game of *Dark Souls* (2011),[21] he has not quite the embarrassment of riches of a barrow hoard at his disposal; he can nevertheless select from one of nine starting "gift" options before play begins. Among the gifts on offer is a simple pendant, whose description reads thus:

"Trinket: No effect, but fond memories comfort travelers." This is the first bit of "flavor text" available to the player. What "story" there is to *Dark Souls* and its sequels is told in large part by item descriptions—sometimes practical, others whimsical—like this.

When the game's designer, Hidetaka Miyazaki, was asked in a 2011 interview with *Famitsu* about his own approach to playing the game, Miyazaki suggested that he would begin a new game by choosing a gift of "either nothing or the pendant" (Stanton 2012). This rather simple and unadorned comment was enough to set off a firestorm of speculation and experimentation by players who were convinced that Miyazaki had hinted at a secret use for the mysterious pendant.[22] For these players, the game's illusion of art and design—its glamour of Poesis, we might say—was so strong that this one more secret— perhaps the greatest of all—would only be natural. Eventually, Miyazaki took pity on fans, putting an end to speculation (for all save the most dogged) and confirming in the lead-up to the game's expansion, *Artorias of the Abyss,* what might have already been clear from the item's "no effect" description: "When it comes to the pendant," he said, "I actually had a little bit of an intention to play a prank" (Stanton 2012).

What would possess players, first, to read into this interview response (like English majors on the scent) some terrible arcana and, second, to lay down uncounted hours in service of the vain testing of outlandish hypotheses in-game, sharing the abortive fruits and missteps of their research findings in the dedicated community spaces online? The answer, I submit, has quite a lot to do with Miyazaki's intuitive grasp—in game design terms—of Tolkien's abovementioned dilemma and the tensions at work therein.[23]

Just as Tolkien claims that fairy stories were not dependent on fairies, I would suggest that Tolkienian slow-gaming need not come packaged with furry-footed hole-dwellers, nor be licensed by Warner Bros. and the Weta Workshop. A good deal of the power and appeal of *Dark Souls* comes not from a borrowed iconography or quotas of fantastic beasts, but from a distinctly Tolkienian *approach* to game design. Returning to Tolkien's theories first outlined in chapter 1, we can recognize choice points of contact between them and the *Souls* games. The critical and popular success of a challenging game such as *Dark Souls* is more than a mere demonstration of Tolkien's continued influence on fantasy gaming—it also suggests that his work might be a valuable touchstone in articulating and exploring the viability of a "slow-gaming" approach to game design and play.

"ELVISH CRAFT" AND UNEXPLAINED VISTAS IN *DARK SOULS*

At the heart of Tolkien's critical essays and his fiction lies the concept of "Faërie," which Tolkien means to represent not only the imaginary *place* built by an author and explored by an audience but also the *condition* of enchantment experienced therein. Faërie, according to Verlyn Flieger's essay in *Tolkien: Maker of Middle-earth,* "may well be the most potent word in Tolkien's imaginative lexicon" (McIlwaine 2018, 35).

Part of Tolkien's spirited defense of fairy story and fantasy is his emphasis on the challenges it poses the artist; fantasy is, he cautions bluntly, "difficult to achieve" (*MC,* 139). Potent as Faërie might be, successfully sustaining it in a work of art is no child's play. The artist cannot simply say "*green sun*" but must "make a Secondary World inside which the green sun will be credible, commanding Secondary Belief." Such an accomplishment may be reserved for the master storyteller only; it "will probably require labour and thought, and will certainly demand a special skill, a kind of elvish craft" (140).

Gamers sense something of this "elvish craft" in From Software's games, attributing it to a kind of gaming auteur theory, or what has been called affectionately "The Miyazaki Touch." Tolkien described the spell woven by a competent sub-creator thus: "He makes a Secondary World which your mind can enter. Inside it, what he relates is 'true': it accords with the laws of that world. You therefore believe it, while you are, as it were, inside" (*MC,* 132). Judging by the *Dark Souls* community's willingness to be trolled by Miyazaki in the case of the pendant, it would seem that his game design work has earned him the status of what Tolkien calls the "successful sub-creator." Tolkien's fantasy framework is taken up in fascinating directions in the *Souls* games.

I have discussed at length Tolkien's memorable metaphor for untold tales in the form of the "unexplained vistas" along or even beyond the edge of his literary canvases. Such vistas—explored and unexplored—feature prominently in the *Dark Souls* series. A player may come upon them unawares: towering cathedral spires, ruined keeps, snowcapped mountain ranges far beyond Lothric Castle, sunlight piercing through the clouds atop the ramparts of the Undead Parish, northern lights of the Boreal Valley. These views offer a break in the action, a breath of fresh air after the claustrophobic dread of dungeon crawling. Sometimes the player looks back on the tortu(r)ous path already traversed, or is momentarily stricken by seeing a familiar landmark or space from a fresh angle. These moments neatly illustrate Tolkien's concept of Recovery, that ability to "clean our windows" grimed with use, which, Tolkien suggests, is one of the chief benefits of fairy story (*MC,* 146).

The sense of interconnectedness to the game world (particularly in the first *Dark Souls*) is frequently cited as one of its most triumphant and unique features. But not all of the game's vistas are ultimately accessible. From Software strikes a delicate balance between richly imagined and cleverly interconnected zones traversable and vistas that remain forever off limits for play, though not, perhaps, beyond the reaches of our imagination.

Lore, too, functions similarly in *Dark Souls*. Beyond an opening cinematic scene, cryptic and cosmogonical, the player is not bombarded with expository info dumps at even narrative intervals. Nor are the people, places, or items you discover in your journeys handily logged in an in-game journal for convenience, a practice now commonplace in role-playing games. To gain an understanding of the world you have entered and the stories it has to tell, you will instead piece together clues from item descriptions, Non-Player Character (NPC) dialogue, and the game's architecture, art, and environments.

The notion of an auteur touch is raised once more in *IGN*'s praise for the expanded content offered in *Artorias of the Abyss:* it "also manages that Miyazaki trick of filling in blanks while suggesting a few new ones" (Stanton 2012). Miyazaki's approach to storytelling shows a marked interest in questions of tradition and story cycles familiar to any medievalist but a hallmark, certainly, of Tolkien's fantasy and his scholarship. When asked about continuity between the first *Dark Souls* and its expanded content, he notes, "There is not a contradiction."

> The lore of [knight] Artorias that prevailed in the original story is very old, so that it is uncertain. . . . Hence by experiencing the story of the additional content there's a partial view of new facts, and the newly unveiled lore will show players another dimension. I suppose this is what lore is like and why it is attractive. (Stanton 2012)

Such musings sound as if they could belong in Tolkien's *Beowulf* commentary.

Interlaced (and often completely optional) NPC story lines likewise grant an impression of depth to the game world, suggesting that this world and its denizens have a life outside the player's purview. Like the Fair Folk of Tolkien's legendarium, the strange inhabitants encountered in the realms of Lordran, Drangleic, and Lothric appear to have their own cares. A chance meeting along the road might set in motion a tragic series of events, or swell the ranks of the merchants and counselors gathering about the Firelink shrine. Or it might not—this meeting is easily missed and once a moment or triggering action is bypassed, it is, within a single play-through, not recoverable.[24]

It is no exaggeration to say that a player might invest fifty hours or more in "beating" *Dark Souls* without having noticed—let alone explored, completed, or exhausted—half of the available NPC story lines. Nor is it feasible or possible for even an expert player to experience all that the game might offer by way of content in a single play-through. This lends a remarkably high degree of replayability to the series. It also facilitates a robust body of online resources and communities where scholars of the game come together to share and compile Wiki-style encyclopedias of information on the game's secrets, mechanics, and lore. The movement of the game's NPCs, flitting in and out of view like the stunning vistas on the horizon, works toward the aesthetic of intrigue and of limitless extensions shared with Tolkien's work.

The world of *Dark Souls* is not one of mystery and wonder only, but also danger and difficulty. In the introduction Tolkien drafted and later abandoned for a proposed edition of George McDonald's *Golden Key*, he rejects the role of cartography in charting the nebulous regions of Faërie: it is a realm with "no known limits, and no maps. Travellers have to do without them—probably the best thing" (*SWM*, 92). It is traveling advice that rings oddly in the ears of readers who may be more familiar with Tolkien's famous claim that he "wisely started with a map" (*Letters*, 177).[25] But the contradiction might be settled by distinguishing between the author on the one hand, and his characters (and readers) on the other.

The author's work of sub-creation, of course, requires labor and thought, planning, craft, and design—and this is what Tolkien is getting at by "started with a map." Like a building constructed from a blueprint, or an essay from a robust outline, this planning stage is felt and appreciated even if it is not openly displayed on the finished product.

It is the experience of the reader that Tolkien emphasizes in his comment about the ascetic virtues of map-less travel through fairyland. But then what of the famous hand-drawn maps that fold out from the covers of Tolkien's tales? These maps, it is true, provide the reader with ballpark estimations and relative distance from land to land. But it is worth noting that they are limited: they offer no guidance, no detailed layout of entrances, exits, and paths in places of "Faërie-within-Faërie"—think Moria, Lothlórien, or the Paths of the Dead.

And, of course, the reader's surrogate in Tolkien's best-known tales is of Hobbit-kind, burdened with a number of cartographic limitations. As Frodo's wanderlust grows in the beginning of *The Lord of the Rings*, he turns to maps, wondering "what lay beyond their edges: maps made in the Shire showed mostly white spaces beyond its borders" (*FR*, I, ii, 43). Later, Gandalf chides Pippin for not studying the maps held in Rivendell. The young Took insists that he just cannot remember what he saw—"Frodo has a better head" for such things (*FR*, II, iii, 283). Unfortunately, such praise for Frodo's memory is misplaced: he recalls being "shown a map of Mordor," but can "only remember it vaguely" (*RK*, VI, ii, 927). In spite of the celebrated maps accompanying Tolkien's texts, many readers, no doubt, empathize most with Sam: "Maps conveyed nothing to Sam's mind" (*FR*, II, iii, 285).

Today's video games come not just with maps, but GPS-style tracking and smart notifications—a far cry from the fanciful hand-drawn *hic sunt leones*. The added convenience is notable and evidently marketable, but limiting in terms of immersion and enchantment, exploration, and bewilderment.

Dark Souls offers no such accommodations: you can eschew a shield for a torch or other light source in dark caverns, drop colored pebbles as breadcrumbs marking your path—or follow Gandalf's advice and "throw yourself in next time" you wonder how deep the rabbit hole goes (*FR*, II, iv, 313). This is frequently frustrating, but it offers that peculiar slow-gaming pleasure, an intimacy with the environs you explore that feels in some ways akin to the long and descriptive passages of landscape found in Tolkien's tales. The challenge of learning these places (you have no other choice if you wish to progress through the game world)—how tunnel connects to tunnel and loops back to the start—can be daunting, but the environment, down to its nooks and crannies, sticks with a player like real places do. The need to forego a map is one of several factors contributing to the perception of *Dark Souls* as a deeply challenging and even punishing game.[26]

The disorientation, fear, wonder—all of these lead the player to take in the game slowly, to savor its atmosphere. By the end, most players willing to brave its perilous realms declare that the game "is too short," paraphrasing Tolkien on *The Lord of the Rings* (*FR*, xxi). The cult success of *Dark Souls* has spread over the past decade; its publisher Bandai Namco announced recently that the series has sold over 27 million copies worldwide. Perhaps it is for Miyazaki as it was for Tolkien, "an unfailing delight" to discover that the fairy tale is in fact an "adult genre . . . for which a starving audience exists" (*Letters*, 209).

EPILOGUE

to coasts and havens unguessed
—J. R. R. Tolkien, "Aldarion and Erendis"

"My father's invented languages," said Christopher Tolkien, "are of more interest than the rather well-tramped field of Anglo-Saxon" (Garth 2020a). After taking up the role of literary executor at Tolkien's death in 1973, Christopher soon resigned his academic post as a fellow at New College in Oxford, spending the rest of his life editing and publishing his father's unpublished and often unfinished tales. With Christopher's passing in January 2020, we may feel that the vault—those seventy boxes of manuscripts and papers that Tolkien left in Christopher's care—from which he brought forth untold treasures has now, finally, closed for good.

The prospect of no "new" works by Tolkien may signal an added impediment to what the author called Recovery in "On Fairy-stories," one of the essential perks or values (alongside Fantasy, Escape, and Consolation) to be gained from fantasy. Recovery, as described in the essay, is the "regaining of a clear view," an opportunity to reenchant our world and to be "startled anew" (*MC*, 146). It is an idea that appears in Tolkien's fiction as well, to my mind most poignantly within the mani-told web of the Túrin saga, when Nienor, recovering from the dragon's curse in Brethil, begins to relearn language, "as one that finds again treasures, great and small, that were mislaid" (*CH*, 217).

It can be hard to do with Tolkien's work, particularly if we agree with Christopher's despairing judgment in the wake of the Jackson film buzz: "Tolkien has become a monster, devoured by his own popularity. . . . commercialisation has reduced the aesthetic and philosophical impact of the creation to nothing" (Garth 2020a). It might be hard enough without the movies, the games, and the limited-time Denny's entrées: many of us long to go back, to recover our own legendary first readings of Tolkien's stories. It is one of the privileges of teaching Tolkien to students; we can absorb some vicarious pleasure in the new discoveries of our students.

Something of an Escape-Recovery loop is present in that symbiosis between the edges of the canvas and the picture within the frame, which has been the subject of this book. For just as untold tales lead us into new imaginative territory "doubly, trebly, and quadruply enchanting," they also point us back to the story told with fresh eyes (*TL*, 157–58).

Perhaps it is our students who should envy us. We have explored the depths—not exhausted them. And we still do not know what became of the Entwives.

I hope that this study, which concludes here, will invite further inquiry and fresh reading. And so we beat on, following in Christopher's footsteps, or (what may be the same thing) in Gimli's: "With cautious skill, tap by tap . . . so we could work, and as the years went by we should open up new ways, and display far chambers that are still dark, glimpsed only as a void beyond fissures in the rock" (*TT*, III, viii, 548).

NOTES

INTRODUCTION

1. Tolkien's fictional scribes also fill their manuscripts with marginalia. Yet Tolkien could also muster some restraint in this regard. Signs of reasonable deference to the margins can be seen elsewhere in the Bodleian catalog, for example, in the drafting of the alliterative *Lay of the Children of Húrin* (McIlwaine 2018, 218).

2. This remark, made in parentheses, comes as part of a discussion between Tom Shippey and Christopher Tolkien on the importance of depth and the challenges Tolkien faced in writing (or at least presenting) the Silmarillion material long after it had crystallized as the "backcloths" drawn about *The Lord of the Rings*. It is a discussion revisited within the pages of this book. See also Lobdell (2005, 167–75).

3. See also George R. R. Martin's 2018 visit to *The Late Show*, wherein he closes his interview with the lascivious regret that "there is no porn in Middle-earth."

4. Dennis Wilson Wise (2016), in "Book of the Lost Narrator," applies the tower allegory to more sympathetic readers of Tolkien who view the 1977 *Silmarillion* as a curio for study rather than a unified literary text. Tolkien's Tower, allegory though it may be, thus demonstrates a remarkable applicability. See also Agøy on the limits of the lost text approach.

5. See Paul Edmund Thomas's (2006) "Towards Quite Unforeseen Goals" for a discussion of how these beliefs are strengthened by Tolkien's creative work on *The Hobbit* and his scholarly work on *Beowulf*.

1. TOLKIEN AND THE "FUNDAMENTAL LITERARY DILEMMA"

1. This was no idle letter: Christopher had been following the development of *The Lord of the Rings* closely and would go on to become Tolkien's literary executor. Perhaps the clearest indication of the difference between *The Hobbit* and *The Lord of the Rings* is in their early audience's change in circumstances. Christopher, away in

RAF training for World War II, received serialized drafts of *The Lord of the Rings* as his father wrote. This was a far cry from *The Hobbit*'s genesis as a bedtime story for Christopher and his siblings.

2. By "near trees" Tolkien suggests the potential in a kind of half-telling, summary, or oblique approach wherein the story (here the tree) is never treated fully and thus cannot be "appropriated" by the reader's mind. This comment connects in some intriguing ways with C. S. Lewis's concepts of literary surprise and narrative lust (*2017*, 24). Tolkien's texts are for many readers preeminently rereadable, yet via untold tales they also maintain a core of insatiable curiosity, a narrative lust forever whetted and unquenched.

3. In "The Books of Lost Tales: Tolkien as Metafictionist," Brljak champions the importance of this letter and argues that Tolkien's solution is found in the "metafictional 'machinery'" of his stories—the mediating conceit that the tales are derived from layered translations and redactions of wholly vanished source texts—which allows for their "telling and untelling . . . in the same breath" (2010, 19). More on Tolkien's play with vanished source texts is discussed in chapter 3 of this book.

4. There is with a body of work as vast and tangled as Tolkien's some difficulty with nomenclature. By legendarium, I refer to the whole mass of writings—published and unpublished—concerned with the invented world of Arda. I find this preferable to the confusion of distinguishing between the legends of The Silmarillion and *The Silmarillion* volume edited by Christopher Tolkien in 1977. Tolkien of course saw the Wars of the Jewels and the Rings as intimately connected parts of the same story, and himself uses the term on occasion—"the legendarium, of which the Trilogy is part (the conclusion)" (*Letters*, 214).

5. Paul Edmund Thomas observes that *The Hobbit*'s "narrator sometimes teases us by revealing some information while holding back other facts, and he makes sure we know that he knows more than he chooses to tell" (2000, 164).

6. Years later, Peter S. Beagle would echo these remarks in "Tolkien's Magic Ring," an appreciation that serves as an introduction to *The Tolkien Reader* (1966). "The true delight of the book," Beagle declares, "comes from the richness of the epic, of which *The Lord of the Rings* is only a few stanzas" (xi). Tolkien, he continues, "is wise enough not to tell all that he knows . . . One can do that with literary creations, but not with anything living. And Middle-earth lives, not only in *The Lord of the Rings* but around it and back and forth from it" (xii).

7. For a discussion of the storied blades taken from the trolls' hoard and their problematic connection to Tolkien's legend of Gondolin, see Renée Vink's "Tolkien the Tinkerer: World-building Versus Storytelling."

8. This echoes the sentiment he had expressed many years earlier regarding the long-winded challenges of philology from the *Year's Work in English Studies* (1927): "Knowing how these little lexicographical chases open vista after vista . . . we can well believe that much self-denial was practiced to keep the notes down to thirteen pages" ("Philology: General Works," qtd. in Bowers 2019, 6).

9. For discussion of the essay's legacy, see, for example, Drout's lecture from Mythcon 42, "'*Beowulf*: The Monsters and the Critics'" Seventy-Five Years Later."

10. One example of this baggage given by Tolkien in the essay is "the catalogue of the heroes of Arthur's court" in *Culhwch and Olwen* (107–8). By contrast, Tolkien's own "catalogue" of knights arriving for the defense of Gondor in *The Lord of the Rings* is put to a grim artistic purpose: it ensures that their deaths, recounted after the Battle of the Pelennor Fields, are not faceless (*RK,* V, i, 770; *RK,* V, vi, 848).

11. Tolkien wrote of the problem on several occasions:

I have been forced to publish up-side-down or backwards; and after the grand crash . . . before the Dominion of Men (or simple history) to which it all led up the mythological and elvish legends of the Elder Days will not be quite the same. But perhaps read, eventually, from beginning to end in the right order, both parts may gain. I am not writing the *Silmarillion,* which was long ago written; but trying to find a way and order in which to make the legends and annals publishable. (*Letters,* 252)

See also the discussion between Shippey and Christopher laid out in the foreword to *The Book of Lost Tales Part I.*

12. Perceptive literary executor that he is, Christopher ends the selection of his father's commentary on the poem with a note of pure untold tales: "the ashes of Beowulf himself are now to be laid in a barrow with much of this same gold . . . and pass down into the oblivion of the ages—but for the poet, and the chance relenting of time: to spare this one poem out of so many. For this, too, almost fate decreed: . . . that shall the blazing wood devour, the fire enfold. Of the others we know not" (*B,* 352–53).

13. Regarding allusions made in *The Lord of the Rings* to Túrin Turambar, a Middle-earth analogue to Sigemund, see chapter 3.

14. See, for example, Michael D. C. Drout's (2013a) lecture, "How to Read J. R. R. Tolkien."

15. In "*Beowulf:* The Monsters and the Critics," Tolkien praises Virgil's deft creation of an impression of depth; his readers say with longing: "Alas for the lost lore, the annals and poets that Virgil knew" (*MC,* 27). Faramir says much the same of Gandalf in his talks with Frodo: his passing means that "much lore" is "taken from the world" (*TT,* IV, v, 670). Gandalf and others frequently cite limited time as an excuse for untold tales, echoing Virgil's Aeneas in prefacing his account of the Fall of Troy. See Shippey on the tantalizingly suggestive adventures in *Sir Gawain and the Green Knight* and their likeness to Bilbo in *The Hobbit* (2003, 92).

16. See David Bratman's entry on Eddison in "The Inklings and Others" for an overview of their encounters (2020, 323–24).

17. See also Drout's discussion of this scene (2013b, 190).

18. For an exploration of the suggestion of oral history and its importance to Middle-earth, see Maria Prozesky's (2006) "The Text Tale of Frodo the Nine-fingered: Residual Oral Patterning in The Lord of the Rings."

19. Perhaps the closest we come to Celebrimbor is in "The History of Galadriel and Celeborn" of *Unfinished Tales.* This material, postdating *The Lord of the Rings,* offers a few fascinating glimpses of Celebrimbor's place in the politics and arts of the Second Age.

20. But for those interested, in "Untold Tales: Solving a Literary Dilemma" I endeavored to chart what I see as some of the most significant depth-marking moves and devices in Tolkien's arsenal. But, as Tolkien might say, those who enjoy close reading only may neglect such an appendix, quite rightly.

21. See the discussion of wise woman Andreth's reticence about the legends of the Fall in the "Athrabeth," and the possible Númenórean influences in "The Tale of Adanel" appended thereto (*MR*, 344).

2. GREAT MATTERS GROWN DIM

1. It seems clear that he saw such forgetfulness as cyclical as well: it does not take long for Orcish cults of Sauron to appear after Aragorn's reign in the aborted Fourth Age tale, *The New Shadow* (*Peoples*).

2. As Andrew Hallam says in "Thresholds to Middle-earth," Tolkien's works "function allegorically as allegories of *reading,* for their characters perform acts of interpretation; they become figures of the modern Reader as they move through the mythic landscape of Middle-earth" (2011, 26).

3. Tolkien significantly increased the distance of time in the revision of the text; early drafts suggested that Aragorn is only a few generations removed from Isildur, or that Eorl the Young rode with the Last Alliance (*TI,* 450). As discussed in this chapter, the wider gulf of time does little to diminish the lasting impact of the old war, but it does, one supposes, add something of the glamor of antiquity so essential to untold tales.

4. Interesting to note first that very little from this germ survives: the names, motives, seconds, weapons, and setting all changed, yet the bones of a wrestling germ still peek through in the later fragments of tag-team swordplay against Sauron—an illustration of the way a striking image often survives in a refashioned and repurposed way in Tolkien's process.

5. A note following "The Disaster of the Gladden Fields" imagines Sauron's rage at the missed opportunity and the seeds of his ultimate downfall: "Nonetheless it proved in the event that the War of the Ring was lost at the Disaster of the Gladden Fields" on account of the "bungling fools" who failed to recover the Ring, having no idea what had transpired on the slopes of Orodruin (*UT,* 270).

6. Recall Hemingway, in his discussion of the iceberg and omission, warning of a damaging "hole" in the story where an author bluffs his knowledge. While Tolkien's methods often sent him in search of "what really happened" as he revised, his untold tales do not appear to adhere to the same rigid standards set by the American—the holes themselves are at times celebrated. For further comparison of the two approaches to omission, see chapter 4.

7. Tolkien was fascinated by unexpected developments and turns of tradition. A telling example from antiquity might be that of Odysseus/Ulysses: a resourceful hero for the Greeks could become a reviled scoundrel for the Romans.

8. For more on this, see Flieger's (2012c) "Tolkien and the Idea of the Book."

9. Tolkien, writing to his son in 1945, counts both "Sam's disquisition on the seamless web of story" and the near repentance of Gollum, which soon follows it among his favorite moments in the story (*Letters,* 110).

10. See also Gergely Nagy's (2006) intriguing investigation of Gollum's subjectivity and speech patterns in "The 'Lost' Subject of Middle-earth." The present reading, with its focus more on Sméagol than Gollum, calls into question the notion that he is "marginal, not in a discursive position of power," unable to "partake in interpretation" (59).

11. See Sam's distinction between the action we hope for in real life and the adventure of stories, or the tavern gossip on the mysterious deaths of Frodo's parents, the sort of thing we would expect to see in a Hitchcock film. Bilbo, in *The Hobbit,* is said to be immensely proud of his small part in The Battle of Five Armies. Tolkien, who more than once likened himself to a Hobbit, said of dragons in "On Fairy-stories": "I desired dragons with a profound desire. Of course, I in my timid body did not wish to have them in the neighborhood. But the world that contained even the imagination of Fáfnir was richer and more beautiful, at whatever the cost of peril" (*MC,* 135).

12. See the draft material in *The War of the Ring* for developments in the tales Gollum remembers (*WR,* 112, 123). At one point Gollum claims that "the tales did not say" anything of Isildur's cut. If this were so, however, it would suggest that the story is completed only when Gollum sees the wound after his capture: he fills in the blanks and begins to formulate a plan of attack. Tolkien was evidently keen to emphasize Gollum's extensive knowledge in the published version.

13. From Gergely Nagy's discussion of Sauron: "But the way he is represented by the other fictional authors is of course also an interpretation, and it is *theirs,* not Sauron's, based on the fictional traditions of representing this being, and the experience they themselves have with his power and effects" (2013, 126). Nagy makes no mention of this particular nickname.

14. As is clear from the middle volumes of *The History of Middle-earth,* Tolkien labored through many different iterations of the Third Age Mount Doom scene, too.

15. One wonders if Sam glimpses the site of the last combat of the Second Age on their trek to Mount Doom: "The path was not put there for the purposes of Sam. He did not know it, but he was looking at Sauron's Road. . . . Out from the Dark Tower's huge western gate it came . . . , and then . . . it ran for a league between two smoking chasms, and so reached a long sloping causeway that led up on to the Mountain's eastern side" (*RK,* VI, iii, 942). Would the bridge or the causeway have been suitable sporting ground for that legendary encounter?

16. Nagy, on the allusion to Túrin in relation to Sam's battle with Shelob, observes that "an embryonic *typological interpretation* is presented by the narrator, with Túrin as type and Sam as antitype, proving the affinity of these texts to each other" (2003, 243). Flieger similarly discusses Frodo's maiming as a "cruel and even less rewarded replication of Beren's lost hand" (2012a, 240).

17. The popular legends of a secret or unstoppable technique in martial arts, like the Italian *botta segreta* in fencing, may be a useful analogue here. It also recalls the advice of Arthur to Gawain before his exchange with the Green Knight. In Tolkien's

translation: "'Take care, cousin,' quoth the king, 'one cut to address, / and if thou learnest him his lesson, I believe very well / that thou wilt bear any blow that he gives back later'" (*Miscellany*, 252).

18. Title of Robert Graves's 1929 autobiography, emblematic of the trench poet's disillusion.

19. Figures like Maglor and Húrin demonstrate that Middle-earth has its share of warrior-poets, something akin to the Norse skalds, yet few of their works remain.

20. Gandalf refuses to tell his companions all of what transpires in his clash with the Balrog (*TT*, III, v, 501). Gimli "will not speak of" his adventures on the Paths of the Dead (*RK*, V, ix, 874).

21. In the essay on "The Palantíri" of *Unfinished Tales*, Gondor's general "waning of interest in or knowledge of ancient history among all but a few even of the high men of the realm" is described (*UT*, 386).

22. Gandalf's language here suggests that Sauron is only vanquished *after* the Ring is cut, but elsewhere it is not so clear.

23. It is noteworthy that Elrond's impressive memory, stretching deep into the First Age, seems at least partly the cause of his initially negative reading; with a fitting sense of nostalgia, both the Alliance's pageantry and results seem to pale in comparison to the memory of the War of Wrath, which ends the First Age.

24. See Tally's (2010) "Let Us Now Praise Famous Orcs."

25. Draft material for this section has Grishnákh replicate Gollum's trademark speech, making all but explicit an acquaintance with Gollum (*TI*, 410).

26. Kocher notes their kinship and function in this sense: Their "memories stretch much farther back, to the first beginnings of life on the planet. Through them he is able to give his story full chronological depth by opening up the longest possible vistas into the past" (1977, 9).

Consider also the philological inspiration behind the Ent name (OE *ent* for giant), as noted in Tolkien's *Letters* (208). This resonates nicely with what the Alliance represents here at the end of the Third Age—the almost unfathomable deeds of heroes larger than life (or at least tall even by Númenórean standards).

27. The surfacing of Númenórean history recalls Hemingway's iceberg—only glimpses remain of the great history buried under the sea. See also Tom Hillman's (2018) blog post "And Thus Was Númenor Avenged" on echoes between Númenor's and Sauron's downfall.

28. This is a common feature of Tolkien's web of story: endlessly referential, moving back and forth between chapters, indices, appendices, and out into other texts as well. This sort of reading as conducting research was a stance Tolkien takes in responding to his own work as well: looking back over old drafts and writing up analyses and footnotes that could later become new stories.

29. In the very same letter of 1954 to Naomi Mitchison, in which Tolkien notes the "clash between 'literary' technique, and the fascination of elaborating in detail an imaginary mythical Age," he reveals his thought on the fate of the Entwives and confirms the suspicion about the Brown Lands: "I think that in fact the Entwives had disappeared for good, being destroyed with their gardens in the War of the Last Alliance

(Second Age 3429–3441) when Sauron pursued a scorched earth policy and burned their land against the advance of the Allies down the Anduin" (*Letters*, 179).

30. This sense of historical precedent in the Alliance adds an additional wrinkle to Saruman's fatal oversight, which is lack of both fore- and hindsight. Here again, the shadow of the past haunts in surprising ways.

31. Not properly Second Age but dealing with the gulf of time between the Alliance and the events of *The Lord of the Rings*—similarly vast and impenetrable.

32. Strider makes his own case for this at the Council, giving a tantalizing glimpse of the Rangers' trade (*FR*, II, ii, 248).

33. Just a sketch might be rendered thus—
Some Branches in the Matter of the Last Alliance

1. Elvish: derived from Elrond, and perhaps Círdan, set down in "books of lore," the verse *Fall of Gil-galad*
2. Mannish:
   a. Big People: Concerning Isildur, scrolls set down in Gondor, Ohtar's account, heroic-elegiac verse of Rohan, Dead of Dunharrow
   b. Little People: Bilbo's special interest in the Dúnedain, his research trips, The Stoors of the Gladden Fields
3. Orcish: *All Not-So-Quiet on the Western Front: Blues Tracks from the Bad Old Days and the Great Siege*
4. Eldest: Treebeard, Bombadil
5. Environments and Artifacts: Brown Lands, Dead Marshes, Ruined Towers (meant to look into Mordor), the pocked and scored earth in Mordor a grim sign of the missiles that slew Anárion, The Ring, Andúril, The Palantíri, blades of Westernesse, Arwen's standard

34. Sam's surprising recitation of the Gil-galad lay is prompted by a nod to our lost tale: "It is told that Elendil stood there watching for the coming of Gil-galad out of the West, in the days of the Last Alliance" (*FR*, I, xi, 185). Strider's "it is told" suggests perhaps that such moments are enshrined in poetic memory and tradition. And, while he offers the Hobbits plenty of sound reasoning for his decision to lead them to Weathertop, it is also the first of many retraced steps as he begins his own quest to "strive with Sauron for the mastery" (*FR*, II, xiii, 368).

35. The Italian adage *traduttore traditore* (translator traitor) comes to mind. Translation, of course, causes trouble in deciphering the password "riddle" on the Gates of Moria. See also Nagy's discussion of retextualization and genre in the "Great Chain of Reading" (2003, 249–50).

36. The bleakness of Tolkien's own unfinished *Fall of Arthur* provides a useful comparison.

37. For Tolkien's discussion of the soup of story, see *MC*, 125–28.

38. As I note in chapter 1, the War of the Ring itself receives this condensed treatment in "Of the Rings of Power and the Third Age," notably eliding—and even misrepresenting—key motives, characters, and events.

39. This authorial vision is, at least in Tolkien's case, itself frequently shifting.

40. They are teased further, but not answered. A note on "The Disaster of the Gladden Fields" further hints at a duel with its parenthetical reference to the "last challenge upon Orodruin" (*UT,* 267). Isildur's scroll makes a chilling reference to the heat of Sauron's hand and Gil-galad's demise (*FR,* II, ii, 252).

41. The invocation of weregild, the Germanic custom of payment as restitution for a killing or wounding, offers a glimpse of the legal customs and codes of conduct among the great in Middle-earth. What does weregild say about Sauron's role in society? Does Isildur then accept weregild and mete out a death sentence on his foe?

42. "Heir of Elendil" and "Heir of Isildur" are both used throughout the text, but are they interchangeable? In this case, with the presentation of Narsil (and the Ring) at the Council, Aragorn and his audience are both focused on administration of the legendary coup de grâce. An interesting corollary in the historical "whodunit" category is discussed at some length in Tolkien's *Beowulf* commentary regarding the attribution of a dragon slaying to Sigemund or to his son (*B,* 290).

43. A curious reversal here, as the broken sword is typically a symbol of defeat (as it is in Elendil's fall)—not wholly vain, indeed, that breaking.

44. It also comes equipped with some impressive untold baggage: What do the runes from the reforging say? What do we know of Telchar, who "wrought it in the deeps of time" (*TT,* III, vi, 511)? How did a blade from the First Age come to Elendil in Númenor?

45. Proto-slasher films, perhaps.

46. For a discussion of "the ripples of Aragorn's open challenge," see Kocher (1977, 47, 74).

3. "STRANGE LUMBER"

1. After the catastrophic Battle of Unnumbered Tears, "the flower of the Eldar withered" and his own House of Hador declined (*CH,* 52). In this way Túrin recalls one of the most compelling antiheroes of the small screen, New Jersey mobster Tony Soprano, who confesses to his psychiatrist: "It's good to be in something from the *ground floor.* I came too late for that and I know. But lately, I'm getting the feeling that I came in at the end."

2. For those looking, "The Choices of Master Samwise" chapter contains other echoes of Túrin's story. Here Sam, like Túrin, inherits a fine sword from a friend (presumed dead), finds himself dogged by the terrible dilemma of choice, and even, in a moment of despair, contemplates suicide: "He looked on the bright point of the sword" (*TT,* IV, x, 732).

3. A few other glimpses emerge prior to 1977. In private correspondence, Tolkien mentions Túrin on a number of occasions, and shared with his old teacher R. W. Reynolds a draft of an alliterative verse Túrin.

4. That Túrin lives on in a naming tradition is itself puzzling. Christopher also observes that in the Qenya Lexicon, Túrin's "sword is given as *Sangahyando* 'cleaver of throngs.'" It lives on "to become the name of a man in Gondor" (*BLT II,* 342).

5. Carl F. Hostetter notes that this dearth might be in some measure explained by the premature end of the House of Hador—no characters in *The Lord of the Rings* can trace their lineage back to Túrin as Elrond or Aragorn could other noteworthy heroes (private correspondence). See also Christopher's note on Tolkien's possible slipup of Túrin for Tuor (*TI*, 6, 15).

6. Nor of course does it include known variants unpublished, including a 170-line fragment in rhyming couplets (*LB*, 130), or those no longer extant (e.g., the erased pencil text overwritten by the *Tale of Turambar* (*BLT II*, 139).

7. For Tolkien's cautionary remarks on this practice, see, for example, *MC*, 14, 45.

8. To which I think we could add a good deal more, including *Macbeth* and certainly *Beowulf*. If, as I argue here, Túrin is Tolkien's great playground for untold tales, it should come as no surprise that we find strong links to *Beowulf*, which was discussed in chapter 1 as Tolkien's principal model. This connection is perhaps most obviously manifest in the alliterative Túrin lay, which has that quality of a "great scene, hung with tapestries woven of ancient tales of ruin." Some of Tolkien's more unorthodox work on *Beowulf*, his fictive reconstructions of fairy tales and courtly ballads in "Sellic Spell" and "The Lay of Beowulf" offer a valuable analogue to his retellings of the Túrin story as well. In the Bodleian Library folder containing his father's unfinished alliterative translation of *Beowulf*, Christopher notes: "This work belongs to my father's time at Leeds University and is closely associated with his alliterative poem 'The Lay of the Children of Húrin,' of the same time" (MS. Tolkien A 29/1).

9. At least one reputable scholar has been known to mutter à la Hugo Dyson, "not another f***ing Túrin."

10. Yet another link between Túrin and *Beowulf* may be seen in the development of "The Hoard": Tolkien has clarified that the original inspiration for this poem (and its early title) is a line from *Beowulf*, *iúmonna gold galdre bewunden*, "the gold of men of long ago enmeshed in enchantment" in Tolkien's translation.

11. To draw comparison with the poems of the Primary World, Tolkien and his colleague E. V. Gordon believed that *The Battle of Maldon* was likely produced when news of the event was still fresh. For more on Tolkien's interest in *Maldon* and its maker, see chapter 4.

12. It appears in a more abbreviated form in *The Silmarillion*: "they saw one going northward in haste, and he was a tall Man, clad in black, and bearing a black sword. But they knew not who he was, nor anything of what had befallen in the south; and he passed them by, and they said no word" (239). The abbreviation suggests a later form of the tale, one in which Túrin, maybe, has become even for the poet an untold tale—the striking scene remains but its significance has faded. Or perhaps the other way round: the scene is cursory because the significance is so plainly obvious.

13. Fireside yarns were an early feature of Tolkien's tales. The Hall of Fire in Rivendell has its antecedent in the Tale-fire of the Cottage of Lost Play (*BLT I*, 17).

14. Compare to the occasionally subtle chapters of *The Lord of the Rings*, such as "The Departure of Boromir."

15. In "The Coming of Túrin into Brethil," Dorlas notes, "By his sword we should have known him, as did the Orcs" (*CH*, 195). There is the suggestion here, as in the case

of the Sword of Elendil, that Orcs have their stories of it, too: perhaps a horror or slasher tradition about the black sword?

16. Tolkien notes this mark of distinction for a small company of heroes: "As for the dragon: as far as we know anything about these old poets, we know this: the prince of the heroes of the North . . . was a dragon-slayer. And his most renowned deed, from which in Norse he derived his title Fáfnisbani, was the slaying of the prince of legendary worms" (*MC*, 16). In his "Dragons" talk: "It was the function of dragons to tax the skill of heroes" (*D*, 48). In the same talk, Tolkien notes the remarkable consolation that tales of such fearsome worms often tell of their defeat.

But it is worth emphasizing that Túrin is the first in Arda, and Glaurung no mere prince but the king of worms. Before the story of Azaghâl, probably most would not have even thought such a feat possible, let alone tried it. In the case of Túrin versus Glaurung, there is no precedent.

17. This nightmare finds a curious complement in *The Hobbit,* where it is Smaug who drifts "from an uneasy dream (in which a warrior, altogether insignificant in size but provided with a bitter sword and great courage, figured most unpleasantly)" (204).

18. Here the allusion to Túrin's strength in "The Choices of Master Samwise" is properly contextualized.

19. The names, numbers, and fates of Túrin's companions on this dragon-slaying venture evolves over time. In the rendition published in *The Children of Húrin,* the most likely eyewitnesses are Túrin's two companions on the hunt, but Dorlas deserts in shame and Hunthor is slain by a falling rock in the lead-up to the confrontation. In draft material explored in *The War of the Jewels,* Túrin's remark on the desertion of his companions (in this case five of an initial six) provides a dim echo of the legend of the seven wounds Morgoth receives from Fingolfin: Turin "woke and looked about in the wan light, and saw that only Dorlas remained by him. 'Seven wounds I hoped to give him,' he thought. 'Well, if it must be two only, then they must go deep'" (153).

20. Apropos the use of parentheses, Tolkien says of his writing in a 1968 BBC interview: "I think rather quickly in very elaborate long sentences, my digression. Sentences by me very largely consist of stuff in brackets" (Lee 2018, 160). This remark survives only in the typist's transcript and so perhaps contains errors.

21. Lewis is quoted in George Sayer's "Recollections of J. R. R. Tolkien" (1996, 22).

22. Perhaps it is meant to represent one of the marginal insertions of Ælfwine or the work of some later redactor. See the discussion of Ælfwine's handling of the *Narn* later in this chapter.

23. For more on this and other verse forms, see Carl F. Hostetter and Patrick Wynne's "Three Elvish Verse Modes" in *Tolkien's Legendarium.*

24. The narrator's excuse here echoes strongly Gandalf's remark to Frodo regarding the history of the Ring and the Last Alliance.

25. The gulf of time between The War of the Ring and the Last Alliance is of course far greater.

26. One additional echoing between the two is the prideful reach for more after a great deed. Recall Beren, who "cut forth a Silmaril. But daring more he essayed to gain

them all. Then the knife of the treacherous Dwarves snapped, and the ringing sound of it stirred the sleeping hosts and Morgoth groaned" (*BL*, 137). And here Túrin: "Then the heart of Turambar rose high within him, and though the Dragon still breathed he would recover his sword" (*CH*, 238).

27. Noteworthy that this talk of smiting fingers foreshadows heroics of the Second and Third Ages as well.

28. Tolkien's *Beowulf* indicates a wider interest in totes and bags. Grendel's *glof*— in Tolkien's translation, "deep was it and strange"—receives considerable discussion in his commentary on the poem (*B*, 74, 343–44).

29. Perhaps sensing our insatiable hunger for more on the sack, or indeed engaging in speculation of his own regarding Mîm's secrets, the narrator chooses to cover Mîm's treachery under the guise of another root-hunt.

30. And then, one day, we do recognize these linguistic markers. Tolkien's efforts to integrate names from his invented languages is both pronounced and effective in the Túrin story.

31. For a Primary World antecedent, we might look to Tolkien's interest in Hrunting, the sword given to Beowulf by Unferth. See his commentary on the episode in the *Beowulf* edition, where Tolkien engages in some lively "guesswork," drawing on the sword as a fragment of a lost tale—a kind of fossil—linking *Beowulf* with older fairy-story traditions of the North (*B*, 210–11).

32. But other curiosities and mysteries remain in *The Children of Húrin*. The role of Finduilas may be one important example. The love triangle formed by Gwindor, Finduilas, and Túrin may recall something of Lancelot's intrusion in Arthur's marriage— once introduced, later poets would have to reckon with in some way. In *The Children of Húrin*, it remains, like much of Nargothrond, underdeveloped. Gwindor's dying words to Túrin—"she alone stands between you and your doom. If you fail her, it shall not fail to find you"—ring strangely (177). Are they meant to suggest an alternate destiny, in which Túrin's Elf-man moniker Adanedhel might have brought about another storied union between Man and Elf?

33. That loss, fittingly, led to further lost tales. As Christopher notes in his commentary, "The orc raid into east Beleriand in which Maedhros saved Azaghâl is nowhere else referred to" (*UT*, 142).

34. See also Richard West's (2000) "Túrin's *Ofermod*: An Old English Theme in the Development of the Story of Túrin."

35. See Shippey's discussion of the connection to the Norse Ægishjálmr (2003, 266–67).

36. For Tolkien's discussion of Norse manuscript history, see *SG*, 26–30.

37. It is likely that Tolkien's literary experiments in tradition and metafiction were in some part inspired by the exciting manuscript discoveries of his day. The 2019 discovery of the *Libro de los Epitomes*, a catalog of works from the sixteenth-century library of Hernando Colon, would have surely piqued his interest as well. Dr. Edward Wilson-Lee notes the "immense importance" of the catalog's discovery, in large part "because it contains summaries of books that no longer exist, lost in every other form than these summaries" (qtd. in Flood 2019).

38. A fair number of these scenes or passages in fact are derived from summary works like the *Grey Annals*—their longer forms no longer extant or never achieved in Tolkien's lifetime.

39. See Christopher's discussion of this development in the essay "The Evolution of the Great Tales" (*CH*, appendix).

40. And there is a case to be made for *The Silmarillion, too.* In spite of its "epitomising form," the 1977 text preserves plenty of curiosities (like Anguirel) as well.

41. For more on eschatology in Tolkien's invented world, see Whittingham (2008) and Larsen (2019).

42. Thus in this story most clearly linked to Tolkien's scholarly interests and inspirations (Kullervo, Sigurd, Beowulf et al.) we find also a strange synthesis of major themes from Tolkien's two most important essays, "*Beowulf*: The Monsters and the Critics" and "On Fairy-stories"—"until the dragon comes" is followed by a remote glimmer of *eucatastrophe* (*MC*, 34).

43. It may also be indicative of Tolkien's late-career preoccupations or, in a certain sense, his commitment *not* to finish *The Silmarillion,* turning to obscure matters of world-building rather than finding suitable form for those most moving untold stories.

44. The "Athrabeth" does speak of some potentially related concerns in its discussion of hope for Men. Of particular interest are Finrod's words on the mystery of the end of Eru's Music: "As may a master in the telling of tales keep hidden the greatest moment until it comes in due course. It may be guessed at indeed, in some measure, by those of us who have listened with full heart and mind; but so the teller would wish. In no wise is the surprise and wonder of his art thus diminished, for thus we share, as it were, in his authorship. But not so, if all were told us in a preface before we entered in!" (*MR,* 319).

45. I recall vividly my own first encounter, in Verlyn Flieger's graduate seminar at the University of Maryland. We were all dumbstruck—and, as if like Eltas, Dr. Flieger would say no more and dismissed us.

46. For discussion of this editorial decision, see Christopher's commentary in *Morgoth's Ring* (204).

47. For one thing the borrowing from a very different text (the *Valaquenta*) causes the kind of editorial/authorial confusion that Christopher remedies so successfully in his later works. For another, notes on the "Athrabeth" suggest that this prophecy was still to end *The Silmarillion,* even if it was recognized as of Mannish derivation (*MR,* 342).

48. A final great irony, Tolkien's strange history of publication may be that Túrin, the story cycle most engaged with divergent tradition, retellings, and unfinished tales, would be the Great Tale that Christopher, in *The Children of Húrin,* presents as essentially complete. This volume would seem to be in a sense the "discovery of the completion of the whole" for his own project as literary executor. In the series of the Great Tales, he strikes a balance between the artificial text of *The Silmarillion* and the full-on scholarly approach to *The History of Middle-earth;* they acknowledge—and even celebrate—the tales' unfinished qualities, present salient scholarly findings on their development, and yet are readable and accessible to a wider audience.

This is what he does with some success in *Beren and Lúthien* and in *The Fall of*

Gondolin; less so, we might say, in *The Children of Húrin,* which started the series. One can understand and even applaud the effort at stitching Túrin's tale together without major lacunae or unscrupulous editorial intervention. Yet we might also bemoan the volume's omissions of the great unfinished alliterative lay, or even a whiff of the developments of the mysterious prophecy of Túrin's role in the end game. Alas, that no second edition will be forthcoming.

49. It stands to reason that an author might wish on some level to devise a happy ending for a character who so dominated his attention.

50. The concept was likely not part of the original talk given at St. Andrews in 1939, but in the 1943 revisions made for publication (*TOFS,* 135). Note that Tolkien's discourse on "untold stories" comes in 1944. Perhaps there and then our hopes of some full treatment of the Dagor Dagorath are dashed.

51. Two quiet details from the *Tale of Turambar* echo/presage the Hunter's famous accessories. First, "Túrin begged Orodreth for a sword," a weapon he had not held since Beleg's death: "rather had he been contented with a mighty club." Then we are told that the new sword "hung from a sable belt" (*BLT II,* 83). In this way it is Túrin's temporary rejection of the sword (something of an ancient equivalent to Michael Jordan's brief hiatus from basketball to pursue baseball) immortalized in the stars. The sword, however, is ready: an early description of the constellation, before it was explicitly identified with Túrin, describes "diamonds on his sword-sheath, and this will go red when he draws his sword at the Great End" (*BLT II,* 281).

4. A PORTRAIT OF THE POET AS A YOUNG MAN

1. A few late examples include Anna Smol's (2019) "Bodies in War: Medieval and Modern Tensions in *The Homecoming*" and Mary Bowman's (2010) "Refining the Gold: Tolkien, The Battle of Maldon, and the Northern Theory of Courage."

2. See also my article "Dialogic War: From the Battle of Maldon to the War of the Ring" (Grybauskas 2011).

3. Smol has also made note of this instance of the omission, raising a number of insightful objections to Shippey's reading of the poem (2019, 279).

4. Hemingway's icebergs extended also to his book-length projects. One particularly noteworthy example is chapter 20 of *Death in the Afternoon,* wherein Hemingway opens with a lament that the book could never contain all that it should. He then proceeds with a kind of lyrical list of all those places, people, and things about which the book says nothing (2003a, 270–78).

5. As Neil Gaiman says of the ways *The History of Middle-earth* sheds light on *The Lord of the Rings:* "It's like being allowed to see a small part of the underneath of the iceberg, or the roots of the tree" (Garth 2020b).

6. Rateliff ultimately doubts the veracity of this assumption.

7. Lines 312–13 in Tolkien's unpublished prose translation of *Maldon* held in the Bodleian actually start identically—"Heart shall be"—but they are crossed out and reworked, suggesting that no one gets it quite right on the first go (MS A 30/2, fol. 135).

8. Shippey makes no mention of the link to the poet, but discusses the dream sequence in terms of its heathen tones and suggests that Tolkien places the famous lines within a dream to "diminish [their] force" (2007, 336–37).

9. In this Totta appears to share something in common not only with the *Maldon* poet but with Tolkien himself, whose heroic romances have seemed to go against the literary grain post–World War I.

10. Richard West observes that "this is [Tolkien's] method" in the creation of *Homecoming*. He also suggests that the poet would be someone "like Totta," but doesn't go all the way with the implication (2018, 348, 345).

11. See also Giuseppe Pezzini's (2018) "The Authors of Middle Earth: Tolkien and the Mystery of Literary Creation."
For more on the omitted epilogue, see Mary Bowman's (2006) "The Story Was Already Written: Narrative Theory in *The Lord of the Rings*."

12. This seems an apt comment on the mysteries of the Túrin in the Great Wrack—and Christopher's hesitance to explain it.

13. As noted in Hammond and Scull's *Chronology,* Tolkien in fact felt that the voice in the dark ought to be omitted from a BBC radio dramatization (2017a, 469).

5. DESTROYING MAGIC, KINDLING FIRE

1. By this time, of course, Tolkien had labored on the project (notwithstanding frequent interruption) for more than half a century. For a recent and illuminating discussion of Tolkien's failure to bring his great work to a conclusion, see John D. Rateliff's (2020a) "The Flat Earth Made Round and Tolkien's Failure to Finish the Silmarillion."

2. According to Wayne Hammond in "The Critical Response to Tolkien's Fiction," reception of *The Lord of the Rings* was "polite compared to some of the criticism that erupted in 1977 upon the long-anticipated (posthumous) publication of *The Silmarillion,* and that later was directed against *Unfinished Tales* and *The History of Middle-earth.* Its force was strong, and is not yet spent" (1996, 229).

3. Ironically, *The Lord of the Rings* is not, in fact, a trilogy. Anticipation for *The Silmarillion* was building long before its appearance in 1977. Readers of the appendices following *The Return of the King* would have salivated over lines like the following: "Of these things the full tale, and much else concerning Elves and Men, is told in *The Silmarillion*" (Appendix A, 1034). Even before the publication of *The Lord of the Rings,* Tolkien's responses to fan inquiries had alluded to *The Silmarillion* and its legends, building a certain anticipation and hype if only by small steps (see, for example, *Letters,* 129). See Makai's (2019) "Beyond Fantastic Self-indulgence: Aesthetic Limits to World-building."

4. See, for example, disappointment in *Unfinished Tales* expressed by Guy Gavriel Kay, who assisted Christopher Tolkien in editing *The Silmarillion.* Kay wrote in a Canadian magazine that "for someone innocently seeking a good read, *Unfinished Tales* emerges as inaccessible, pedantic and perhaps ultimately saddening. Where has the magic gone? One feels at times like an archeologist, digging amongst the dusty rubble

of a once-glorious civilization . . . Broken shards of pottery . . . the dry dust of scholarly footnotes replacing the gleam of enchanted swords" (qtd. in Hammond 1996, 230).

5. For a discussion of the distinctions between world-building and sub-creation, see Izzo's (2019) "Worldbuilding and Mythopoeia in Tolkien and Post-Tolkienian Fantasy Literature."

6. Martin's saga does, on the other hand, begin to show some unfortunate parallels to Tolkien in its apparently interminably unfinished state.

7. See Shippey's (2018) *Laughing Shall I Die* for a lively discussion of the western as a story cycle.

8. For Hitchcock's famous description of the MacGuffin, see his interview with François Truffaut (1984, 138).

9. See Verlyn Flieger's discussion of the Ring and the Falcon in "Sometimes One Word Is Worth a Thousand Pictures" (2011, 53).

10. This is satirized beautifully in Mel Brooks's (1987) *Star Wars* spoof, *Spaceballs:* "Forget the Ring. I found it in a Crackerjack box!"

11. Legend has it that The Beatles approached Stanley Kubrick about a film treatment of *The Lord of the Rings,* but the director dismissed the project in these terms.

12. He does hum a few bars of a "Lay of Lúthien" while the Hobbits sleep in the extended cut.

13. Ralph Bakshi's 1978 animated film opens likewise, though it makes the interesting/budget-conscious decision to represent the Last Alliance victory in live-action silhouette—like shadows of the past, one supposes—thus distinguishing it from the animation of the rest of the film.

14. George Lucas is no doubt an influence on Jackson, just as Tolkien's stories helped to pave the way for Lucas and his most famous cinematic "sub-creation" of the twentieth century.

15. See Aubron-Bülles (2012) for some discussion of Tolkien's technique and Jackson's abundance of options.

16. See Richard Lawson (2012) in *The Atlantic.*

17. I first tried to articulate this theory of slow-gaming in a graduate school paper of 2010. I was largely unsuccessful; it received that emblem of graduate-level mediocrity, the B+.

18. Tolkienian inspiration is revealed in several ways. The town's smith, for instance, boasts of a mithril sword he once forged for the king.

19. See Moore (2013).

20. One possible exception here is its touted "Nemesis" system, which provides a charming glimpse of the tenuous power structures of Mordor's Orc population and reminds us, importantly, that Orcs have stories to tell, too.

21. September 22, to be exact—Bilbo's birthday. A spiritual successor to 2009's *Demon's Souls, Dark Souls* would go on to become one of the most critically acclaimed titles in recent memory, spawning two sequels, a Lovecraftian spin-off of sorts, *Bloodborne,* and the Sengoku-era samurai fantasy, *Sekiro,* mentioned in an epigraph to this chapter. A dedicated fanbase for all these titles remains active today.

22. Some fragmentary record of speculative experimentation with the pendant in various corners of the game world is maintained on the *Dark Souls* Wiki for posterity, https://darksouls.wiki.fextralife.com/Pendant. It reads eerily like a latter-day page from the Book of Mazarbul.

23. While finely delineating Miyazaki's direct engagement with Tolkien's work is not a part of this chapter's objective, his wide reading in western fantasy is worth noting. A brief description of his library, given in an interview, notes that "a shelf is packed with novels—old classics of fantasy and science fiction" (Mielke 2016).

24. The scene (discussed at some length in chapter 3) in *The Fall of Gondolin,* when Túrin comes crashing through the trees, momentarily crossing paths with his better-fated cousin Tuor, stands out in expressing Tolkien's interest in interlacement, chance meeting, and the strange points at which stories converge and diverge.

25. Most recently taken up into the social media teasers designed to drum up early buzz for the forthcoming Amazon Studios production.

26. It recalls in some ways the popular impression of *The Silmarillion*—widely owned but rarely read beyond the first few pages.

WORKS CITED

Agøy, Nils Ivar. 2007. "Viewpoints, Audiences, and Lost Texts in *The Silmarillion*." In The Silmarillion—*Thirty Years On*, 139–63. Edited by Allan Turner. Zurich: Walking Tree.

Aubron-Bülles, Marcel. 2012. "'The Lord of the Gaps': How Tolkien's Mastery of a Literary Technique Would Make Ten Hobbit Films Possible—and They Still Wouldn't Be Enough." *The Tolkienist,* Oct. 11. https://thetolkienist.com/2012/10/11/the-lord -of-the-gaps-how-tolkiens-mastery-of-a-literary-technique-would-make-ten-hob bit-films-possible-and-they-still-wouldnt-be-enough/#disqus_thread.

Bakshi, Ralph, dir. 1978. *The Lord of the Rings*. United Artists.

Beagle, Peter. 1966. "Tolkien's Magic Ring." In *The Tolkien Reader,* ix–xvii. New York: Del Rey Books.

Blizzard Entertainment. 2012. *Diablo III*. Blizzard Entertainment.

Blizzard North. 1997. *Diablo*. Blizzard Entertainment.

———. 2000. *Diablo II*. Blizzard Entertainment.

Bloom, Harold. 2008. "Introduction." In *Modern Critical Interpretations: The Lord of the Rings—New Edition,* 1–2. New York: Infobase Publishing.

Bowers, John M. 2019. *Tolkien's Lost Chaucer*. Oxford: Oxford Univ. Press.

Bowman, Mary R. 2006. "The Story Was Already Written: Narrative Theory in *The Lord of the Rings*." *Narrative* 14, no. 3: 272–93.

———. 2010. "Refining the Gold: Tolkien, The Battle of Maldon, and the Northern Theory of Courage." *Tolkien Studies* 7: 91–115.

Bratman, David. 2018. "*Smith of Wootton Major* and Genre Fantasy." In *A Wilderness of Dragons: Essays in Honor of Verlyn Flieger,* edited by John D. Rateliff, 25–41. Wayzata, MN: Gabbro Head.

———. 2020. "The Inklings and Others: Tolkien and His Contemporaries." In *A Companion to J. R. R. Tolkien,* edited by Stuart D. Lee, 317–34. Hoboken, NJ: Wiley Blackwell.

Brljak, Vladimir. 2010. "The Books of Lost Tales: Tolkien as Metafictionist." *Tolkien Studies* 7: 1–34.

Brooks, Mel, dir. 1987. *Spaceballs.* MGM.

Chase, David. 1999. "The Sopranos." *The Sopranos,* Jan. 10. HBO.

Corriea, Alexa Ray. 2014. "Why Shadow of Mordor's Undead Elven Hero and Sexy Sauron Are Such a Big Deal." *Polygon,* July 28. https://www.polygon.com/2014/7/28/5945029/middle-earth-shadow-of-mordor-celebrimbor-sexy-sauron.

Drout, Michael D. C. 2011. ""*Beowulf:* The Monsters and the Critics" Seventy-Five Years Later." *Mythlore: A Journal of J. R. R. Tolkien, C. S. Lewis, Charles Williams, and Mythopoeic Literature* 30, no. 1: 5–22.

———. 2013a. "How to Read J. R. R. Tolkien." Lecture, Carnegie Mellon Univ., Pittsburg.

———. 2013b. "The Tower and the Ruin: The Past in J. R. R. Tolkien's Works." In *Tolkien: The Forest and the City,* edited by Helen Conrad-O'Briain and Gerard Hynes, 175–90. Portland, OR: Four Courts Press.

Drout, Michael D. C., Namiko Hitotsubashi, and Rachel Scavera. 2014. "Tolkien's Creation of the Impression of Depth." *Tolkien Studies* 11: 167–211.

Dunsany, Lord. (1908) 2000. "The Sword of Welleran." In *Fantasy Masterworks: Time and the Gods.* London: Millennium.

DuPlessis, Nicole. 2018. "'Changed, Changed Utterly': The Implications of Tolkien's Rejected Epilogue to *The Lord of the Rings.*" *Tolkien Studies* 15: 9–32.

Eddison, E. R. (1922) 1991. *The Worm Ouroboros.* New York: Dell Publishing.

———. 2014. *Mistress of Mistresses.* London: HarperCollins.

Fawell, John. 2005. *The Art of Sergio Leone's* Once Upon a Time in the West. Jefferson, NC: McFarland and Company.

Flieger, Verlyn. 2011. "Sometimes One Word Is Worth a Thousand Pictures." *Picturing Tolkien: Essays on Peter Jackson's* The Lord of the Rings, edited by Janice M. Bogstad and Philip E. Kaveny, 46–53. Jefferson, NC: McFarland.

———. 2012a. "A Cautionary Tale: Tolkien's Mythology for England." In *Green Suns and Faërie: Essays on J. R. R. Tolkien,* 237–41. Kent, OH: Kent State Univ. Press.

———. 2012b. "A Post-Modern Medievalist." In *Green Suns and Faërie: Essays on J. R. R. Tolkien,* 251–61. Kent, OH: Kent State Univ. Press.

———. 2012c. "Tolkien and the Idea of the Book." In *Green Suns and Faërie: Essays on J. R. R. Tolkien,* 41–53. Kent, OH: Kent State Univ. Press.

Flood, Alison. 2019. "'Extraordinary' 500-Year-Old Library Catalogue Reveals Books Lost to Time." *Guardian,* Apr. 10. https://www.theguardian.com/books/2019/apr/10/extraordinary-500-year-old-library-catalogue-reveals-books-lost-to-time-libro-de-los-epitomes. From Software. 2011. *Dark Souls.* Bandai Namco.

Garth, John. 2020a. "Christopher Tolkien Obituary." *Guardian,* Jan. 20. https://www.theguardian.com/books/2020/jan/20/christopher-tolkien-obituary.

———. 2020b. "'He Lets Us Walk the Road as JRRT Walked It': Neil Gaiman's Tribute to Christopher Tolkien." *John Garth,* Nov. 22. https://johngarth.wordpress.com/2020/11/22/he-lets-us-walk-the-road-as-jrrt-walked-it-neil-gaimans-tribute-to-christopher-tolkien/.

Gordon, E. V., ed. 1937. *The Battle of Maldon.* London: Methuen.

Greene, Graham. 1950. "'The Third Man' as a Story and a Film." *New York Times,* Mar. 19. http://movies2.nytimes.com/books/00/02/20/specials/greene-astory.html.

Gregory, Joel. 2011. "The Lord of The Rings: War in the North *Review.*" *Official PlayStation Magazine,* Dec. 6. https://web.archive.org/web/20140828225345/http://www.official playstationmagazine.co.uk/review/the-lord-of-the-rings-war-in-the-north-rev_ew/.

Grybauskas, Peter. 2011. "Dialogic War: From *The Battle of Maldon* to The War of the Ring." *Mythlore* 29, no. 3: 37–56.

———. 2012. "Untold Tales: Solving a Literary Dilemma." *Tolkien Studies* 9: 1–19.

———. 2020. "A Portrait of the Poet as a Young Man: Noteworthy Omission in *The Homecoming of Beorhtnoth Beorhthelm's Son.*" *Tolkien Studies* 17: 163–78.

Hallam, Andrew. 2011. "Thresholds to Middle-earth: Allegories of Reading, Allegories for Knowledge and Transformation." *Mythlore* 30, no. 1: 23–42.

Hammond, Wayne G. 1996. "The Critical Response to Tolkien's Fiction." *Mythlore* 21, no. 2: 226–32.

Hammond, Wayne G., and Christina Scull. 2017a. *Chronology. The J. R. R. Tolkien Companion and Guide.* London: HarperCollins.

———. 2017b. *Reader's Guide Part I. The J. R. R. Tolkien Companion and Guide.* London: HarperCollins.

Hemingway, Ernest. (1929) 1957. *A Farewell to Arms.* New York: Scribner.

———. 1958. "The Art of Fiction no. 21." Interview by George Plimpton. *The Paris Review* no. 18 (Spring). https://www.theparisreview.org/interviews/4825 /the-art-of -fiction-no-21-ernest-hemingway.

———. 1983. "The Art of the Short Story." Quoted in Paul Smith, "Hemingway's Early Manuscripts: The Theory and Practice of Omission." *Journal of Modern Lit-erature* 10, no. 2: 276.

———. 1998. "The Snows of Kilimanjaro." In *The Complete Short Stories of Ernest Hemingway,* 39–56. New York: Scribner.

———. 2003a. *Death in the Afternoon.* New York: Scribner.

———. 2003b. *A Moveable Feast.* New York: Scribner.

Hillman, Tom. 2018. "And Thus Was Númenor Avenged." *Alas, Not Me,* Feb. 16. http:// alasnotme.blogspot.com/2018/02/and-thus-was-numenor-avenged-rk-6iii947.html.

Hollander, Lee M., trans. 2006. *The Poetic Edda.* Austin: Univ. of Texas Press.

Holmes, John R. 2007. "The Battle of Maldon." In *J. R. R. Tolkien Encyclopedia: Schol-arship and Critical Assessment,* edited by Michael D. C. Drout, 52–54. New York: Routledge.

Honegger, Thomas. 2007. "*The Homecoming of Beorhtnoth*: Philology and the Liter-ary Muse." *Tolkien Studies* 4: 189–99.

Hostetter, Carl F., and Patrick Wynne. 2000. "Three Elvish Verse Modes." In *Tolkien's Legendarium: Essays on* The History of Middle-earth, edited by Verlyn Flieger and Carl F. Hostetter, 113–39. Connecticut: Greenwood Press.

Izzo, Massimiliano. 2019. "Worldbuilding and Mythopoeia in Tolkien and Post-Tolkienian Fantasy Literature." In *Sub-creating Arda: World-building in J. R. R. Tolkien's Work, Its Precursors, and Its Legacies,* edited by Dimitra Fimi and Thomas Honegger, 31–55. Zurich: Walking Tree.

Jackson, Peter, dir. 2001. *The Fellowship of the Ring.* New Line Cinema.

———, dir. 2012a. *The Hobbit: An Unexpected Journey.* Warner Bros.

———. 2012b. "An Unexpected Journey." Note on *Facebook,* July 30. https://www .facebook.com/notes/peter-jackson/an-unexpectedjourney/10151114596546558/.

Kane, Douglas Charles. 2011. *Arda Reconstructed.* Bethlehem: Lehigh Univ. Press.

Keats, John. 1820. "Ode on a Grecian Urn." https://www.poetryfoundation.org/poems /44477/ode-on-a-grecian-urn.

King, Stephen. 2016. "On Being Nineteen (And a Few Other Things)." In *The Gunslinger,* xi–xix. New York: Scribner.

Kocher, Paul H. 1977. *Master of Middle-earth.* New York: Ballantine.

Larsen, Kristine. 2019. "'While the World Lasted': Eschatology in Tolkien's 1930s Writings." *Journal of Tolkien Research* 7, no. 1.

Lawson, Richard. 2012. "'The Hobbit': Like One Bad Video Game." *The Atlantic,* Dec. 12. https://www.theatlantic.com/culture/archive/2012/12/the-hobbit-movie-review /320567/.

Lee, Stuart D. 2018. "Tolkien in Oxford" (BBC, 1968): A Reconstruction." *Tolkien Studies* 15: 115–76.

———. 2020. "*Lagustreamas:* The Changing Waters Surrounding J. R. R. Tolkien and *The Battle of Maldon.*" In *The Wisdom of Exeter: Anglo-Saxon Studies in Honor of Patrick W. Conner,* edited by E. J. Christie, 157–75. Medieval Institute Publications.

Le Guin, Ursula K. 1975. "The Rule of Names." In *The Wind's Twelve Quarters,* 80–92. London: HarperCollins.

———. 1979. "The Staring Eye." In *The Language of the Night: Essays on Fantasy and Science Fiction,* edited by Susan Wood, 171–74. New York: GP Putnam's Sons.

———. 2008. "The Fiction Issue 2008." Interview by Steve Lafreniere. *VICE.* https:// www.vice.com/en_us/article/jmdq48/ursula-k-le-guin-440-v15n12.

Leone, Sergio, dir. 1966. *The Good, the Bad, and the Ugly.* United Artists.

Lewis, C. S. *(1937)* 2013. "*A World for Children: J. R. R. Tolkien, The Hobbit: or There and Back Again.*" First published *Times Literary Supplement. Republished in The Paris Review.* https://www.theparisreview.org/blog/2013/11/19/c-s-lewis-reviews-the-hobbit -1937/.

———. 2017. "On Stories." In *On Stories: And Other Essays on Literature. London:* HarperCollins.

Lobdell, Jared. 2005. *The Rise of Tolkienian Fantasy.* LaSalle, IL: Open Court.

Lucas, George, dir. 1977. *Star Wars.* 20th Century Fox.

MacDonald, Keza. 2019. "*Sekiro: Shadows Die Twice* Review: A Samurai Sword Through the Heart." *Guardian,* Apr. 12, 2019. https://www.theguardian.com/games/2019 /apr/12/sekiro-shadows-die-twice-review-playstation-xbox-software-activision.

Makai, Péter Kristóf. 2010. "Faërian Cyberdrama: When Fantasy Becomes Virtual Reality." *Tolkien Studies* 7: 35–53.

———. 2019. "Beyond Fantastic Self-indulgence: Aesthetic Limits to World-building." In *Sub-creating Arda: World-building in J. R. R. Tolkien's Work, Its Precursors, and Its Legacies,* edited by Dimitra Fimi and Thomas Honegger, 57–92. Zurich: Walking Tree, 2019.

Martin, George R. R. 2013. *A Song of Ice and Fire.* New York: Bantam.

———. 2017. "About Those Spinoffs. . . ." *Not a Blog*, May 14. https://georgerrmartin.com/notablog/2017/05/14/about-those-spinoffs/.

———. 2018a. "Imaginary History: PW Talks with George R. R. Martin." Interview by Lenny Picker. *Publishers Weekly*, July 16. https://www.publishersweekly.com/pw/by-topic/authors/interviews/article/77516-pw-talks-with-george-r-r-martin.html.

———. 2018b. Interview on *The Late Show with Stephen Colbert*, Nov. https://www.youtube.com/watch?v=4RaehHesOTE&feature=emb_logo.

McIlwaine, Catherine. 2018. *Tolkien: Maker of Middle-earth*. Bodleian Library, Univ. of Oxford.

McKillip, Patricia A. 1996. *The Forgotten Beasts of Eld*. New York: Magic Carpet Books.

Mielke, James. 2016. "'Dark Souls' Creator Miyazaki on 'Zelda,' Sequels and Starting Out." *Rolling Stone*, Oct. https://web.archive.org/web/20161005123700/http://www.rollingstone.com/culture/news/dark-souls-creator-miyazaki-on-zelda-sequels-w443435.

Monolith Productions. 2014. *Middle-earth: Shadow of Mordor*. Warner Bros. Interactive Entertainment.

———. 2017. *Middle-earth: Shadow of War*. Warner Bros. Interactive Entertainment.

Moore, Bo. 2013. "Why *Diablo*'s Auction House Went Straight to Hell." *Wired*, Sept. 20. https://www.wired.com/2013/09/diablo-auction-house/.

Nagy, Gergely. 2003. "The Great Chain of Reading: (Inter-)Textual Relations and the Technique of Mythopoesis in the Túrin Story." In *Tolkien the Medievalist*, edited by Jane Chance, 239–58. New York: Routledge.

———. 2004. "The Adapted Text: The Lost Poetry of Beleriand." *Tolkien Studies* 1: 21–41.

———. 2006. "The 'Lost' Subject of Middle-earth: The Constitution of the Subject in the Figure of Gollum in *The Lord of the Rings*." *Tolkien Studies* 3: 57–79.

———. 2013. "A Body of Myth." In *The Body in Tolkien's Legendarium*, edited by Christopher Vaccaro, 119–32. Jefferson, NC: McFarland.

Njal's Saga. 1975. Translated by Magnus Magnusson and Hermann Pálsson. Baltimore: Penguin Books.

O'Brien, Tim. 1990. "How to Tell a True War Story." In *The Things They Carried*, 67–85. New York: Broadway Books.

Pezzini, Giuseppe. 2018. "The Authors of Middle Earth: Tolkien and the Mystery of Literary Creation." *Journal of Inklings Studies* 8, no. 1: 31–64.

Prozesky, Maria. 2006. "The Text Tale of Frodo the Nine-fingered: Residual Oral Patterning in *The Lord of the Rings*." *Tolkien Studies* 3: 21–43.

Rateliff, John D. 2002. "Classics of Fantasy: *The Forgotten Beasts of Eld*." In *Wizards of the Coast*. http://web.archive.org/web/20021015111224/http://www.wizards.com/default.asp?x=books/main/classics2.

———. 2006. "And All the Days of Her Life Are Forgotten: The Lord of the Rings as Mythic Prehistory." In The Lord of the Rings *1954–2004: Scholarship in Honor of Richard E. Blackwelder*, edited by Wayne G. Hammond and Christina Scull, 67–100. Marquette Univ. Press.

———. 2009. "'A Kind of Elvish Craft': Tolkien as Literary Craftsman." *Tolkien Studies* 6: 1–21.

———. 2020a. "The Flat Earth Made Round and Tolkien's Failure to Finish the Sil-marillion." *Journal of Tolkien Research* 9, no. 1, Article 5. https://scholar.valpo.edu/journaloftolkienresearch/vol9/iss1/5.

———. 2020b. "Dr. Havard's 10%." *Sacnoth's Scriptorium,* May 22. https://sacnoths.blogspot.com/2020/05/dr-havards-10.html.

Rérolle, Raphaëlle. 2012. "Tolkien, l'anneau de la discorde." *Le Monde,* July 5. https://www.lemonde.fr/culture/article/2012/07/05/tolkien-l-anneau-de-la-discorde_1729858_3246.html.

Richardson, Ben. 2011. "GDC 11—*War in the North* Hands-on." *Gamefront,* Mar. 10. https://www.gamefront.com/games/gamingtoday/article/gdc-11-war-in-the--north-hands-on.

Rushdie, Salman. 2003. "Arms and the Men and Hobbits." *Guardian,* Jan. 3. https://www.theguardian.com/books/2003/jan/04/film.salmanrushdie.

Sayer, George. 1996. "Recollections of J. R. R. Tolkien." *Mythlore: A Journal of J. R. R. Tolkien, C. S. Lewis, Charles Williams, and Mythopoeic Literature* 21, no. 2: 21–25.

Shippey, Tom. 1979. "Creation from Philology." In *J. R. R. Tolkien, Scholar and Story-teller: Essays in Memoriam,* edited by Mary Salu and Robert T. Farrell, 286–316. Ithaca, NY: Cornell Univ. Press.

———. 1992. "Tolkien as a Post-war Writer." In *Proceedings of the J. R. R. Tolkien Centenary Conference, 1992,* edited by Patricia Reynolds and Glen H. GoodKnight, 84–93. Altadena: Milton Keynes Tolkien Society.

———. 2001. *J. R. R. Tolkien: Author of the Century.* Boston: Houghton Mifflin.

———. 2003. *The Road to Middle-earth.* New York: Houghton Mifflin.

———. 2007. "Tolkien and the *Homecoming of Beorhtnoth.*" In *Roots and Branches: Selected Papers on Tolkien,* 324–39. Zurich: Walking Tree.

———. 2010. "Tolkien's Two Views of *Beowulf:* One Hailed, One Ignored." *Lord of the Rings Fanatics Plaza,* July 25.

———. 2018. *Laughing Shall I Die: Lives and Deaths of the Great Vikings.* London: Reaktion Books.

Smith, Paul. 1983. "Hemingway's Early Manuscripts: The Theory and Practice of Omission." *Journal of Modern Literature* 10, no. 2: 268–88.

Smol, Anna. 2019. "Bodies in War: Medieval and Modern Tensions in *The Homecoming.*" In *"Something Has Gone Crack": New Perspectives on J. R. R. Tolkien in the Great War,* edited by Janet Brennan Croft and Annika Röttinger, 263–83. Zurich: Walking Tree.

Snowblind Studios. 2010. "War in the North: Untold Story Trailer." YouTube Video, 1:37, Nov. 18. https://www.youtube.com/watch?v=kDnwgqLiLFs.

———. 2011. *The Lord of the Rings: War in the North.* Warner Bros. Interactive Entertainment.

Stanton, Rich. 2012. "*Dark Souls'* Miyazaki Talks *Artorias of the Abyss.*" *IGN,* Nov. 2. https://www.ign.com/articles/2012/11/02/dark-souls-miyazaki-talks-artorias-of-the-abyss.

Tally, Robert T. 2010. "Let Us Now Praise Famous Orcs: Simple Humanity in Tolkien's Inhuman Creatures." *Mythlore: A Journal of J. R. R. Tolkien, C. S. Lewis, Charles Williams, and Mythopoeic Literature* 29, no. 1: 17–28.

Thomas, Paul Edmund. 2000. "Some of Tolkien's Narrators." In *Tolkien's Legendar-ium: Essays on The History of Middle-earth,* edited by Verlyn Flieger and Carl F. Hostetter, 161–81. Westport, CT: Greenwood Press.

———. 2006. "Towards Quite Unforeseen Goals." In *The Lord of the Rings 1954–2004: Scholarship in Honor of Richard E. Blackwelder,* edited by Wayne G. Hammond and Christina Scull, 57–66. Milwaukee: Marquette Univ. Press.

Tolkien, J. R. R. (1937) 1994. *The Hobbit.* Boston: Houghton Mifflin.

———. 1953. *The Homecoming of Beorhtnoth Beorhthelm's Son.* Vol. 6, *Essays and Studies.* Edited by Geoffrey Bullough, 1–18. London: John Murray.

———. (1962) 2014a. *The Adventures of Tom Bombadil.* Edited by Christina Scull and Wayne G. Hammond. London: HarperCollins.

———. (1967) 2005. *Smith of Wootton Major.* Edited by Verlyn Flieger. London: HarperCollins.

———. (1984) 2002b. *The Book of Lost Tales,* Part II. The History of Middle-Earth I. Edited by Christopher Tolkien. New York: Houghton Mifflin Harcourt.

———. (1985) 2002c. *The Lays of Beleriand.* The History of Middle-Earth I. Edited by Christopher Tolkien. New York: Houghton Mifflin Harcourt.

———. 1999. *Farmer Giles of Ham.* Edited by Christina Scull and Wayne G. Hammond. New York: Houghton Mifflin.

———. 2000. *The Letters of J. R. R. Tolkien.* Edited by Humphrey Carpenter, with Christopher Tolkien. Houghton Mifflin. Boston.

———. 2001a. "Leaf by Niggle." In *Tree & Leaf,* 91–118. London: HarperCollins.

———. 2001b. "The Rivers and Beacon-hills of Gondor." Edited by Carl F. Hostet-ter. *Vinyar Tengwar* 42: 5–31.

———. 2001c. *The Silmarillion.* Edited by Christopher Tolkien. New York: Houghton Mifflin.

———. 2002a. *The Book of Lost Tales,* Part I. The History of Middle-Earth I. Edited by Christopher Tolkien. New York: Houghton Mifflin Harcourt.

———. 2002d. *The Lost Road.* The History of Middle-Earth I. Edited by Christopher Tolkien. New York: Houghton Mifflin Harcourt.

———. 2002e. *Morgoth's Ring.* The History of Middle-Earth III. Edited by Christopher Tolkien. New York: Houghton Mifflin Harcourt.

———. 2002f. *The Peoples of Middle-earth.* The History of Middle-Earth III. Edited by Christopher Tolkien. New York: Houghton Mifflin Harcourt.

———. 2002g. *The Return of the Shadow.* The History of Middle-Earth II. Edited by Christopher Tolkien. New York: Houghton Mifflin Harcourt.

———. 2002h. *Sauron Defeated.* The History of Middle-Earth II. Edited by Christopher Tolkien. New York: Houghton Mifflin Harcourt.

———. 2002i. *The Shaping of Middle-earth.* The History of Middle-Earth I. Edited by Christopher Tolkien. New York: Houghton Mifflin Harcourt.

———. 2002j. *A Tolkien Miscellany.* New York: Houghton Mifflin/Quality Paper-back Book Club.

———. 2002k. *The Treason of Isengard.* The History of Middle-Earth II. Edited by Christopher Tolkien. New York: Houghton Mifflin Harcourt.

———. 2002l. *The War of the Jewels.* The History of Middle-Earth III. Edited by Christopher Tolkien. New York: Houghton Mifflin Harcourt.

———. 2002m. *The War of the Ring.* The History of Middle-Earth II. Edited by Christopher Tolkien. New York: Houghton Mifflin Harcourt.

———. 2005a. *The Fellowship of the Ring. The Lord of the Rings.* London: HarperCollins.

———. 2005b. *The Return of the King. The Lord of the Rings.* London: HarperCollins.

———. 2005c. *The Two Towers. The Lord of the Rings.* London: HarperCollins.

———. 2006a. "*Beowulf:* The Monsters and the Critics." In *The Monsters and the Critics and Other Essays,* edited by Christopher Tolkien, 5–48. London: HarperCollins.

———. 2006b. *Finn and Hengest.* Edited by Alan Bliss. London: HarperCollins.

———. 2006c. "On Fairy-stories." In *The Monsters and the Critics and Other Essays,* edited by Christopher Tolkien, 109–61. London: HarperCollins.

———. 2006d. "On Translating Beowulf." In *The Monsters and the Critics and Other Essays,* edited by Christopher Tolkien, 49–71. London: HarperCollins.

———. 2006e. "A Secret Vice." *The Monsters and the Critics and Other Essays.* Edited by Christopher Tolkien. London: HarperCollins.

———. 2006f. "Sir Gawain and the Green Knight." In *The Monsters and the Critics and Other Essays,* edited by Christopher Tolkien, 72–108. London: HarperCollins.

———. 2006g. *Unfinished Tales of Númenor and Middle-earth.* Edited by Christopher Tolkien. London: HarperCollins.

———. 2007. *The Children of Húrin.* Edited by Christopher Tolkien. New York: Houghton Mifflin.

———. 2008. *Tolkien on Fairy-Stories.* Edited by Verlyn Flieger and Douglas A. Anderson. London: HarperCollins.

———. 2009. *The Legend of Sigurd & Gudrun.* Edited by Christopher Tolkien. New York: Houghton Mifflin Harcourt.

———. 2011. *Beowulf and the Critics.* Edited by Michael D. C. Drout. Arizona: ACMRS.

———. 2013. *The Fall of Arthur.* Edited by Christopher Tolkien. New York: Houghton Mifflin Harcourt.

———. 2014b. *Beowulf: A Translation and Commentary.* Edited by Christopher Tolkien. New York: Houghton Mifflin.

———. 2015. *The Story of Kullervo.* Edited by Verlyn Flieger. London: HarperCollins.

———. 2017. *Beren and Lúthien.* Edited by Christopher Tolkien. New York: Houghton Mifflin Harcourt.

———. 2018a. "Dragons." In *The Hobbit 1937–2017: A Commemorative Booklet,* edited by Christina Scull and Wayne G. Hammond, 39–62. *The Hobbit Facsimile Gift Set.* London: HarperCollins.

———. 2018b. *The Fall of Gondolin.* Edited by Christopher Tolkien. New York: Houghton Mifflin.

———. 2019. *Il Ritorno di Beorhtnoth Figlio di Beorhthelm.* Translated by Giampaolo Canzonieri. Milan: Bompiani.

———. N.d. MS. Tolkien 5. Tolkien Papers. Bodleian Library, Univ. of Oxford.

———. N.d. MS. Tolkien A 29/1. Tolkien Papers, Bodleian Library, Univ. of Oxford.

———. N.d. MS. Tolkien A 30/2. Tolkien Papers, Bodleian Library, Univ. of Oxford.

Truffaut, François. 1984. *Hitchcock*. New York: Simon & Schuster.

Twain, Mark. 1898. *Following the Equator*. Hartford, CT: American Publishing Company. https://www.gutenberg.org/files/2895/2895-h/2895-h.htm.

Vink, Renée. 2019. "Tolkien the Tinkerer: World-building Versus Storytelling." In *Subcreating Arda: World-building in J. R. R. Tolkien's Work, Its Precursors, and Its Legacies*, edited by Dimitra Fimi and Thomas Honegger, 177–97. Zurich: Walking Tree.

Virgil. 1952. *The Aeneid*. *The Poems of Virgil*. Translated by James Rhoades. N.p. Encyclopedia Britannica.

Walker, Steve. 2009. *The Power of Tolkien's Prose: Middle-earth's Magical Style*. New York: Palgrave Macmillan.

West, Richard C. 2000. "Túrin's *Ofermod*." In *Tolkien's Legendarium: Essays on* The History of Middle-earth, edited by Verlyn Flieger and Carl F. Hostetter, 235–45. Westport, CT: Greenwood Press.

———. 2018. "Canute and Beorhtnoth." In *A Wilderness of Dragons: Essays in Honor of Verlyn Flieger*, edited by John D. Rateliff, 335–58. Wayzata, MN: The Gabbro Head.

Whittingham, Elizabeth A. 2008. *The Evolution of Tolkien's Mythology: A Study of the History of Middle-earth*. Jefferson, NC: McFarland.

Wilson, Edmund. 1965. "Oo, Those Awful Orcs." In *The Bit Between My Teeth: A Literary Chronicle of 1950–1965*. New York: Farrar, Strauss and Giroux.

Wise, Dennis Wilson. 2016. "Book of the Lost Narrator: Rereading the 1977 *Silmarillion* as a Unified Text." *Tolkien Studies* 13: 101–24.

INDEX

Paris Review, 93
Peoples of Middle-earth, The (Tolkien), 76;
    Ancalagon, 76; Andreth, 76–77; "Athra-
    beth Finrod ah Andreth," 77; Dagor Dag-
    orath, 76, 78; Last Battle, 76; Túrin, 76
Pippin: conversation with Gandalf, 18–19,
    119–20; *The Fellowship of the Ring,* 39,
    119–20; held captive by Orcs, 38–39; *The
    Return of the King,* 49; and the Ring, 38–
    39; *The Two Towers,* 19, 38; the War of the
    Ring, 18–19
PlayStation Magazine, 113
Plimpton, George, 93
Polygon, 114
"Post-Modern Medievalist, A" (Flieger), 30
Power of Tolkien's Prose, The (Walker), 3
Pulp Fiction, 104

Quenta Noldorinwa (Tolkien), 75, 78; Man-
    dos, 75; Túrin, 75
Quenta Silmarillion (Tolkien), 75–76

Rateliff, John D., 3, 94, 103
Red Book of Westmarch, 24, 30, 34, 55–56, 97
Return of the King, The: Alliance, 29; appen-
    dix, 31, 113; Aragorn, 23, 55, 47–48; Baldor
    the hapless, 23, 26, 106; battle of the Horn-
    burg, 48; Captains of the West, 22, 49, 57;
    Cracks of Doom, 34; Dunharrow, 28–29;
    the Eagles, 49; Elrohir, 47; Elrond, 47;
    Elves, 47; footnotes, 23; Frodo, 33–34, 49;
    Gandalf, 49, 113; Gimli, 29, 34, 48; Gollum,
    31, 33–34; Isildur, 47; Legolas, 48; Mal-
    beth the Seer, 47; Oathbreakers, 47; Paths
    of the Dead, 13, 23, 29, 47, 106; Pippin,
    49; Rohirrim, 28–29; Sam, 33–34; Sauron,
    48–49; Strider, 47–49; summoning of the
    Dead, 47; supplementary material, 4; Tale
    of Years, 28, 45; Théoden, 47; War of the
    Ring, 29; Wild Men of the Woods, 29
Return of the Shadow, The (Tolkien), 91
Reynolds, R. W., 51
Ring of Power, 104; destruction of, 22; forg-
    ing, 106–7; Frodo and, 34, 50; Gollum and,
    31, 32, 33; Isildur and, 30, 32–33, 35–36, 38,
    40, 45, 107; as the One Ring, 30, 105; Orcs
    and, 38–39; Pippin and, 38–39; Sam and,
    33; Sauron and, 30, 32, 33, 36, 38, 57
Rivendell, 50; libraries of, 21, 31, 37, 56
role-playing games (RPGs), 110–20
Royal Air Force, 49

Samwise Gamgee, 22, 24, 26, 30, 79, 97; battle
    with Shelob, 51, 55; at the Cracks of Doom,

34; *The Fellowship of the Ring,* 33, 35, 37,
    44, 47, 84; and the Ring, 33; *The Return of
    the King,* 34; at the Stairs of Cirith Ungol,
    94; *The Two Towers,* 29, 30, 32, 51
Saruman, 18; downfall, 41; *The Hobbit,* 110;
    *Unfinished Tales of Númenor and Middle-
    Earth,* 46
Sauron, 22, 28, 31, 39, 41, 78; the Black Hand,
    32; "The Disaster of the Gladden Fields,"
    27–28, 32, 45–47; the Eye, 49; fall, 27, 36,
    45, 48, 107; *The Fellowship of the Ring,* 33,
    38; the Mouth, 49; *The Return of the King,*
    48, 49; the Ring, 30, 32, 33, 36, 38, 57; tor-
    turing Gollum, 32, 33; *The Two Towers,* 48
Sauron Defeated (Tolkien), 24
Scavera, Rachel, 3, 52
"Secret Vice, A" (Tolkien), 7
Sekiro, 99
Shadow of Mordor, 110
Shelob, 39, 55; *The Two Towers,* 28, 51
Shippey, T. A., 2–3, 5, 86, 88, 89, 90, 94
Shire Records, 43
Silmarillion, The (Tolkien), 8–9, 44–45, 52,
    60, 65, 74, 77–78, 99–101; appendices, 103;
    Elendil's sword, 22; Fëanor, 20; Heir of
    Isildur, 22, 46; Isildur, 45; "Of the Rings of
    Power and the Third Age," 22; publication
    history, 9, 37, 51, 99–100; reception of,
    100; writing style, 21
Sir Gawain and the Green Knight, 5, 11, 14, 26
Sketch of the Mythology (Tolkien), 51, 75, 78;
    Morgoth, 75; the End, 78; Túrin, 75
slow-gaming, 111–16
Smith, Paul, 93
Smith of Wootton Major (Tolkien), 7, 11, 105,
    111
Snowblind Studios, 113
"Snows of Kilimanjaro, The" (Hemingway),
    18, 23
Song of Ice and Fire, A (Martin), 102–3
"Staring Eye, The" (Le Guin), 101
Star Wars series, 108–9
"Story of Kullervo" (Tolkien), 51, 52
Strider, 46–47, 49; *The Fellowship of the
    Ring,* 31, 33, 36–37, 44; first meeting with
    Gollum, 46–47; history of Weathertop, 44;
    The Lay of Leithian, 59; at The Prancing
    Pony, 36–37, 105; *The Return of the King,*
    47–49. See also Aragorn
"Sword of Welleran, The" (Dunsany), 15

Tale of Turambar and the Foalókë (Tolkien),
    52, 57–58; Battle of Lamentation, 52; Beleg,
    53, 58–59, 61; Brodda, 53; Dírhaval lay, 54,